This is an analysis of English studies in higher education, addressed in particular to practitioners in the field – teachers and students. As Heather Murray states in her introduction, those who work in English are likely to have a stronger sense of critical history than of disciplinary history. She contends that, in order to understand and reform the discipline of English studies, it is necessary to shift the focus of examination 'down and back' – to look at ordinary and often taken-for-granted disciplinary practices (such as pedagogy), and to extend the historical frame.

Murray begins with an examination of some important historical moments in the development of the discipline in Canada: the appointment in 1889 of W.J. Alexander as first professor of English at the University of Toronto; the twenty-five-year experiment early in this century in rhetorical and dramatic education for women that the Margaret Eaton School of Literature and Expression represented; and the entry of 'theory' into the English-Canadian academy. The second section examines some of the common features and routines of English departments, such as curriculum design, seminar groups, tests and assignments, essay questions, and the conference, in order to establish the critical/political principles that underpin study and teaching in the academy today. In this section, Murray also focuses on the role of women as students and teachers of English. The final section surveys the literature available for further research on the discipline and for constructing a history of English studies in Canada.

Theory/Culture

HEATHER MURRAY is an associate professor in the Department of English at the University of Toronto.

THEORY/CULTURE

Editors:
Linda Hutcheon, Gary Leonard,
Janet Paterson, and Paul Perron

HEATHER MURRAY

Working in English:
History, Institution, Resources

UNIVERSITY OF TORONTO PRESS
Toronto Buffalo London

© University of Toronto Press Incorporated 1996
Toronto Buffalo London
Printed in Canada

ISBN 0-8020-2853-5 (cloth)
ISBN 0-8020-7350-6 (paper)

Printed on acid-free paper

Canadian Cataloguing in Publication Data

Murray, Heather, 1951–
Working in English

(Theory/culture)
Includes index.
ISBN 0-8020-2853-5 (bound)
ISBN 0-8020-7350-6 (pbk.)

1. English philology – Study and teaching (Higher) –
Canada – History.   I. Title.   II. Series.

PR51.C2M87 1996   420'.071'171   C95-93311B-2

1001429279

This book has been published with the help of a grant from the Humanities
and Social Sciences Federation of Canada, using funds provided by the Social
Sciences and Humanities Research Council of Canada.

University of Toronto Press acknowledges the financial assistance to its
publishing program of the Canada Council and the Ontario Arts Council.

This book is dedicated
to the memory of my father

Donald Wellesley Murray

who was always interested in how and why
people do the work they do.

Contents

Acknowledgments

This book is embedded in a series of discussions which have been widespread in the discipline of English studies in the last ten years, so that my acknowledgments are for the most part equally general. I am grateful to a number of organizations for opportunities to present this work: the Association for Teaching and Learning in Higher Education, the Association of Canadian College and University Teachers of English (ACCUTE), the Atlantic Association of University Teachers of English, the 'Boundaries in/of Literature' conference (McMaster University), the 'Canons and Culture' conference (Concordia University), the 'Cultural Practices' conference (Ontario Institute for Studies in Education), the GRIP group (Group for Research into the Institutionalization and Professionalization of Literary Studies) (Carnegie-Mellon University), the 'English Studies and the Canon' conference (McMaster University), Inkshed, the MLA Commission on the Status of Women in the Profession, the 'Resistance to Theory' conference (University of British Columbia), the 'Rhetoric of Controversy' conference (University of Waterloo), as well as the OISE Curriculum Studies Group, the departments of English at Concordia, Cornell, Guelph, and University of Western Ontario, the graduate program in English at the University of Ottawa, the writing workshop at York University, and the humanities programs of York and Vanier College, Montreal. Of the panels and symposia in which I've participated at Toronto, I have especially enjoyed the invitations by FACT (the graduate students' Feminism and Critical Theory group) and the English Students' Union. I am indebted to participants in these and other forums. My gratitude goes, above all, to ACCUTE, its members, and its annual conference, for helping me to think about English and its institutions. At the moment of the writing of this preface, ACCUTE, like the other scholarly organizations in the humanities, faces funding cuts which could be devastating and, at the least, will seriously impair ACCUTE's ability to function as the centre of the discipline in Canada. To give the title of my book a twist it did not originally have: attention to our history, institutions, and resources is more necessary now than ever before if we are to continue working in English.

Several sections of this book have appeared in print. 'Resistance and Reception' was published in *Signature*; 'Close Reading, Closed Writing,' in *College English*; 'From Canon to Curriculum,' in the *University of Toronto Quarterly*; 'Charisma and Authority,' in *Theory/Pedagogy/Politics: Texts for Change*, edited by Donald Morton and Mas'ud Zavarsadeh (U Illinois P, 1991); while the two bibliographies have appeared in *English Studies in Canada*. An excerpt from the chapter on W.J. Alexander appeared in my article 'English Studies in Canada and the Case of Post-colonial Culture' in *Essays on Canadian Writing*, and some material from 'Women in English' appeared in my article 'Women in the Disciplines' in the *CAUT Bulletin*. I am grateful to all the editors and publishers involved for permission to reprint here. For the sake of consistency, this previously published material is reprinted with only minor alterations, although some addenda have been incorporated into the annotated bibliography. Archival material is cited courtesy of the Archives of Ontario, the Thomas Fisher Rare Book Library, University of Toronto, and the University of Toronto Archives; I thank Mavor Moore for permission to cite the Dora Mavor Moore papers at Toronto, and Eaton's for permission to quote from the Margaret Eaton School material contained in the Eaton Collection at the Archives of Ontario.

Portions of this work and the necessary conference travel have been supported by the Social Sciences and Humanities Research Council of Canada (postdoctoral fellowships program); the York University Graduate Research Development Fund and the Part-Time Research and Travel Fund; the Queen's University Arts Research Council; the University of Toronto Humanities and Social Sciences Committee Grant-in-Aid program; and Trinity College's Cassady Fund.

I am grateful to the many departmental chairs who answered my queries and assisted me in locating material for the bibliographies of English studies in Canada. Margery Fee brought several items to my attention; Stephen Bonnycastle and Barry Rutland lent material from their files; the inter-library loan staff of the University of Toronto Library tracked down many items; and Lisa Pottie provided a careful checking of the citations. For the book overall, I have received helpful advice from the anonymous readers for University of Toronto Press and the Canadian Federation for the Humanities; the anonymous reader of the Press's Manuscript Review Committee; the late John Robson; and the series editors Linda Hutcheon and Paul Perron. Gerry Hallowell and Rob Ferguson of the Press have helped to see this book through to its conclusion, and Ken Lewis has provided careful copy-editing.

And thanks to David Galbraith for encouragement throughout, in this and other projects.

WORKING IN ENGLISH

1

Introduction: Working in English

This book operates from one basic contention – that in order to understand and reform the discipline of English, it is first necessary to shift the focus of examination *down* and *back*. This crudely spatializes what could be put in other terms: that we have a great deal to learn about the day-to-day operations and practices of English studies; and that present examinations will be much more effective when grounded in a history that includes both disciplinary developments and their cultural (in this case, English-Canadian) contexts. Section 2 of this book ('Institution') provides six studies that take this first point as their mandate. They are framed, on the one side, by a 'History' section, which offers three analyses of disciplinary formation in English Canada, while the two chapters in the closing 'Resources' section are intended to suggest future research directions and to provide some of the necessary source material for more comprehensive historical studies.

The 'History' section begins with a chapter on the appointment of W.J. Alexander in 1889 as professor of English at the University of Toronto. The public controversy over the appointment of Alexander shows the discipline as we know it today in a process of active formation and supports the contention (made by Gerald Graff, among others) that there is no harmonious and unproblematic past in English studies to which our own age is a messy and troublesome successor. Alexander's appointment is a disciplinary crux, a moment when some roads are taken and others not; the direction chosen would have extensive ramifications for the development of English studies throughout the country, since the University of Toronto produced a number of widely used teaching texts and was for many years the sole domestic trainer of the professoriate. In addition, looking at the particular outlines of

Alexander's own scholarly work (an early attempt to blend an aesthetic with a historical study) may help us to identify some prominent, and even distinctive, features of literary criticism as it has developed in English Canada. (The question of Alexander's pedagogic and intellectual legacy is pursued as well in chapter 4.)

Consideration of the discipline's cast-off directions informs chapter 3, '"We Strive for the Good and the Beautiful": Literary Studies at the Margaret Eaton School of Literature and Expression.' Some twenty years after Alexander's appointment (and roughly the same number of years after the admission of women to the modern languages program at the University of Toronto), an independent women's academy for the study of literature, expression, dramatic arts, and physical culture was opened in Toronto. Often dismissed as a finishing school (when it is remembered at all), the Margaret Eaton School in fact aimed to provide a career-oriented training for women, and to offer an alternative to a university education perceived as impersonal and unintegrated. While somewhat anxiously maintaining a version of the Toronto curriculum in the 'University English Topics,' the women of the MES also turned their attention to contemporary literature, developed iconoclastic teaching methods, and continued the study of rhetoric and oratory, which had been dropped in the universities of eastern and central Canada, whose inclinations were more specifically 'literary.' I suggest that it is helpful to have models of earlier experiments in English studies when rethinking disciplinary directions today; and the history of the Margaret Eaton School may help as well to provide some background for continuing contemporary discussions about the recasting of literary as 'rhetorical' study.

Chapter 4, 'Resistance and Reception: Backgrounds to Theory in English Canada,' is an attempt to 'read' the contemporary state of theory backwards, into the discipline's past. This chapter surveys recent accounts of the resistance to theoretical inquiry in the literary disciplines, to assess their suitability to the Canadian situation; and the interestingly uneven response to 'theory' (and its associated curricular challenges) is seen in correspondence to the discipline's residual, dominant, and emergent forms (in Raymond Williams's terms). In this chapter, English studies in Canada is viewed as a sedimentation of past disciplinary developments, in turn composed of both widespread critical shifts and local innovations: this 'sedimentation,' the concurrent existence of a variety of modes of work and pedagogic practice, may be viewed as one of the strengths of the discipline in Canada and its departments.

If section 1 attempts to move the examination of English studies *back* (and to develop a specifically English-Canadian analysis), the second 'Institution' section tries to move it *down*. Here the focus is on common contemporary practices, some of which, like Poe's 'purloined letter,' are often invisible because they are omnipresent.

Chapter 5, 'Women in English,' initiates this section since the gender structuration of English studies is one of its predominant features. A brief history of English as a 'feminine' discipline, and of women's activities in it, is contraposed to women's seemingly paradoxical disciplinary marginality, which persists despite the more equitable hiring practices of the 1980s and 1990s, and the fact that women remain the consistent majority of students. How are we to account for this? In this chapter I contend that across-the-board analysis of the position of women (as students and teachers) in higher education is insufficient to detect the mechanisms which ensure women's exclusion; rather, a discipline-specific analysis is needed to uncover the distinctive beliefs and paradigms that keep women in place. While the situation of women in English is clearly a concern of this entire book, these considerations emerge more explicitly in chapters 8 and 10, in which some specific exclusionary practices are examined.

Chapter 6, 'Close Reading, Closed Writing,' is concerned with another disciplinary anachronism. It shifts to a concrete pedagogic example, the 'close reading' essay assignment or examination question. The specifically New Critical underpinnings of the 'close reading' have been subject to a sustained attack; probably few would adhere to these principles now, if they did in the first place. Yet the 'close reading' assignment is not only common; it is a sort of 'touchstone' or test which ascertains which students have decoded not only the text but the discipline itself. It therefore has a particular indexical value for understanding the state of English studies and the odd mimetic series (minds like poems) we have inherited from the 'practical criticism' experiment of I.A. Richards (a consideration which recurs in chapter 9).

'From Canon to Curriculum,' the seventh chapter, is an attempt to redirect the continuing debate over the 'canon' by criticizing some of its terms. First, I argue, a 'canon' is a method of heuristic organization and not a principle upon which curricula are actually structured (although 'canon' may be an effect). And further, if it is through the curriculum (and not 'canon' *per se*) that the university's socially reproductive role is maintained – as George Grant has suggested – progressive academics need to move away from text-centred discussion. But there are difficulties in shifting the debate from 'canon' to 'curriculum' as this seems to demand an educational vocabulary which most of us lack. This chapter concludes by offering some resources from contemporary curriculum theory which have a particular applicability to the English department situation.

An eighth chapter, 'Reading Readers,' reverts to some of the concerns of 'Women in English' while relating the gender structure of the English department more expressly to the classroom situation. This chapter poses the question of how statements made by students (and women students in particular) are 'read' by their instructors; and explores the ramifications of a professorial tendency to take student questions as socially or even psychologically symptomatic, rather than as comments having a literary or theoretical import. The engendered situation of woman student and male instructor, and the pedagogic paradigm in which a 'first' text is replaced or displaced in order to clear the way for a critical supplement, replicates a literary structure economically illustrated by Wordsworth's 'She dwelt among the untrodden ways.'

Chapter 9, 'Charisma and Authority in Literary Study and Theory Study,' continues the examination of classroom dynamics with a study of the operations of the seminar group. Because it operates as an idealized pedagogic situation, the seminar also facilitates a 'misrecognition' of pedagogic power relations (to use Bourdieu's term). The more general concern of this chapter is whether 'theory' works counter to or within the particular structure of charismatic authority prevalent in the 'soft' disciplines; and it concludes with a program for a more 'conditional' (both provisional and situational) teaching practice.

The tenth chapter, 'Does Controversy Have a Rhetoric?' looks at the rhetorical and conventional limitations placed on academic debate in its most common manifestations, the conference and the published critical correspondence. Here the gender structure of intellectual inquiry is strikingly evident, in the establishment of a triangulation where 'woman' initiates a male-to-male theoretical discourse (as Mary Jacobus has noted), or where 'woman' is the position to which one critic tries to push an opponent. Some recent interchanges over indeterminacy (or 'deconstruction,' loosely defined) are used as examples; what characterizes these debates (precisely because they are organized in order to exclude 'controversy') is an uncanny and unsettling recurrence of their expelled terms.

While the first ten chapters share a topical and theoretical orientation, the studies are discrete and have little overlapping citation. For this reason (and because the bibliographies of some chapters are designed to provide resource guides to often unfamiliar material), citations are listed separately for these first ten chapters.

The last two chapters of *Working in English* provide the 'Resources' section, which is part of the book's historical frame. Chapter 11, 'English Studies in Canada to 1945: A Bibliographic Essay,' is an annotated guide to material pertaining to the discipline's formative years, listing some two hundred print sources. While it is not a disciplinary history, this chapter does attempt to contextualize the items and to provide a rough chronology. 'English Studies in Canada, 1945–1991: A Handlist' lists 370 items; the handlist format has been chosen instead of the essay in this case because of the number of items and because readers will be more familiar with the discipline's recent years. These bibliographies are not complete – I have not comprehensively surveyed nineteenth-century newspapers or unindexed periodicals, for example, nor have I listed archival holdings. They are intended to encourage and facilitate further work in this area, and in the field of Canadian intellectual history more generally.

The above is the pattern of organization of these chapters as they are arranged for the reader. As in any book, there is a second ordering principle at work, which is more or less invisible (or may be visible in the gaps and shifting foci of *Working in English*). This is the order in which the problems which motivate these chapters occurred to me, or turned into other ones. It may be worth detailing this process, as it tracks a particular theoretical trajectory, and one which I think others have shared.

The 'Institution' chapters were the first to be written, and they had a double impetus. Originally attempts to theorize my own learning and teaching experiences ('Close Reading, Closed Writing' is an example), they are also responses to developments of the day. The 're-reading' work of *Re-Reading English* and related publications offered a form of examination not available elsewhere, as these writers turned their attention to the nuts-and-bolts of English studies in the universities and the schools: 'A' and 'O' level reading lists, examination questions, and the assessment of grades, for example. This seemed to provide a useful counterbalance to the inquiry being undertaken in the United States – the long-running debate over 'professionalism' and the later discussion of academic 'commodification,' for example – for it seemed that neither category provided a sufficiently broad base for institutional analysis. (The 'professionalism' debate, in particular, operated with little reference to specific professional practices such as hiring and tenuring, and its 'high' centre of examination reduced students to a blur in the professional picture.) I did find myself, however, later tackling an offshoot of the 'professionalism' debate: the discussion over the definition of 'interpretive communities,' which is examined in 'Does Controversy Have a Rhetoric?' Social reproduction theory seemed to provide a way to think more broadly about social formation through the humanities disciplines – as well as the question of who is 'in' and who is 'out' – and this informs 'Charisma and Authority in Literary Study and Theory Study,' which considers the continuing thorny question of the politics (or political efficacy) of literary theory.

The three other 'Institution' chapters are motivated by some key disciplinary disputes. 'From Canon to Curriculum' is an intervention into the 'canon' debate, which I feel to be vitally important but at a frustratingly stalled stage. 'Women and English' and 'Reading Readers,' of course, draw heavily on my own experiences as a student and teacher, but were particularly occasioned by evidence of the slow change (and, in some respects, the erosion) of the status of women in higher education. (And in the case of 'Reading Readers,' the chapter was motivated by my concern over the ethics of the 'psychoanalytic' classroom.) I have attempted to bring some of the 'material' components of the engendered institution into a relationship with more 'impressionistic' aspects of critical and disciplinary paradigms; thus the double-jointed motion of these two chapters.

'Resistance and Reception' links this first sort of work to the historical and bibliographic studies which frame the 'Institution' section. I wished to work further on one lacuna in the institutional analysis; while it was 'Canadian' in the sense of operating from Canadian experience and a nationalist perspective, it took as a point of reference histories and theories developed specifically for an English or U.S. context, albeit trying to inflect these on the basis of local evidence and experience. However, a more fundamental address to this question appeared to be required. What was the history of English studies in this country? Are the materials available to gain this understanding? I began to collect citations and to read the available material, with the goal of ascertaining what could be done. The results are published in the bibliographic essay and handlist. A second question then occurred: were there sources of sufficient density that more focused, synchronic studies could be undertaken? The first two chapters of this book (which were the last to be written) are archivally based attempts to analyse specific disciplinary 'moments': they bring some further questions in their wake.

This is a study about English studies; its focus is narrow, and its address is especially to practitioners of English (teachers and students), most of whom will have already taken part in debate on these and similar topics, and will be able to provide their own context for the chapters to follow. But it may be worthwhile, at this point, drawing out some other considerations which are not developed here explicitly, and which arise from the last chapters written; this may help, as well, to locate this study within other emergent areas of work.

Chapter 1, on the appointment of Alexander, raises the question of the adequacy or applicability of theoretical and historical accounts developed in an English, European, and U.S. context (a concern to which I have alluded above). To take only one example: both traditional and revisionist accounts of the 'rise' of English studies in England generally assume a particular timetable based on the development of English studies at Oxbridge; but 'English' in Canada (and indeed in the United States) was in place almost fifty years before its transatlantic counterpart was well developed. If we are to generate analyses in which the 'rise' of English studies is seen not just as a series of disciplinary mutations, but as a response to social and political transformations, then the geographic shift must bring a pronounced alteration to the historical frame as well. What is needed, then, is a specific study of English and its institutions in the colonial situation; which leads to a second point. To date, there has been little analysis of the institution of English undertaken from a postcolonial perspective; and that work with few exceptions (Gauri Viswanathan's is one) tends to provide a simplified model in which 'English' is merely a transparent (and unproblematically transferred) container for the values of the colonizer culture. But the institutionalized study of 'English' is equally as complicated and contradictory as the 'English' literary texts produced in the same colonial circumstances, as illustrated by the continuingly chiasmic relationship of left and right, nationalism and anglicism, in the Alexander appointment controversy. The entire question of the 'institutionalization' of English may require revision as that first term loses its stability: for the boundary between the academy and the 'public' can be as fluid as it is rigid, permitting certain forms of osmosis of opinion and influence, while resolutely preventing others.

The question of the institutionalization of 'English' in this country is further complicated by the fact that, in the nineteenth century and indeed to this day, much of what we call 'English studies' took place outside the academy or in parallel academic forums (of which the

Margaret Eaton School was one). At present, our understanding of the role of 'English' (or the humanities) in the education of women and workers is incomplete, in large part because the institutions which they themselves generated or controlled have received little attention. As a result, there is a popular misconception that the discipline has a coherent past, which can be broadly conceived as 'liberal-humanist' or 'conservative' (terms which, rather bizarrely, have come to mean the same thing). If this book offers any one conclusion, it is that reductionist versions of the discipline's past stand in the way of new work for the future – work in, on, and through 'English.'

What does it mean to 'work in English'? While we often speak of 'working' in a foreign language, in the sense of having a sufficient linguistic understanding to carry on outside of a first tongue, that is not the connotation of 'working in English,' where comprehension of the language is taken for granted and linguistic or language-based issues are for the most part relegated to an unliterary elsewhere. Does 'working in English' identify a field or specialization (in the way that a person might announce, 'I'm in computers') or delineate a location of work or even an employer (one works in, and is nominally hired by, an English department)? At this point, the definition of 'work' seems to waver: are we assuming an activity in which many people have participated at one point or another (working in *English* involves writing, reading critically, and discussing works of literature), or is the restriction to a narrower band of people (*working* in English meaning occupation of a waged position)? (And are secretaries in the department, for example, working in English? For a great deal of the work *of* English could not happen without them.) As is often the case, students present an interesting definitional test. There is, I think, little doubt in the minds of English majors that what they are doing is work ('I can't go. I've got to get some work done'). And instructors also break down the year's assignments into a course 'workload' – three essays, a test, a seminar report, and so on. 'Work,' on this definition, is more specifically categorized as the written production of assessable material and excludes other tasks which students themselves might classify as 'work' (reading *Ulysses* for Monday). This perception may also operate the other way and often does: that instructors are 'paid for reading' seems to put them in an enviable position, and suggests that a broader band of activities is counted (not just articles and reviews, but committees and preparation and keeping up with one's specialty). (This bifurcation between student and professorial work occupies part of 'Close Reading, Closed Writing.') Graduate students are suspended between these two definitions of work, which accounts in large measure for the contradictions and difficulties of graduate life. Positioned as both students and professors (many are junior instructors; all are potentially professionals), yet lacking the formal signs of professorial admission, graduate students are switched back and forth between two definitions of 'work.' Difficulties in justifying the work of English (mounting a defence of the humanities, or conducting effective funding lobbies) may well come from the ambiguity or amorphousness of the definition of 'working in English.'

When people 'work in English' in whatever manner, what is actually produced? To say it is a written product – articles, even essays or book reports – is to account for only a minority of the hours spent by those who 'work in English.' (And feminist labour analysts can explain the pitfalls of defining work too narrowly in terms of 'productive' labour alone.) This book will explore, at various points, the suggestion that the 'work' of English studies is really socially reproductive, and in a specific way: whereas it may appear that the job of the professoriate is to reproduce itself (to train many students, of whom the most qualified will go on to graduate study), this socially reproductive role should be defined more broadly, with English located in an educational system which at all levels functions to produce continuing class and gender stratifications. In this case, the 'work' of English studies may be to normalize or naturalize procedures which take place, more violently and visibly, in other disciplines and in the primary and secondary systems. (I take up this question again in 'Charisma and Authority.') This book will also present a less dystopian picture by exploring a disciplinary countermotion: for while the above may (arguably) be the 'work' of English, often the work of English doesn't work, and people can use English ('work' it) for very different ends. A related approach would be the one taken by Evan Watkins in *Work Time: English Departments and the Circulation of Cultural Value* (a book which appeared after the 'institution' chapters were complete, but which I have subsequently found very useful). Watkins argues that what is generated but, more importantly, circulated by English departments is not a series of cultural *values* but the category of cultural *value* itself.

Watkins's redefinition of this work as circulation rather than production stems in part from his suspicion of the concept of 'institutionalization.' (Briefly put, he objects that the 'institutionalization' of critical tasks within the academy cannot be paralleled to the incorporation and then transformation of craft skills in the factory setting [13–14].) I have clustered, however, a number of critical questions under the heading of 'Institution' to make one simple point: that the 'work' we do in English partakes of a series of received practices which may be referred to the setting of the English department in the university and the education system, in turn funded and to an extent legislated (at least in Canada) by the state. Thus 'institution' has a double sense, referring to habits, conventions, and customs, but also to the bodies within which activities take place. A revived sense of the definitional possibilities is currently being provided by two Canadian projects. HOLIC/HILAC ('Towards a History of the Literary Institution in Canada / Vers une histoire de l'institution littéraire au Canada'), based at the University of Alberta, has also published several volumes of proceedings (Blodgett and Purdy; McLaren and Potvin, for example). This project overlaps to a degree with undertakings throughout Quebec, but centred at Université Laval, to provide a discursive and material analysis of Quebec literary institutions (see, for example, Lemire, and Robert). However, in the case of *Working in English*, the focus of examination is not literary or critical institutions (or institutionalization) but a pedagogic institution. There is, however, clearly an overlap in these systems; and exploring their intersections now seems to me a useful direction for further work.

But for the present purpose, there seemed to be an advantage in placing the pedagogic aspects of 'work in English' in sole view, at least temporarily. English (for reasons which I will later explore) is a discipline which has been, paradoxically but quite characteristically, both inward-turned and lacking in self-reflexivity. Those who work in English are much more likely to have a strong sense of critical history than of disciplinary history; but we need to turn onto our own day-to-day practices the close, between-the-lines, and sceptical reading skills customarily reserved for texts. That will allow us to 'work in English' in an additional way, by taking the discipline itself, past and present, as a subject of scrutiny. I hope *Working in English* will make a contribution to this endeavour.

Works Cited

Blodgett, E.D., and A.G. Purdy. *Prefaces and Literary Manifestoes / Préfaces et manifestes littéraires.* With S. Tötösy de Zepetnek. Edmonton: Research Institute for Comparative Literature, 1987.

– *Problems of Literary Reception / Problèmes de réception littéraire*. Edmonton: Research Institute for Comparative Literature, 1988.

Bourdieu, Pierre, and Jean-Claude Passeron. *Reproduction in Education, Society and Culture*. Trans. Richard Nice. London: Sage, 1977.

Graff, Gerald. *Professing Literature: An Institutional History*. Chicago: U Chicago P, 1987.

Grant, George. 'The University Curriculum.' *Technology and Empire: Perspectives on North America*. Toronto: House of Anansi, 1969. 111–33.

Lemire, Maurice. *La Vie littéraire au Québec*. Laval: Presses de l'Université Laval, 1991.

McLaren, I.S., and C. Potvin, eds. *Questions of Funding, Publishing and Distribution / Questions d'édition et de diffusion*. Edmonton: Research Institute for Comparative Literature, 1988.

Robert, Lucie. *L'Institution littéraire au Québec*. Vie des lettres québécoises. Laval: Presses de l'Université Laval, 1989.

Viswanathan, Gauri. 'Currying Favour: The Beginnings of English Literary Study in British India.' *Social Text* 19/20 (Fall 1988): 85–104.

– *Masks of Conquest: Literary Study and British Rule in India*. New York: Columbia UP, 1989.

Watkins, Evan. *Work Time: English Departments and the Circulation of Cultural Value*. Stanford, Calif.: Stanford UP, 1989.

Widdowson, Peter, ed. *Re-Reading English*. London: Methuen (New Accents), 1982.

Williams, Raymond. 'Base and Superstructure in Marxist Cultural Theory.' *Problems in Materialism and Culture*. London: Verso, 1980. 31–49.

PART I: HISTORY

2

The Appointment of W.J. Alexander

In 1889 the University of Toronto appointed William John Alexander as its first chair in English, bringing to five the number of such positions in the country. (Charles Moyse and William Tweedie were at McGill and Mount Allison respectively; Archibald MacMechan would take up the Munro Chair at Dalhousie, which Alexander had vacated; and James Cappon had been awarded the same position at Queen's only months before.) Thus – some thirty years before the Oxbridge rise of English studies – the discipline in English Canada was well established, taking on the contours familiar to us today in the development of a specialized literary-aesthetic study. The establishment of such chairs, in the narrow space of a decade, seems to present a particularly compacted and coherent point of disciplinary origin. But English studies in English Canada was not born in the 1880s, but made, in a series of local contestations, choices, and accommodations. For the 'choice' of W.J. Alexander was one of many other similar decisions taking place across North America, in a shift from the philological or rhetorical to the literary, from a general to specialist study.[1] But there was nothing preordained about this, or any other decision: what is fascinating, in retrospect, is not only the difficulty with which that selection was made (for, as today, what was to be chosen was both a candidate and a disciplinary direction), but the public nature of the controversy. The case of the appointment of Alexander provides a well-documented – because especially public – record of one such moment of disciplinary formation.

At first (hindsight) glance, W.J. Alexander seems to have been a 'natural' choice for this crucial position: a humane, learned, and open-minded man, well fitted by talent and accomplishment, whose later achievements validated Toronto's decision. Born in Hamilton, he matriculated with highest honours into the program at University College, where he studied English, French, and history. Before completing a Toronto degree, he won a Gilchrist Scholarship to University College, London, to study in the more specialized honours course in English language and literature. Alexander completed a first B.A. in English in 1875, adding an additional degree in physiology the next year (Alexander and MacGregor [4]). According to A.S.P. Woodhouse and R.S. Harris, at London he came under the influence of Henry Morley and the inspiration of J.W. Hales, two men with different approaches: 'Morley extended the range and detail of literary history; Hales advanced the close study of texts ...' (Woodhouse and Harris 12). After winning one of the university's three exhibitions, Alexander taught for two years at Prince of Wales College in Charlottetown (now the University of Prince Edward Island), before undertaking graduate work at the newly founded Johns Hopkins University. 'As no advanced instruction in English Literature proper was to be obtained in any University, either in America or Europe,' Alexander later wrote, 'I determined to continue in private my more direct study of the subject, and to avail myself of university assistance in gaining a wider knowledge of other literatures, especially those of the classical languages, – which I deemed the best preparation for the study of any literature, – and also in gaining a better acquaintance with scientific philology' (Alexander *Testimonials* 6). Alexander therefore studied Anglo-Saxon, classics, and philology, gaining a fellowship in Greek and publishing his thesis on participial paraphrases in Attic prose in the *American Journal of Philology* in the fall of 1883. After one further year of advanced study, in German language and literature at Heidelberg, he took up the Munro Chair of English Language and Literature at Dalhousie.

Alexander's own work was an innovative 'coupling of a close study of texts with historical method,' which could be attributed to the combined influence of his two London mentors (Woodhouse and Harris 12). He developed a detailed program for the new discipline, propounding a specifically literary study at all educational levels; as early as 1880, in an address to the Ontario Teachers' Association, he had deplored the fact that not enough prominence was given by educators to the reading of literature ('The First'). In his two inaugural addresses at Dalhousie and Toronto, he would develop a distinct programmatic for English literary studies, extending J.W. Hales's influential formulation of English as – to use Chris Baldick's term – the 'poor man's classics' (Baldick 62).[2] Whereas Hales advocated English study in 'schools whose pupils are not destined to proceed from them to a University, or to a life of studious leisure and opportunity' (Hales 310), Alexander made a similar case for university English studies in an emergent culture. While promoting a specifically literary study, he interpreted this term widely, to include not only belles-lettres but history and expository prose; literature, as defined in the first inaugural, is 'written thought' (4). Poaching a term from contemporary debates on modern language instruction, in the second inaugural he advocated a 'natural method' for the study of English, in which students would first gain a close knowledge of central texts, and then contextualize them with a study of literary and intellectual history, encountering criticism only in the higher years (25). Thus Alexander attempted to extend to the classroom the combination of textual and historical study which characterized his own work. Malcolm Wallace has noted that he initiated a 'revolutionary development' in the teaching of English from the chair he would hold until 1926:

He established the English and History course with supplementary work in either the classical or modern languages and also in philosophy. The writing of English essays became an important part of the course, though he had little faith in formal courses in composition ... He required from his students minute technical studies, some demonstrated capacity for literary analysis and for coherent presentation of ideas, but always behind the exercises of training was the assumption that art and literature constituted a unique approach to the understanding and enjoyment of life. (5)

Alexander's continuing activity as critic, anthologist, and educational adviser meant that his ideas spread far beyond the confines of the University of Toronto. How English developed in the universities in Canada, and in the public school system in Ontario, is in many respects dependent on the trajectory of Alexander's career. However, having acknowledged the particularities, one may also view Alexander as a representative, even a symptomatic, man. Similarly, the process of his selection was thoroughly embedded in the cultural and educational debates of the day.

The search for a chair of English may be placed squarely in a fifteen-year history of appointment controversies at Toronto, of which the cumulative effect would be the student strike of 1895. The Senate Reform Act of 1873 specified that alumni must be represented, and elected by fellow graduates. For the most part Canada Firsters, either by party membership or sympathy, these younger 'nativists' (as they were then called) had unsuccessfully opposed the nomination of English and history professor Daniel Wilson, who was a Scot, to the university's presidency, and would continue to battle for Canadian hiring and the admission of women. (The conservative Wilson would find himself confronting education minister George Ross, in a famously adversarial relationship, on the same issues.) This polarization was mirrored in the opinions of the larger public, who took a keen interest in the explosive university politics of the day.

As today, new appointments took on an especial, even inflated, significance because they were rare: while relatively fortunate by comparison to other Canadian colleges in being a state-funded institution, the University of Toronto was in a position of chronic penury, especially throughout the 1880s. The fact that appointments were made by the Ontario government, since Toronto was the provincial university, added a further, political dimension. Thus not only 'internal' criteria – staffing needs and scholarship – were at stake in any given case, but also such 'external' questions as the autonomy of the university. The classics appointment in 1880 is a case in point, and it continued the chain reaction initiated by the hotly debated promotion of Wilson to the presidency earlier that year. The government appointed Maurice Hutton of Oxford to the chair of comparative philosophy while Wilson was abroad, causing even the non-nativist *Canada Educational Monthly* to editorialize that the appointment had been handled in a particularly 'maladroit' fashion ('University Appointments' 425). While underfunding meant that little hiring took place throughout the first part of the 1880s, a posting in political economy and constitutional history in 1888 had similar results; although several Canadians applied, Premier Sir Oliver Mowat filled the position while travelling in England, selecting William James Ashley, again an Oxonian. (As before, there seems to have been little consultation with the university; and although Wilson would later be blamed for the choice, he in fact favoured a candidate from the United States [Hoff 60].) With the appointment a *fait accompli* (and Ashley, once arrived, was popular with the students), nationalist sentiment and discontent with government intervention spilled into the next event, the search for a chair of English. While Alexander's eventual appointment, as will be shown, temporarily appeased most modernists and traditionalists, nationalists and internationalists, a controversy over the replacement for the metaphysician George Paxton Young directly followed. In a history which Tory Hoff has traced, the applicants in a widely advertised search in the area of the mental sciences were eventually narrowed to James Hume, a follower of Young, and James Mark Baldwin from Princeton. Here both disciplinary and nationalist issues were again at work, with the traditional idealism of one candidate contraposed to the other's specialization in the new field of psychology. The government's compromise, offering the professorship to Baldwin and a more conditional appointment to Hume, left the underlying problems unresolved.

Soon two issues would cross in a way that ignited significant revolt. Daniel Wilson's death in 1892 created a lectureship in history, which was awarded to George Wrong, son-in-law of the prominent Liberal, and university chancellor, Edward Blake. This was converted to a professorship after only two years. While Wrong was liked by the students – and he would become an important scholar – his promotion was considered a prime case of academic pork-barrelling. Also in 1892, James Mavor was brought from Scotland to assume the chair in political philosophy opened with Ashley's move to Harvard. He soon made himself thoroughly unpopular through his high-handed treatment of students and his censorship of the activities of the Political Science Club, culminating in a refusal to allow the workers' advocate Alfred Jury and the socialist T. Phillips Thompson to talk on the labour question.[3] The campus newspaper, *Varsity*, connected the cases of Wrong and Mavor with a general criticism of the university administration; the resignation of the editors was demanded and refused; the popular classicist William Dale was forced to resign his professorship for defending the students; and the strike was on (see Bothwell; and Ferns and Ostry). This unprecedented student boycott scandalized Victorian Canada, and was resolved only with the establishment of a royal commission. While the students had anticipated an investigation into university practices, the commission instead passed a judgment on student misbehaviour. But the strike of 1895 may be viewed as the pinnacle of a series of political and pedagogic struggles.

The process that led to the appointment of W.J. Alexander was one such contestation. At work were both general concerns – 'nativism' in hiring, university-government relations, the growth of the new humanities and social science disciplines, the rise of specialization – and some particular disciplinary questions. The state of English studies was at stake, in debates over the goals and objects of the discipline, the uses of criticism, the development of a specifically 'literary' rather than more generally 'rhetorical' instruction, and the pedagogic merit of contemporary texts. Interests and interventions would be sometimes singular, and sometimes conflated.

Until the time of the appointment, English at the University of Toronto was really a question of the skills and inclinations of Sir Daniel Wilson, who had taken up the joint chair of English and history thirty-five years before. Although he had many literary interests – a poet himself, Wilson had authored studies of Chatterton and Shakespeare, and introduced reviews of Canadian literature to the pages of the Canadian Institute's journal – his approach to English was shaped by his training as an antiquarian and his later interest in linguistics. Further, Wilson's primary concern with ethnohistory and, after 1880, his duties as the university's president meant that English was increasingly sidelined as a study; and even the sessional lecturer, D.R. Keys, had to do double-duty in the modern languages, instructing first in Italian, then Gothic (Fee 206). English instruction was discontinuous and unspecialized, and students in the general course studied rhetoric and literary history with no firsthand classroom exposure to texts (see Harris 21–7). By 1883 the *Canada Educational Monthly* was calling for new appointments in the languages, noting that 'it is no credit to this province that provision for the teaching of Anglo-Saxon has been so long delayed' ('Modern Languages' 452–3), and decrying the university's reliance on sessionals. Editor Graeme Mercer Adam noted with favour the installation of Leslie Stephen at Cambridge, and recommended the following:

Now that English Literature is beginning to take its rightful place in the educational institutions of Canada, of what service would it not be to have in our University Chairs a few modern men of culture and enthusiasm in letters? This is nowadays an imperious want; and we could name three or four Canadian scholars whose services should be instantly had, if not as additional and permanently appointed Professors of English Literature in our Colleges, then as occasional lecturers and exponents of the subject. English Literature has of late years had the benefit of so much critical thought and expository skill, and so many modern minds have enriched the field of letters by their research and analytic talent, that the subject presents new worlds of thought and interest to the student which have scarcely hitherto been dreamed of. Hence the need of well-equipped lecturers and of modern, sympathetic expositors. ('English Literature Lectureships' 248)

The *Educational Journal* concurred, noting that a recent convention of provincial high school teachers had petitioned for revisions to the university's English curriculum ('Study of English' 168). Pressure for change was coming from within the university as well, as evidenced by an article in the *Varsity* the next year. The writer envisaged inclusion of the language departments in a 'thorough re-organization of the curriculum,' and offered the following rationale:

The study of languages should have a two-fold object. *First*, the acquirement of the faculty of scientific procedure, and *second*, the assimilation of the finest thoughts of different nations. Philology affords opportunity for the one and literature for the other. The former is entirely neglected, and of the latter, except perhaps English, we hear nothing. Even in English the lectures seem to be consecrated chiefly by age. ('Modern Language Department' 233)

Echoing a common complaint among the students about the dull surveys commonly assigned, the critic added that 'it is rank folly to give such works as Craik and Demogeot, fictitious importance as affording any knowledge of literature, which alone can be gained by intercourse with the authors themselves' (233). Attention focused more specifically on English in an editorial prediction at the end of the year: 'Evidently the day is not far distant when more importance will be attached to this subject, and when no man will be entitled to rank as a first-class English scholar who cannot read with ease any literary composition in his mother tongue from Beowulf to the Idyls [sic] of the King' (*Varsity*, 18 Dec. 1884: 91).

   Despite public agitation for a position, the university's financial situation made the chances of an appointment remote, until there occurred a fortuitous act of mismanagement on the part of the city. The University of Toronto rented College Park (now Queen's Park, site of the Ontario legislature) to the city, which appears to have defaulted on the lease. The university was anxious to break the arrangement, as the rent was too low; but a court settlement allowed the city to remain, with the stipulation that it endow two chairs at $ 3,000 per annum each. However, as Wilson noted at the time, the city wanted to dictate the chairs, 'with a view of extending the benefits of the National University to the wage-earning classes who have not hitherto shared in an equal degree with the rest of the community its educational advantages' (Diary, 14 Sept. 1888).[4] Wilson's own suggestion was for chairs in English language and literature and applied electricity, although other members of the university administration appear to have had different views. Wilson in part prevailed, and one month later, in his 1888 convocation address, he was able to look forward 'with sincere gratification to the supply of a long-felt want in the founding of a chair of English language and literature,' which he felt would benefit not only the university but Ontario public and high schools as well (*Address ... 1888* 8). He had no hesitancy in announcing that language study was the basis for literary work: 'we must aim at a system of study which in its honor work shall embrace the Moeso-Gothic of Uphilas, the Icelandic, the Anglo-Saxon of Alfred and the Saxon Chronicle, and the Middle English of writers from the Ormulum and Layamon's "Brut" to Langland and Gower; as well as the influence of the Scandinavian and the Romance languages on the English grammar and vocabulary' (8). Already attempting to pre-empt those who would press for a more 'literary' appointment, Wilson also began to actively recruit candidates. A somewhat cryptic diary entry states that he 'undertook to write to Dr. Hair [?] and sound him as to accepting the new English Chair with possible succession to the Presidency! It is a little like arranging for my funeral' (Diary, 12 Nov. 1889).[5] (In fact, Wilson had been told only a few weeks before that his cataract condition was irreversible and he would soon be blind.) He wrote to the eminent Cambridge philologist W.W. Skeat for recommendations, and this generated one application from an Anglo-Saxonist, Fred Hursley of Owen's College (later the University of Manchester), whose candidacy Wilson would support.[6] Later, in discussions with the minister of education, he would try to narrow the field to ensure a 'tolerable certainty of getting the best man that has offered,' although he would remain disappointed as a whole with the candidates (attributing their weakness to Canada-only advertising and to the brevity of the search), and would maintain that Ross was 'scared by the "native" cry fostered by a designing wouldbe professor' (Diary, 21 Jan. 1889).

For any candidate, the process of application was complex, as evidenced by a flurry of letters written throughout the fall and winter by Charles G.D. Roberts, possibly the 'designing wouldbe professor' of Wilson's account. An honours graduate in mental and moral philosophy and political economy from the University of New Brunswick (with awards for his achievements in classics), Roberts was now overworked and underpaid at King's College in Windsor, Nova Scotia. Roberts had applied for the chair of political science at Toronto earlier in the year but withdrew to compete, unsuccessfully, for the new position in English at Queen's which was awarded to Cappon. As Roberts had learned by the time of his next attempt, candidates needed to appeal not only to the university and to the public, but to the minister of education and even the provincial premier. In Roberts's case, it was necessary to be doubly skilful in generating support, since the possibility of a raise at King's meant that he could not apply directly but must have his name put forward. In October he declared to fellow-poet William Lighthall his intent to try for the job (Boone 89), although rumour had it that 'Dr. Wilson is "still hunting" in England to get hold of a man for the Toronto Chair, which is to be established at once':

My friends think that our chance is by appealing, through the press, to *Canadianism*, – agitating for the appt. of a *Canadian* (*my* name merely *understood*, not expressed), & so giving Ross an excuse for following his inclinations, – which are for a *Canadian*. (quoted in Boone 92)

'I feel that if I do succeed,' Roberts added, 'it will only be through energetic efforts on the part of my friends.'

These 'energetic efforts' were in large part coordinated by Roberts. He convinced the poet Charles Mair to 'put in a spoke for him' (quoted in Adams 59), and asked Archibald Lampman to write a letter 'to one of the big papers, Ottawa or Toronto' (quoted in Boone 97). George Taylor Denison, founder of Canada First and a leader of the Imperial Federation movement, appears to have written directly to Premier Sir Oliver Mowat (Boone 100), while parliamentary librarian and former *Mail* editor Martin J. Griffin was asked for his support, which may 'produce a marked effect' on Wilson (quoted in Boone 101). The writer Agnes Maule Machar ('Fidelis'), who would soon praise Roberts's program for English studies in an article in *Canada Educational Monthly*, also wrote an effusive letter to Ross, recommending Roberts for his international reputation, his patriotic spirit, and his ability to inspire students 'with a *genuine & enduring love* of literature for its own sake' (Machar to G.W. Ross., n.d., Archives of Ontario, Ministry of Education Papers [hereinafter ME], RG-2, Minister's Papers, D-7, box 4, 'English Department'). Roberts prevailed on others to organize on his behalf, including King's College colleague William Hammond and Andrew Stevenson, a former *Varsity* writer and one-time colleague at the *Week*. So he also wrote to fellow-poet William Wilfred Campbell, who was in turn encouraged to lobby Agnes Ethelwyn Wetherald, the novelist and *Globe* columnist:

In regard to Toronto, I think you could be *much* help. *Stevenson* thinks so, decidedly. He is one of my strongest supporters. Your reputation is high in Toronto, and your advocacy would carry weight. A letter from you, over your own name, to the Toronto *Globe and Mail* would influence popular feeling, – and you would be in no bad company in so doing, as there have been a number of earnest & important letters on my behalf. *Entre nous*, *Varsity* is *ardently* for me. A letter from you (I might whisper in your ear) to your brilliant admirer Miss Wetherald would probably secure to me her able support. In this contest all our engines must be marshalled, for the forces of the Philistines are all arrayed against us. (quoted in Boone 100)[7]

However, as Roberts was to note in another letter to Lighthall just before Christmas: *'Dom. Illusd.* is advancing a new candidate, Alexander of Dalhousie. He is a good man, by the way' (quoted in Boone 98).

Alexander's name was first mentioned, along with Roberts, in the December 1 issue of the *Dominion Illustrated News,* which notes that 'the call on the University of Toronto to give its new chair of English Language and Literature to a native Canadian is getting general throughout the country' (1 Dec. 1888: 343); one week later, the *Illustrated* had 'yet to see the paper that has not chimed in with the general feeling in favour of having born Canadians for the chairs of our universities and colleges in all cases where other things are equal,' and was self-congratulatory for having been the first to put forward the names of both Alexander and Roberts (8 Dec. 1888: 354–5). However, the editor of the paper, Jean Talon Lesperance (who was also the literary columnist under the name 'Talon'), was a self-declared friend of Alexander's, and in that same issue came out strongly in Alexander's favour, despite the fact that Roberts was one of the most frequent correspondents to the *Dominion Illustrated* and was mentioned multiply in almost every issue. Alexander's candidacy was launched with a lengthy précis of his Dalhousie inaugural address, under the title 'The Study of Literature'; the *Illustrated* would also give a favourable advance review to his Browning book (26 Jan. 1889: 55).[8] But, as Alexander details in his 'Reminiscences,' both he and his wife, Laura Morrow Alexander, had some reservations about the proposed position: her family was from Nova Scotia, and their Halifax years were happy. On the other hand, a number of Alexander's closest colleagues were leaving Dalhousie, and he was deeply attached to Toronto from his undergraduate days:

So I became an applicant. To increase my chances, it seemed desirable to publish some lectures on Browning which I had written two years before. I entered into negotiations with Ginn & Co of Boston. I set to work to gather & print testimonials ... All this added an element of excitement to life. (27)

This excitement was increased by a letter from George Munro, the founder of the Dalhousie chair, who offered an immediate advance of

$1,000 per year if Alexander would withdraw his candidacy. 'I hesitated about rejecting Mr. Munro's offer for an utter uncertainty at Toronto' (28), Alexander recalled; but receiving Munro's consent to postpone his decision until the new year, he and his wife spent Christmas in Toronto, ostensibly to examine more closely the position at Toronto but also to speak to men with influence:

> I remember scarcely anything about that visit except my calls in the interest of my candidacy on various persons – especially Sir Daniel Wilson, Sir Oliver Mowat ... and G.W. Ross. In those days the appointment was in the hands of the government. I got along excellently with Sir Daniel; he told me, before I left, that all his influence should be in my favour. Upon Mowat I conjecture that I made a favourable impression. With regard to Ross's support I was very doubtful. On the whole, I determined to take the risk and refuse Mr. Munro's offer. (29)

It is easy to see why the *Dominion Illustrated* considered Roberts and Alexander the two candidates 'chiefly in view' (1 Dec. 1888: 343). Each was a Canadian, holding a position in a well-respected eastern college. Roberts's reputation as a poet, man of letters, and anthologist would be balanced by Alexander's substantial academic career. Roberts had just completed a college edition of Shelley and was writing a manual for teachers of English (see Boone 90), but Alexander's *Introduction to the Poetry of Robert Browning* was scheduled to appear in February.[9] Each had a well-formulated and well-known program for the future of English studies: Roberts's 'The Teaching of English' had appeared in the *New York Outlook* and the *Christian Union*, while Alexander's Dalhousie inaugural had been published in Halifax and made more widely known by the *Illustrated*.[10] Roberts's correspondence makes it apparent that he had considerable literary and journalistic connections, but Alexander was also well placed in academic circles, the nephew of a former University College principal, and the brother-in-law of Bryon Edmund (later Sir Edmund) Walker, who, although new to Toronto, held influence as general manager of the Bank of Commerce and was involved in the affairs of the university. Alexander's *Testimonials* contained the strongest possible references, cannily chosen for their range, including enthusiastic recommendations from the three institutions where he had taught, as well as letters from the president of Johns Hopkins, from a theologian, a metaphysician, and the famous philologist Basil Gildersleeve.

This was, however, by no means a two-way race; at various points in the proceedings other candidates were favoured, and all had their proponents.[11] The incumbent for the position was D.R. Keys, an Anglo-Saxonist and the much overworked sessional lecturer who had undertaken, as he ruefully pointed out, the job 'for which three men are now thought necessary' (Keys *Testimonials* 6). Keys gained a B.A. in modern languages and English from Toronto, coming first in the modern languages, and augmented his education with study abroad: some months of English and Anglo-Saxon at 'Leipsic' (presumably Leipzig), a summer course in old and modern French at the University of Geneva, and another in Italian at Florence. (He had also studied law for one year at Columbia.) In his *Testimonials*, Keys outlined his practical qualifications in English:

Since 1884 I have had entire charge of this department, and, in addition to the lectures required by the curriculum, have prepared special courses on the development of the English drama, the representative English prose writers of the nineteenth century, the characteristics of Elizabethan prose, and the comparative grammar of the Teutonic languages ... To Anglo-Saxon I have devoted much private study, reading Beowulf, the Chronicles, and the works of Alfred and AElfric, besides working at Middle English, and making a special study of Icelandic, with a view to determining its influence upon our literature. (5)

Should readers of the *Testimonials* miss the similarity, Keys directly related his qualifications to the portrait of the ideal candidate drawn by Wilson in his fall address. Perhaps concerned that he seemed more suited to a position in the modern languages, Keys also noted that a recent chair in English at Oxford had been filled by 'a tutor from a German university': 'The example of Sainte-Beuve, followed by Scherer, Matthew Arnold, and Lowell, has demonstrated that a first class critic should be familiar with the spirit of modern literature, and must acquire that familiarity in the languages themselves' (4).

Tangential qualifications were abundant in this competition, as shown in the case of another candidate, John Seath. Seath earned a B.A. in natural sciences from Queen's College, Belfast, before moving to Canada to teach high school and receiving his Toronto B.A. *ad eundem* in 1864. Made an inspector of high schools in 1884, he was a member of the Central Committee of the Board of Education, which oversaw examinations and curriculum and acted in an advisory capacity to the minister. He was also at that point the president of the Modern Language Association of Ontario. Despite his Scots birth, Seath's involvement in local organizations caused him to be considered a local candidate (and he considered himself a nativist); Daniel Wilson would later suspect that 'the High School men were keen to have Mr. Seath appointed to the Chair of English, and the Minister would not have been unwilling to comply' (Diary, 15 Feb. 1889).

William Houston, the third local candidate, had trained as a teacher at the Toronto Normal School at its first session in 1864, received a B.A. from Toronto in 1872, and an M.A. two years later, joining the editorial staff of the *Globe* immediately upon his university graduation.[12] At the time of his application, he was the librarian of the Ontario legislature. Houston, like many alumni of the day, maintained close ties with the university: he was a radical member of the senate and fond of writing long and provocative letters to the newspapers on educational matters. He championed the entry of women to the university and then engaged, throughout 1885, in an intense debate with those who felt that the range of literary texts should be restricted for study by women. (In that same year, impatient with the slow pace of educational change, he developed a 'Proposed English Curriculum,' which was published in the *Varsity* and put before the senate.) Next, in an episode anticipating the events of 1895, he invited A.F. Jury to address the University College Historical and Political Science Association.[13] In response to attacks, Houston cheerfully accepted the charge of revolutionary sympathies, saying that 'the world will stand a good deal of agitation and revolution before all social and political wrongs are righted ...' and irreverently quipped that Jury had preached a better sermon than could be heard from many pulpits (*Presbyterian Review*, 6 May 1886: 141). Houston's beliefs (which occasioned the enmity of Daniel Wilson) may have been an impediment to his application; but they also inspired strong loyalties, and he had developed good connections through his journalistic work, including a close friendship with George Brown before the *Globe* editor's death. (After Houston had twice failed to get a political science appointment at Toronto, George Ross had suggested him for a lectureship in law, although Wilson turned this down [Wilson diary, 19 April 1888].)[14] According to *Saturday Night*, his testimonials for the position 'proved him possessed of a great many friends; nearly every public school inspector recommended him for the position' (2 Feb. 1889: [2]). Roberts may have shared Stevenson's support, for Daniel Wilson fingered him (along with alumnus and lecturer Charles Whetham) as Houston's principal supporter (Diary, 9 Feb. 1889).[15]

One other candidate completes the field, although he does not appear in the press coverage and his application arrived too late for consider-

ation (perhaps supporting Wilson's view that the position was insufficiently advertised). While Archibald MacMechan's letter to George Ross
is dated the day after Alexander's appointment was announced, his
application gives a sense of the qualifications and strategies of these
early members of the discipline (Letter, MacMechan to G.W. Ross, 31
Jan. 1889, ME, RG-2, Minister's Papers, D-7, box 16). MacMechan was
raised (like Alexander) in Hamilton and did his first degree at Toronto.
Entering modern languages in 1880, MacMechan audited a wide variety
of courses, and especially admired the charismatic George Paxton
Young (see MacMechan *Reminiscences*); he was also an amusing chroni-
cler of student literary life for the *Varsity* under the pen-name 'Bohemian.' After gaining first-class honours in English, French, and German
(and second-class in Italian and ethnology), MacMechan taught high
school for several years before entering, in 1886, the doctoral program at
Johns Hopkins. Here he specialized in German and English (largely
Anglo-Saxon and Middle English), and wrote a dissertation on 'The
Relation of Hans Sachs to the *Decameron.*'[16] In his *Testimonials* for the job
(MacMechan forwarded the *Testimonials* he had already assembled for
the Queen's position for which he, like Roberts, was an unsuccessful
candidate), he described the results of this training:

I call attention to the specific scientific and philological side of my training
because I regard it as the necessary step to a thorough understanding of the literature ... I believe that the time has come for an historical and comparative study
of English literature which shall lift it out of the field of mere aestheticism into the
dignity of a real science. The aesthetic study must be continued, the study of particular authors must be dwelt on with emphasis and with devotion for truly great
names, but, from the first, the student must be taught to compare, to examine, to
weigh ... The student must learn to look at every period and every poetic monu-
ment as far as possible from within, *i.e.*, from the vantage-ground of the period
producing it. He must then learn to compare periods. To instruct worthily from
this point of view, accurate scientific training is indispensable, and for this reason
I lay special stress on my Johns Hopkins course. (MacMechan *Testimonials* 4–5)

'At the same time,' MacMechan was careful to add, 'I regard philology
not as an end in itself, but as a means towards the wider comprehension
of literature ... Everything seems to point towards this as the method of
the future' (5).[17]

The interest of the press in the posting was immediate, and by 6
November the *Toronto World* (in columns interspersed with accounts of

the latest horrors of Jack the Ripper) took a strong stand which helped to set the tone for the debate which followed. The newspaper began by quoting another portion of Daniel Wilson's fall convocation address: 'On the appointment to every vacant chair depends the intellectual development of a whole generation in the department which it represents; and the cry that would narrow the choice to graduates of a single University, or the natives of a Province, is alike short-sighted and contemptible.' In reply to Wilson, the *World* retorted that only the second-rate Oxford and Cambridge man would be willing to come to the colonies for a small salary, and inquired: 'Has not the University turned out a man who could fill the chair as well as a second-rate graduate of an English university?' (1). Thus, in the opening volley of the exchange, the *World* raised the question of the hiring of Canadian nationals – which was to underpin the debates over this and other appointments – as well as the issue of the hiring of Toronto graduates, and began a series of *ad hominem* attacks against Wilson: if the university had produced no candidate worthy of the post, what did that say about Wilson as the English professor and, indeed, the university's president? The *World* pushed the point in doggerel verse:

> Who is the friend of all that race,
> That know just where's their proper place,
> And do not lack in proper grace?
>> Sir Daniel.

> Who, when a humble scribe aspired
> To reach a goal that he desired,
> Him with both feet then quickly fired?
>> Sir Daniel.

> Who looks askance with envious eye
> At all Canucks who dare apply
> For any 'sit' which seems too high?
>> Sir Daniel.

> And who, when questioned as to how
> He will avoid another row,
> Exclaims, 'Ye cannot enter now'?
>> Sir Daniel.

(*Toronto World*, 6 Nov. 1888: [1])

A few weeks later, the *World* was able to provide a fuller, and in some respects prescient, version of the situation, just before Alexander's application was filed:

It is certain now that the long talked of and much needed chair of English is to be established. The applicants from Canada are limited to four in number, Wm. Houston, D.R. Keys, John Seath and Charles Roberts. The claims of this latter gentleman are being pushed by his friends on the ground that he is a literary man, a poet of no mean order, and thoroughly in sympathy with Canada and Canadians. Mr. Houston claims to have the solid support of the teaching community throughout the Province. Mr. Seath claims the same support. Mr. Keys has his record as a lecturer for the past five years in the department of English at the University. These candidates are all pulling on different ropes, each of which is attached to a leg of the chair of English. The result will probably be foreseen. The chair will become disintegrated and the four gentlemen will fall back into their original positions of would-be professors. (1 Dec. 1888: 1)

For the *World*, far less important to get a literary man – or a poet or a pedant – than to hire on the merits of the candidates, although the *World*'s criteria for these were vague: 'by all means let us have a man of individuality' who would make an impact on students (1 Dec. 1888: 1).

While the question of a nativist hiring runs through all the debates, in many contributions the literary issues emerge more clearly. Over the next few months, some will advocate a literary person; others a critic, linguist, philologist, or Anglo-Saxonist; others, an all-round man of culture. And some are searching for the person who embodies all areas of expertise. So extensive is the debate that it in turn becomes a subject of commentary. 'Wanted, a Professor!' cries an anonymous observer in a comic yet incisive treatment of the contretemps, writing in the literary periodical the *Week* in the new year. The writer notes the accumulation of an almost impossible set of requirements, but where is such a paragon to be found, except in the person of Max Müller (and would Max Müller really want to move to Toronto?). Surely the first qualification should be proficiency in English, and not only etymological, philological, and rhetorical command:

In addition to this it is necessary that he should have a thorough and familiar acquaintance with English literature in all its stages, not merely as having made a study of its great works and being able to criticize its various periods and the characteristics of its leading representatives, but also as being really imbued with its spirit as the result of constant contact with its contents. (118)

Again in the *Week*, in an article entitled 'A Professor of the English Language and Literature,' 'A.M.' (possibly Archibald MacMurchy) suggests that the advanced state of Canadian scholarship may allow these competing interests to be mutually satisfied.[18] 'Graduates of fifteen or twenty years' standing, who have not watched the progress of Teutonic scholarship specially, would be astonished to learn what an entirely different aspect the study of English and the German languages, generally, has assumed' (843). Scholars in England have lagged behind in a discipline changing under the impact of philological and comparative study; so while the university has often, to the dissatisfaction of the public, 'sent for' Englishmen without conducting proper searches, an Englishman, 'A.M.' felt, might not be the most appropriate candidate in this case.

Students also entered the debate, with an exchange of editorial pieces and letters in the *Varsity*. The paper declared itself for Roberts by mid-November, noting 'the claims of nationality' and the opportunity to hire 'our foremost *littérateur*' (17 Nov. 1888: 20); and in the same issue, Andrew Stevenson reminded readers that the twofold nature of the subject matter demanded a versatile instructor: 'We have had enough of analysis and criticism by themselves; let us have as well some construction and criticism' (17 Nov. 1888: 20). When it was later rumoured that Alexander would be offered the job, 'Sigma' (quite possibly Stevenson under another name) deplored the prospect of a classicist in the position, in a letter which echoes the polemic and phrasing of Roberts's essay on 'The Teaching of English': 'Men saturated with the principles of the synthetic classical languages ... keep on trying to put the new wine of living English into the old bottles of the classical tongues.' Again 'Sigma' stresses the need for a professor who combines a 'scientific knowledge' of English, literary ability, and the power to inspire students (27 Jan. 1889: 77). In raising the question of the relationship of English study to literary production, the student correspondence glosses what may appear a missing component of the debate: the question of the teaching of Canadian literature. Even the 'nativists' in the controversy assume that Canadian literature is insufficiently evolved to be taught at the university; one purpose of English study, therefore, is to train those who will produce it. Thus the 'nativists' and boosters of Canadian literature emphasize literary talent and pedagogic 'inspiration' as crucial qualifications.[19]

The campus correspondence appears sketchy, but that is because the *Daily Mail* provided the primary forum for alumni opinion, with a sustained exchange of letters and editorials appearing from December through February.[20] (The public interest in academic literary culture is indicated by the fact that this was only one of several such issues being covered. The publication of Wilson's address to the Modern Language Association of Ontario also set off a flurry of letters; in addition, the *Mail* was reviewing the other papers presented, and the MLAO's resolutions for the reformation of modern language teaching.) The interchange relating to the proposed appointment begins with 'Onlooker,' who has written several recent letters to the editor on the general topic of scholarly standards, and now turns to the question of 'The New Professorship':

If no Canadian is competent to fill the professorship of English literature in Toronto University, it must be either because he lacks energy and ability to master the subject or because he has never been taught it. If he has not been taught it, the fault would seem to lie at the door of the university professoriate who were brought to Ontario years ago ... (27 Dec. 1888: 3)

Here 'Onlooker' has doubled the charge made by the editors of the *World*; if no home-grown candidates are worthy, this is not only proof of Wilson's inadequacy as professor and president, but a more general indication of the past inefficacy of hirings from abroad. To this 'An Ontario Schoolmaster' replies that the root of the problem may be inadequate schooling at the lower levels. An Englishman educated at a public school, 'Schoolmaster' wistfully notes, would have had the advantage of a splendid library and 'class-reading [which] covered the greater part of Milton, several plays of Shakespeare, much of Spencer [*sic*], and such collections as the Golden Treasury in poetry, with prose masterpieces as well' (29 Dec. 1888: 4). 'How can we compete,' the writer laments, 'as long as we confine ourselves to the reading of a hackneyed poem of Coleridge's one year, and a dull piece of Cowper the next?' (4). But responsibility for this situation, 'Onlooker' writes back, should also be placed at Daniel Wilson's door, for 'English literature would have been taught years ago in both High School and Public schools if Toronto University had been fully alive to her responsibilities' (2 Jan. 1889: 6).

The relationship of curricular reform to the proposed hiring is made clearer by a new correspondent, 'Caveant.' The chair is a difficult one to fill because the study of English has been 'revolutionized':

The ideal – and at once the impossible – professor of English is one who is master of all the tributary languages. But it is not too much to demand that he should be a linguist as well as a *littérateur*. It is not visionary to hold that a Professor of English suitable for the Provincial University should be deeply read in the Latin and Greek classics, that he should be familiar with the great languages of modern culture, that he should have studied the earlier stages of English itself, and that he should be familiar with the cognate Teutonic languages, especially the Germanic and Scandinavian. Add to this good literary taste and a power to impart knowledge, and you have an ideal which is high, it is true, but not impossible. If the professor have a pure and elegant diction, free from American twang or Scottish burr, Irish brogue, or English lisp, so much the better. (15 Jan. 1889: 5)

This may well be the letter mocked by the *Week*, and a *Mail* respondent signed 'Literature' also wonders whether this is reasonable. ('All that would be a good outfit for a comparative philologist; but this is to be a Chair of English Literature ...') For 'Literature,' a sound classical training is the best foundation. The public interest in the debate is also noted: 'there has been no appointment made for a long time that interests so many university men and the public; and if an incompetent man or a literary character be appointed, they will want to know the reason why' (19 Jan. 1889: 9).

The letter from 'Literature' is a good example of the partisanship underlying this keen interest, with its coded detractions of Seath ('Literature' values classics over composition-teaching) and Roberts (the 'literary character'). The debate became increasingly heated after the announcement of the appointment. 'Baltimore' (who Wilson figured to be Houston supporter Charles Whetham) considers the candidacy of Alexander part of a scheme to control the presidency of the university and (alluding, in all probability, to the position of Alexander's brother-in-law) states that a certain bank, with ties to the minister of education, stands behind the plot. The announcement of the appointment two days later only increased the letters. For 'Torontoniensis' (identified by Wilson as Andrew Stevenson) clearly 'no man of Canadian education, and especially no graduate of Toronto, need apply for vacant chairs' (9 Feb. 1889: 7), and this elicits defences from Daniel Wilson and George Paxton Young, with Wilson comparing their record favourably on this score to McGill, Queen's, and Trinity. Next 'Torontonensis' (with an amended spelling) reappears along with 'Torontonensis No. 2' to refute Wilson's statistics; on the same day, Wilson apologizes for maligning Queen's, although he cannot resist mentioning that *their* newly appointed English chair is non-Canadian. 'Studiosus Literarum' deplores Wilson's lack of faith in Toronto graduates, but admits that confidence may not be warranted (his friend, William Houston, is excepted) since Wilson himself was responsible for their education. 'Studiosus' reveals that the university graduates who grade matriculation exams often have to be coached in the correct answers. 'A.M.' adds that Wilson is entirely unqualified to make appointments in the first place, since he lacks a degree and is fifteen to twenty years behind in each of the disciplines he practises.

Wilson's diary has little detail about the appointment – he appears to have been more occupied during the late fall and early winter by the minister's proposed, and for Wilson impracticable, changes to the University Act – but his February entries show him meeting these challenges with gusto. 'When the ostrich has got his head in the sand, he is full persuaded that nobody can see him,' wrote Wilson, referring to the anonymous letters of 'Baltimore' and 'Torontoniensis.' 'Yet I may be unjust, and so had better dismiss the paltry slanderer with his quietus, and so leave him under a cloud' (Diary, 9 Feb. 1889). Days later, when 'Torontonensis' (now with a different spelling) reappears with 'Torontonensis 2,' Wilson is scathing: 'Here in to-day's *Mail* comes Torontonensis with an eye (i) knocked out, and with him his alter ego. A worthy pair! It is a nuisance to have to waste time over such contemptible slanderers.' The letter from 'Studiosus Literarius' [*sic*] had, Wilson felt, inadvertently aired some of the 'secrets of the education office examination conclave' headed by Seath, who Wilson considered a pedant: 'The grand device of a grammar that has no practical bearing on the daily use of language either in speaking or writing would have flourished in luxuriant bloom had they succeeded. No wonder they attack me bitterly' (15 Feb. 1889).Wilson shared the opinion of letter-writer 'Eighty-Three,' who says that the grumblers are simply friends of the defeated candidates and that no one could reasonably object to Alexander, who is 'Canadian, with Canadian education, overlaid with Old World culture' (*Mail*, 18 Feb. 1889: 5).

The debate in the *Daily Mail* is brought back to literary terrain with a letter from 'Outsider.' Setting up his argument neatly with quotes from Matthew Arnold, he charges that most of the letter writers 'betray an almost entire absence of any real standard of criticism.' For this writer, the professor of English literature

must be neither a mere philologist nor aesthetic sentimentalist, nor a pedagogue whose highest idea of style is that of a pedantic accuracy: he must be, above all

things, a man of wide culture, who brings to the study of literature a comprehensive grasp of the principles of literary criticism. A knowledge of those principles, it is safe to say, has not yet found its way into Canada. (20 Feb. 1889: 5)

The literary focus is not maintained for long, and in the same issue 'Torontonensis' and 'E.T.H.' offer further evidence of Wilson's adversion to
Toronto graduates. As the debate moves to a crescendo, 'Torontonensis'
gives more details of Wilson's injustice in past appointments; 'Collegensis' and the publisher John E. Bryant suggest that 'Torontonensis' has little support among members of the university; 'M.A.' hopefully suggests
that the debate may lead to a general change of policy and 'the dawn of
the new day' (22 Feb. 1889: 5); and the *Mail* announces its refusal to publish anything else on the topic.

It must have come as a relief to Daniel Wilson to announce the decision at the end of January:

Announcement to-day of the appointment of W.J. Alexander B.A., Ph.D., to the
Chair of English Language and Literature. Fred Hursley, a good Anglo-Saxon
scholar, strongly recommended by Skeat of Cambridge, and I believe a really
able man, but the Minister had not the moral courage to entertain the thought of
an Englishman; so I believe we have got the best man available and one that I
have reason to hope will not discredit us. We have, moreover, escaped the
chances of a wretched creature, who employed all the unscrupulous tactics of a
skilled ward politician in the detraction of his opponents – especially for Keys –
and in enlisting a phalanx of political allies on his behalf. So the agony is over
and I am contented. (Diary, 30 Jan. 1889)

It is ironic that while this crisis was quieted, another was brewing.
George Paxton Young's defence of Wilson was one of the last public gestures of his life: eleven days after his letter appeared, he suffered a
stroke, and four days later was dead. The new posting in mental sciences would create a controversy that more than equalled that over the
chair of English literature.

The appointment of W.J. Alexander was greeted in other quarters
with more enthusiasm than Wilson could muster. The *Toronto World*
announced itself well pleased, although it may have made this decision
primarily on nationalist grounds as indicated by its headlined
announcement of 'The New Chair of English: Awarded to Dr. W.J. Alexander of Dalhousie College N.S. – an Old Hamilton Boy' (30 Jan. 1889:
1). For the *Empire*, the presence of a Canadian in the chair would 'induce

a closer scrutiny of the qualifications of our own men another time' (31 Jan. 1889: 4). On the other hand, the *Canada Educational Monthly*, while equally pleased by the appointment, used the announcement as an opportunity to take a parting shot at the nativists: 'The field is wide, the common heritage magnificent, the culture and refinement of the English gentleman is not confined to any special part of our Great Empire. Canada is simply Britain in the West. No one owing allegiance to our Gracious Queen can possibly be a "Foreigner" in Canadian academic halls' ('Chair of English Literature' 71). The *Week* viewed the appointment of Alexander as the best possible solution and one that would satisfy all sides: the Canada-Firsters would be pleased by Alexander's background, but his higher training abroad would also reassure those who were 'doubtful whether the opportunities afforded by Canadian institutions and environments can be relied upon to impart the high degree of culture and erudition which should be deemed essential to the occupant of so important a chair ...' (8 Feb. 1889: 147). The pedagogically inclined *Educational Journal* was pleased by the selection of one whom they considered, above all, a teacher ('Chair of English' 317). While the *Varsity* forthrightly admitted that their choice was Roberts, they congratulated Alexander and pronounced him 'the best man available' ('The New Professor' 84). The students continued to press for curricular reform and offered their own version of an English course which would feature contemporary authors and be synthetic rather than strictly chronological:

... while we are thus gradually taking up the old authors, let us continue our study of the new, thus making the course resemble an arithmetical progression, commencing at Junior Matriculation from the base of Modern Literature and gradually increasing, till the fourth year becomes a synopsis of the sum total of English Literature. Thus the interest would be made continuous and unbroken, and the subject would be presented in a form most adapted for a large and comprehensive view. ('New English Course' 84)

The controversy was thus abandoned – or, more accurately, subsumed into another – as within weeks there were letters in the press and denunciations in the provincial legislature that Wilson was attempting to strike a secret deal for a successor in metaphysics.

Charles G.D. Roberts applied for the job left vacant by Alexander at Dalhousie, but then withdrew from the competition; he failed to win a similar post at Yale and would soon leave the academy, and indeed Canada, altogether, for some decades of a roving writerly life in the

United States and Europe. D.R. Keys continued as one of the two instructors in the English Department until the appointment of Malcolm Wallace added a third, and was finally promoted to associate professor after almost twenty years as a lecturer (Harris 31–2). The support John Seath received was evident in his election to the university's senate in the next balloting; he continued his career as a school inspector and text editor, becoming the province's superintendent of education in 1906 and, briefly, president of the Ontario Educational Association. William Houston continued in a distinguished career as both an educator and a *Globe* journalist; he would remain a university senator for thirty-five years and an enthusiastic supporter of groups and causes from the Dickens Fellowship to the Suffrage Association. Archibald MacMechan was awarded the Munro Chair at Dalhousie left vacant by Alexander.

Once appointed, Alexander had his work cut out for him. As A.S.P. Woodhouse wrote:

... he set himself almost single-handed to shape and teach the whole range of necessary courses in literature, as well as to give guidance to the study of English in the schools. He had to rescue the teaching of literature from the dead hand of linguistic analysis, to free it from the mere cramming of irrelevant information and unattached literary history, and to show how the subject could be presented as a thing of ideas, of beauty and of power. (Woodhouse 'Critic' 9)

In retrospect, Alexander fulfilled as closely as was possible the warring mandates of the many interested participants and observers in the controversy over his appointment.[21] Maintaining the traditional emphasis on gentlemanly learning, he also supported the newly emergent research ideal imported into North America *via* Johns Hopkins.[22] While rigorously trained as a classicist, he was also the first Canadian professor of English to be educated specifically in the subject; a philologist and Anglo-Saxonist, he wrote and lectured on recent writers and included them in anthologies. While he did not teach Canadian literature (a lack for which he was upbraided by J.D. Logan in *Aesthetic Criticism*), he was an enthusiastic supporter of its growth and a founder of the Canadian Society of Authors. In many respects a traditionalist, he expanded the 'canon' of the day with anthologies ranging from ballads to free verse, and supported women in English as both students and instructors. Thus Alexander's appointment was 'crucial' in several senses: he gave important direction to literary studies at Toronto and in Canada, but his appointment also marks a paradigmatic crux or crossroads.

It may be worth remembering, should the appointment of Alexander seem too weighted with disciplinary inevitabilities, what was lost in the transitions and exchanges of the controversy. For the 'public' debate was composed of the contributions of overlapping circles of male alumni and administrators in turn drawn from the small minority of sons of the business and land-owning classes who attended university in that day.[23] And the degree to which the establishment of a chair in English did, or did not, serve working-class education is an issue that drives disciplinary debate to this day.

Notes

1   Competitions for jobs at Queen's, Toronto, and Dalhousie occurred within the space of a few months. The surveys of English departments published first in the *Dial*, and then in a collection edited by William Morton Payne, give a sense of both local divergences and a general disciplinary shift in the United States for the same period.

2   Alexander repeated his Dalhousie inaugural at Toronto, with some expansions. However, it would be incorrect to assume from this that Alexander's ideas remained unmodified; the replication of talks is probably attributable to the fact that the Alexanders' infant daughter, Emily, died almost immediately after they arrived for the start of term. While Alexander did adhere to a core set of principles, a series of introductions and guides for study written over the years show him grappling with the problems and practicalities of English literature teaching throughout the educational system.

3   The *Varsity*, throughout the 1880s, complained about the university's restrictions on student speech and assembly; both Daniel Wilson and James Mavor (who had replaced the liberal Ashley) were increasingly interventionist. In 1890, for example, Wilson had prevented the Boston suffragist Kate Taunsett Wood from addressing the women undergraduates (Wilson diary, 22 Oct. 1890); while Mavor forced the students in the Political Science Club to submit their meeting programs for approval. In 1892 several students who criticized the administration were expelled.

4   Minister of Education Ross addressed the city's concerns in an interview with *Saturday Night*: 'The School of Science will be thoroughly a workingman's institution ... Mayor Clarke is satisfied that if the $6,000 goes to the University the government will in this way provide the education he is so anxious to see the masses obtain' (3 Nov. 1888: 1). The School of Science, of course, did not become a 'workingman's institution'; but this allusion to

streaming in higher education marks the perceived class specificities of arts and practical education.

5 Wilson's original diary has been destroyed, and the only extant version is a transcription by his biographer, H.H. Langton. Education Minister Ross may also have attempted to recruit candidates: an equally cryptic letter implies that Ross had instructed Wilson to offer the chair to a Dr Schurman [?] who might also be a fitting successor to the presidency (Wilson to Ross, 13 Nov. 1888, Archives of Ontario, Ministry of Education Papers [hereinafter ME], RG-2, Minister's Papers, D-7, box 14, Wilson file).

6 Little detail is available for this candidate. Only MacMechan's (late) application is contained in the Ministry of Education records; files for other candidates were presumably forwarded to the university, where they would have been destroyed in the University College fire of 1890.

7 Laurel Boone, editor of the Roberts letters, identifies 'Stevenson' as Orlando John Stevenson, later to be a professor of English at the Ontario Agricultural College (Guelph), with whom Roberts developed a friendship. As O.J. Stevenson had not yet entered university, it seems the more likely reference would be Andrew Stevenson, who was actively involved in the public debates about the appointment. A famous university essayist and journalist (who fought for the admission of women), Stevenson joined, for a time, the staff of the *Week*, and then became a school teacher. In later years, an instructor at the Stratford Collegiate Institute, he wrote *The Teacher as a Missionary of Peace*, which may be the first Canadian tract advocating anti-racist education.

8 The *Dominion Illustrated* promised excerpts from Roberts's 'The Teaching of English' (19 Jan. 1889: 35), but these did not appear.

9 Roberts's *Adonais and Alastor* appeared in 1902; the manual appears never to have been completed.

10 Pomeroy says that 'The Teaching of English' appeared in a journal which she identifies, variously, as the *New York Outlook* and the *New Outlook* (100).

11 And rumours abounded. At one point, for example, it was suggested that expatriate writer Grant Allen be nominated for the chair, as reported in the *Illustrated* (29 Dec. 1888: 411).

12 Biographical information for Seath and Houston is drawn principally from the graduate record clipping files in the University of Toronto Archives, A-73–0026.

13 'A College Is Known by Its Teachers' headlined the *Dominion Churchman*, excoriating the university for inviting 'a well-known infidel, who is, as they usually are, a Communist, and a foe generally to social order' (quoted in *Presbyterian Review*, cited below); while the more moderate *Presbyterian Review* felt it was unjust to blame the university when the fault lay with the

club, 'led by a graduate whose sympathy with agitation and revolutionary measures sometimes overmasters his judgements' (*Presbyterian Review* 15 April 1886: 116).

14 This may have been evidence of the influence of his supporters rather than personal regard by Ross. *Saturday Night*, in covering the appointment controversy, stated that Houston was 'no great favorite with the Minister of Education' (2 Feb. 1889: [1]).

15 Stevenson's *Varsity* writings show him supporting the hiring of a Canadian *littérateur*; but after the appointment was made, he shifted his attention to the status of Toronto graduates.

16 MacMechan's letter of application gives a catalogue of specialized study in English in the '80s. He listed the relevant courses taken in his three years at Johns Hopkins: in first year 'Beowulf, Anglo-Saxon Poetry, Anglo-Saxon Prose, Historical English Grammar, Early English, Anglo-Saxon Dialects, Early Scottish Literature'; in second year, 'Middle English Grammar, Piers the Plowman, Anglo-Saxon Poetry, Chaucer and Shakespeare'; with a final year of 'English Philology, Anglo-Saxon Poetry' (MacMechan to G.W. Ross, 31 Jan. 1889, ME, RG-2, Minister's Papers, D-7, box 16).

17 Robin Harris says that Arthur [*sic*] Stevenson was also a candidate for the position (30), although I have found no other evidence for this.

18 The principal of the Toronto Grammar School, who followed Mercer Adam as editor of the *Canada Educational Journal*, MacMurchy would also write one of the first handbooks of Canadian literature.

19 This view was shared by many of the poets themselves (Roberts being an exception). Writing in 1891, for example, Archibald Lampman was of the opinion that 'it will probably be a full generation or two before we can present a body of work of sufficient excellence as measured by the severest standards, and sufficiently marked with local colour, to enable us to call it a Canadian literature' (Lampman 27).

20 A complete listing of the *Mail* letters is given under 'Works Cited' below. Occasional items also appeared in the other Toronto papers (which generally took a moderate nationalist stance on the question). Further, correspondence extended across the papers. For example, a *Varsity* letter criticizes the *Educational Journal*, in turn editorializing on a *Globe* letter; the *Educational Journal* responds to a piece in the *Mail*; the *Week* satirizes the *Mail* writers, and so on.

21 Laura Morrow Alexander also made her mark on Toronto, founding the Social Service Department of Toronto General Hospital in addition to raising eight children.

22 McKillop notes that Alexander's support was crucial in gaining assent, in 1897, for the development of the doctorate at Toronto (McKillop 93).

23 Gaffield et al. estimate that, as late as 1901, only one-half of 1 per cent of all
Canadians aged between fifteen and twenty-four attended university (11).
While entrance was not limited to the elite (sons of farmers were numerous
among entrants), the university functioned to *produce* the elite which dictated
'public' life.

Works Cited

Note: When a work has been put on fiche by the Canadian Institute for Historical Microreproductions, the citation is followed by the CIHM number.

'A.M.' [Archibald MacMurchy?]. 'A Professor of the English Language and
Literature.' *The Week* 5, 53 (29 Nov. 1888): 843–4.
Adams, John Coldwell. *Sir Charles God Damn: The Life of Sir Charles G.D. Roberts*.
Toronto: U Toronto P, 1986.
Alexander, W.J. 'Reminiscences [written at time of his wife's death].' Alexander
Papers, box 1, file 5. Thomas Fisher Rare Book Library, University of Toronto.
– *The Study of Literature: Inaugural Address Delivered at the Convocation of
Dalhousie University, Halifax, N.S., Oct. 28th, 1884*. Halifax: Office of the Nova
Scotia Printing Co., 1884. [CIHM 08835]
– *The Study of Literature: Inaugural Lecture Delivered in the Convocation Hall, Octo-
ber 12th, 1889*. Toronto: Rowsell and Hutchison, 1889. Rpt. *Canada Educational
Monthly and 'School Magazine'* 11, 11 (Nov. 1889): 337–43. Rpt. *The Week* 6, 52
(1889): 823–4; 7, 1 (1889): 9–10. Rpt. as 'A Lecture on Literature.' *Select Poems
1908*. Toronto: Copp, 1907. vii–xxiv. [CIHM 01350]
– and J.G. MacGregor. 'Letter Concerning the Gilchrist Educational Fund:
Together with an Appendix Containing the Names of Gilchrist Scholars from
Canada.' N.p.: n.p., 1895. [CIHM 29095]
Baldick, Chris. *The Social Mission of English Criticism, 1848–1932*. Oxford: Claren-
don P, 1983.
Boone, Laurel, ed. *The Collected Letters of Charles G.D. Roberts*. Fredericton, N.B.:
Goose Lane, 1989.
Bothwell, Robert. *Laying the Foundation: A Century of History at University of
Toronto*. Toronto: Department of History, University of Toronto, 1991.
'The Chair of English.' *Educational Journal* 2, 20 (1 March 1889): 317.
'The Chair of English Literature.' [Editorial.] *Canada Educational Monthly and
'School Magazine'* 11, 2 (Feb. 1889): 71.
'The Claims of Nationality.' *Varsity* (17 Nov. 1888): 20.
'English Literature Lectureships.' [Editorial.] *Canada Educational Monthly and
'School Magazine'* 5, 5–6 (May–June 1883): 248.

Fee, Margery. 'English-Canadian Criticism, 1890–1950: Defining and Establishing a National Literature.' Diss. U of Toronto 1981.

Ferns, Henry, and Bernard Ostry. *The Age of Mackenzie King*. Toronto: James Lorimer, 1976.

'Fidelis' [Agnes Maule Machar]. 'The True Principles of Teaching English.' *Canada Educational Monthly and 'School Magazine'* 11, 2 (Feb. 1889): 46–8.

'The First of the Three R's.' [Editorial note.] *Canada Educational Monthly and 'School Magazine'* 11, 9 (Sept. 1889): 423–4.

Gaffield, Chad, Lynne Marks, and Susan Lashin. 'Student Populations and Graduate Careers: Queen's University, 1895–1900.' *Canadian Society: Essays in the Social History of Higher Education*. Ed. Paul Axelrod and John G. Reid. Kingston and Montreal: McGill-Queen's UP, 1989. 3–25.

Hales, J.W. 'The Teaching of English.' *Essays on a Liberal Education*. Ed. F.W. Farmer. London: Macmillan, 1867. 293–312.

Harris, Robin S. *English Studies at Toronto*. Toronto: U Toronto P, 1988.

Hoff, Tory. 'The Controversial Appointment of James Mark Baldwin to the University of Toronto in 1889.' Thesis, Carleton U, 1980.

Houston, William. 'Proposed English Curriculum.' *Varsity* (25 Oct. 1885): 5–6; (31 Oct. 1885): 17–18.

Lampman, Archibald. 'Two Canadian Poets: A Lecture, 1891.' *Masks of Poetry: Canadian Critics on Canadian Verse*. Ed. A.J.M. Smith. Toronto: McClelland and Stewart, 1962. 26–44.

McKillop, A.B. 'The Research Ideal and the University of Toronto.' *Contours of Canadian Thought*. Toronto: U Toronto P, 1987. 78–95.

MacMechan, Archibald. *Reminiscences of Toronto University*. [I. The Convocation Hall. II. Professor George Paxton Young.] [Halifax]: n.p., n.d. Dalhousie University Archives.

'The Modern Language Department.' *Varsity* (8 March 1884): 233.

'Modern Languages at University College, Toronto.' [Editorial.] *Canada Educational Monthly and 'School Magazine'* 5, 11 (Nov. 1883): 452–3.

'The New English Course.' *Varsity* (2 Feb. 1889): 84.

'The New Professor.' *Varsity* (2 Feb. 1889): 84.

Payne, William Morton, ed. *English in American Universities, by Professors in the English Departments of Twenty Representative Institutions*. Boston: D.C. Heath and Co., 1895.

Pomeroy, E.M. *Sir Charles G.D. Roberts: A Biography*. Toronto: Ryerson, 1943.

Roberts, Charles G.D. 'The Teaching of English.' *Christian Union* 37, 16 (1888): 488–9.

Stevenson, Andrew. *The Teacher as a Missionary of Peace*. N.p.: n.p., 1904.

'The Study of English at the Provincial University.' *Educational Journal* 2, 11 (15 Oct. 1888): 168.

'The Study of Literature.' *Dominion Illustrated* 1, 23 (8 Dec. 1888): 353–4.

Testimonials in Favour of William John Alexander, B.A. (Lond.), Ph.D. (J.H.U), Munro Professor of English Language and Literature in Dalhousie College and University, Halifax, N.S., and Formerly Fellow of the Johns Hopkins University, Candidate for the Professorship of English in the University of Toronto. Halifax: Nova Scotia Printing Co., 1888. [CIHM 24672]

Testimonials of Archibald MacMechan, B.A. (Toronto). Submitted with an Application for the Chair of English at Queen's College, Kingston. N.p.: n.p., [1888]. [CIHM 16318]

Testimonials of David Reid Keys, B.A. (Toronto), Candidate for the Chair in English Literature, University of Toronto. Toronto: n.p., 1889. [CIHM 01485]

Toronto Daily Mail [letters on the Toronto appointment]: 'Onlooker' 18 Dec. 1888: 3; 'Onlooker' 26 Dec. 1888: 3; 'Onlooker' 27 Dec. 1888: 3; 'An Ontario Schoolmaster' 28 Dec. 1888: 4; 'Onlooker' 29 Dec. 1888: 9; 'Onlooker' 31 Dec. 1888: 3; 'Onlooker' 2 Jan. 1889: 6; 'Caveant' 15 Jan. 1889: 5; 'Literature' 19 Jan. 1889: 9; 'Baltimore' 28 Jan. 1889: 5; 'Torontoniensis' [*sic*] 9 Feb. 1889: 7; Daniel Wilson 11 Feb. 1889: 5; George Paxton Young 11 Feb. 1889: 5; 'Torontonensis No. 2' 14 Feb. 1889: 3; 'Torontonensis' 14 Feb. 1889: 3; Daniel Wilson 14 Feb. 1889: 3; 'Studiosus Literarum' 15 Feb. 1889: 5; Daniel Wilson 15 Feb. 1889: 5; 'A.M.' 18 Feb. 1889: 5; 'Eighty-Three' 18 Feb. 1889: 5; 'Outsider' 20 Feb. 1889: 5; 'Torontonensis' 20 Feb. 1889: 8; 'E.T.H.' 20 Feb. 1889: 8; 'Torontonensis' 22 Feb. 1889: 5; John E. Bryant 22 Feb. 1889: 5; 'M.A.' 22 Feb. 1889: 5; 'Collegensis' 22 Feb. 1889: 5.

'University Appointments.' *Canada Educational Monthly and 'School Magazine'* 11, 9 (Sept. 1880): 425.

Wallace, Malcolm W. 'Memoir' [of W.J. Alexander]. *University of Toronto Quarterly* 14, 1 (1944): 1–8. Rpt. *In Memoriam: William John Alexander (1856–1944)*. Toronto: U Toronto P, 1944.

'Wanted, a Professor!' *The Week* 6, 8 (25 Jan. 1889): 117–18.

Wilson, Daniel. *Address at the Convocation of the University of Toronto and University College, October 19, 1888*. Toronto: Rowsell & Hutchison, [1888?]. [CIHM 25979]

– Diary. Transcribed by H.H. Langton. Langton Family Papers. B65-0014/004, University of Toronto Archives.

Woodhouse, A.S.P. 'Critic and Teacher.' *University of Toronto Quarterly* 14, 1 (1944): 8–33. Rpt. *In Memoriam: William John Alexander (1856–1944)*. Toronto: U Toronto P, 1944. 8–33.

– and R.S. Harris. 'English Study in the English-Language Universities.' *Encyclopedia Canadiana*. Toronto: Grolier, 1957. 4: 12-16.

3

'We Strive for the Good and the Beautiful': Literary Studies at the Margaret Eaton School of Literature and Expression

Writing in the *University of Toronto Monthly* in March 1907, D.R. Keys, then professor of English at University College, recalled a ceremonial opening on 7 January for which a 'distinguished and highly sympathetic audience' had assembled. In his opening remarks, the lieutenant-governor of the province 'dwelt upon the artistic beauty of the structure, recalling his visit to Athens'; while the dean of Toronto's faculty of arts, Ramsay Wright, 'welcomed the institution as another younger daughter of the University, and referred to the Greek ideal of expression and education.' Nathanael Burwash, the chancellor of Victoria College, spoke on the aims of this new institution, and 'literature was well-represented' by the addresses of Professors William Clark of Trinity and W.J. Alexander of University College (125). In what was to prove the last public gesture of his life, department store magnate Timothy Eaton handed to educator Emma Scott Raff a large silver key which contained a small golden latchkey to the 'Kalokagathon,' the new quarters of the Margaret Eaton School of Literature and Expression. The *Monthly*'s reporter reflected on the emblematic nature of the scene:

We hope that the favourable auspices under which the school was opened will continue to influence its work, and that the gifted Principal will be a very *Fors Fortuna clavigera*, bearing not only the silver key, symbol of eloquence, but the inner golden key, betokening that power of literary interpretation by which alone the works of the world's greatest geniuses give forth their highest value. (126)

The significance of the building itself was equally apparent to Professor Keys, who enthused in the following way:

It has been said that if every memorial of the Greek race save the Parthenon had perished, it would be possible to gain from that relic of the past a clear and true impression of the spiritual condition and quality of the Greeks ... Toronto now has a replica in the Kalokagathon, or Greek Theatre, erected on North Street to be the home of the Margaret Eaton School of Literature and Expression. Quietly and unobtrusively, like the work of the school for which it forms a fitting abode, this wonder of Athenian architecture has been reproduced in the Athens of Canada. (124)

This 'simple, beautiful temple of classic design' (*Toronto Star*, 20 March 1933: 3) – quickly dubbed the 'Greek Temple' by taxi drivers – stood out even among the plenitude of italianate villas, romanesque churches, and renaissance-style warehouses built in turn-of-the-century Toronto. For architectural historian Eric Arthur, the MES was 'the swan song of the Greek revival in Toronto,' and he added that 'were it not for the so typical Toronto cottages on each side and the shabby Hydro pole, the central building might be the headquarters, somewhere in Asia Minor, of a mysterious and unrecorded cult' (Arthur 230). 'Anything more unlike a school for young girls could hardly be imagined' (230), Arthur concluded, but his comments stand in an interesting contrast to Keys's observations: for the complete suitability of this form to its function was apparent to the audience and participants at the opening some sixty years before.

The Margaret Eaton School, a women's academy of literature, rhetoric, dramatic arts, and physical culture, existed in various forms for forty years.[1] It had at its peak, part-time and full-time, one thousand course enrolments a year, and was located two blocks from the University of Toronto, with which it had continuing relations, gaining adjunct status in the 1930s. The fact that the Margaret Eaton School has dropped so entirely from historical awareness is both startling and entirely symptomatic, but the school was known in its day in several spheres.[2] It was (especially in its later organization) the country's primary proponent of women's physical culture and athletics in the first part of this century, and was sympathetic to the modern dance. It founded one of Canada's first little theatres, introduced Toronto audiences to the works of the Irish Literary Movement, and provided the most extensive dramatic arts training of the day.[3] But the school also undertook a multi-directed literary studies program, which developed in some distinct and interdisciplinary directions during the years 1907–25. An interesting example of women's educational experimentation, the Margaret Eaton School is also part of a legacy of extra-university attempts – in women's seminaries and academies, in mechanics' institutes, and in public reading groups, for example – to develop models or counter-models for English study. In particular, the Margaret Eaton School was innovative in two branches of literary study which had been dropped in the universities of the day – rhetoric and oratory – and it developed a curriculum in which both contemporary literatures and oral forms found a distinctive place.[4]

The literary program of the Margaret Eaton School was determined by the overall orientation of the school, in turn attributable to its historical situation and to the particular training and inclination of its principal, Emma Scott Raff (later Nasmith). A number of women's postmatriculate academies were founded in Canada before university coeducation, running in parallel to the universities and sometimes enjoying a loose affiliation. (The Brookhurst Academy and the Wesleyan Female College are two examples from Ontario in the 1860s and '70s [Prentice 258–83].)[5] The MES, however, was founded significantly later and well after the entry of women to English-Canadian universities, and may more properly be classed with the many conservatories and schools of expression which sprang up in North America in the late nineteenth century, fuelled by the renewed popularity of Delsartism and the ever constant quest for female accomplishment.[6] Unlike other such institutions, the MES developed in an increasingly academic manner, nurturing ties with the university and with Victoria College, and eventually taking over some aspects of Victoria's instruction.

Why was this educational supplement needed when women had been admitted to the University of Toronto a quarter-century before? There are several reasons, and the first lies in the narrow range of vocations and professions for which university-educated women were equipped. Lack of prerequisite training and encouragement meant that women clustered in arts faculties in the pre–First World War years, avoiding for the most part the new science and social science subjects (LaPierre 227–8). They remained in small (in fact, declining) numbers in the faculties of medicine and law; and while a Faculty of Household Science was founded at Toronto in the year of the school's opening, programs in nursing and social work remained to be developed. In addition, the arts degree outfitted women for fewer occupations than it did their male peers, who could proceed from the B.A. to the clergy, civil service, or business world, or to graduate training, in which women were still a rarity. By desire or default, most women convocates aimed for secondary school teaching, with library and, increasingly, secretarial work providing the alternatives. Thus the Margaret Eaton School was able to attract entrants through its express aim to provide a 'professional and practical education for women' (*Calendar*, 1908–9; E,* series 8, box 12, file X8/4).

A second reason for the rise of the Margaret Eaton School is found in the attitudes to the newly arrived women in the universities of the day. The early years of this century saw a significant backlash against women students, and one year after the opening of the MES, the senate of the University of Toronto voted overwhelmingly to segregate them, citing as one reason their 'predominance' in the modern languages and making a spurious case for 'the special needs of women's education' ('Report' 287). Charlotte Ross, the literature and rhetoric instructor at the Margaret Eaton School, was one of the alumnae who banded together to fight the senate's decision. They detected the potential inequalities in the plan and noted that women were in the modern languages, not through fear of difficult subjects, but for reasons of 'practical utility' since this training offered a means of earning a living ('Reply' 289). Women's needs, they affirmed, would better be met through equality in both arts and professional education, and by the hiring of female staff. They were successful in overturning the senate's decision, but the chilly climate remained. (Thus, while some progressive men supported the MES, at least some of the university's interest in its 'younger daughter' must be attributed to the school's function as a perceived prototype for a women's college.)[7]

Another reason for the development of an alternative school for women follows directly from the first two. Once women were admitted to the universities and the dust of debate had settled, little further thought was given to their specific needs or to the curricular revision that would accommodate their interests. Thus, while making public cases for the success of coeducation (as the alumnae did), many university women in the early decades of this century doubted that their aspirations could be fulfilled by a system that remained resolutely masculinist. What was needed, Virginia Woolf would write some years later in *Three Guineas*, was

an experimental college, an adventurous college ... The aim of the new college ... should be not to segregate and specialize, but to combine. It should explore the

---

* See 'Abbreviations' below.

ways in which mind and body can be made to co-operate; discover what new combinations make good wholes in human life. (Woolf, *Three Guineas* 39–40)

For many women educators of the day – like their literary sisters – this modernization often took the form of a distinctively post-Victorian revival of Greek ideals, and a vernacularization (and 'feminization') of classical study.

Emma Scott Raff shared the goal of an integrated and experimental women's education. Born in Owen Sound, she had trained under the artist George Reid and at the Boston School of Expression in a Delsartist program aimed at uniting literary understanding, voice expression, and physical movement; later, she was an eclectic auditor of classes in philosophy, psychology, and dramatic literature at Toronto. She would be remembered by Lorna Sheard, a graduate of the Margaret Eaton School who became a proponent of the little theatre in Canada. Sketching Scott Raff for her fellow Heliconian Club members in 1970, Sheard recalled the magnetic personality of their colourful forerunner:

Hers was a noble, classical type of beauty. She always gave the effect of great simplicity of style. Yet, as I remember her in the [early] '20s, she favoured flowing robes (usually of peacock blue or moss green) metal girdled, and festooned with long ropes of amber, or carved wooden beads. In that tripping, high-heeled period she often wore some simple sort of suede sandal ... We, who were privileged to know her, recognized that she had been very unusually, and variously, endowed: an artist, a fine teacher, and an astute business woman. ('Nov. 8 1970 Heliconian Club,' typescript, H, MU 8092, file 11)[8]

A widow and sole-support mother in turn-of-the-century Toronto, this energetic and enterprising woman used her multifarious talents in a variety of ways: teaching physical culture and eurhythmics at Victoria College as director of its Annesley Hall gymnasium; coaching in voice expression at the Toronto College of Music and the Conservatory; giving lectures on travel and art ('Six Mornings in Florence with Ruskin'), readings from *Macbeth,* and dramatic presentations of passages from *Parsifal.* Encouraged by Nathanael Burwash – and discouraged by difficulties she encountered in having expression accredited as a separate department at Victoria – in 1901 she opened a small studio, the original School of Literature and Expression.[9] Burgeoning enrolments, Raff's considerable energy, and the persuasive powers and generosity of Margaret Beattie Eaton (who carried on a life-long love affair with the theatre) resulted in the opening of the school's new quarters, which contained a recital hall, a studio, and classrooms. On the architrave were the words that would soon be freely translated as the school's motto: τὸ καλοκαγθόν – 'We Strive for the Good and the Beautiful.' [10]

The goal of the Margaret Eaton School was to provide what Emma Scott Raff termed 'a three-fold education for women':

We ... believe that any education to be of value must be threefold in nature – a training of the mental, a training of the moral and a training of the physical forces. So we begin our threefold training first in the Gymnasium; for the preparation of the body as an instrument of expression we work for the freedom of the body, then for natural adjustment of its parts. Secondly – In the classroom for a knowledge of the best in Literature. An intelligent conception of the text must form the basis of all satisfactory interpretation in the studios for Vocal Expression of that best [sic] – we stimulate thought. The voice receives the most careful and intelligent training for purity of tone and is made responsive to thinking and feeling. (Calendar, 1908–9)

All aspects of the school pointed to this Greek ideal – the design of the building, the shallow stage designed for the presentation of tableaux, the clothing of its (dress reformist) principal, even the caretaker's nickname of 'Hermes' (Toronto Star, 22 March 1933: 4). For Lorna Sheard, Scott Raff's dream had been 'a school where students could have university english and french along with their dancing & dramatic training'; it finally 'materialised complete with a building with Greek pillars, Greek lamps & Greek dance tunics and barefoot students of the dance' (5; 'Transcript of Nov. 11 meeting, Heliconian Club, c. 1970,' H, MU 8092, file 4). This appreciation of classical training as the highest form of study was shared by many women of the early twentieth century, as indicated by the fleeting vision of 'J–H–' (Jane Harrison) in A Room of One's Own, and by Woolf's wistfully titled 'On Not Knowing Greek.' Woolf's encomium in that essay – that 'every line of its literature ... admit[s] us to a vision of the earth unravaged, the sea unpolluted, the maturity, tried but unbroken, of mankind' (11) – makes clear that the 'classics' were not simply a container for ideals of personal development and public duty, and not only a form of male education to which women wished entry, but represented the very idea of a liberal education. Further, the turn-of-the-century discovery of Sapphic fragments, as well as Jane Harrison's probing of archaic and, she suggested, pre-patriarchal cults and rituals (see Peacock), offered the possibility of a woman-centred adaptation of classical myths and training. A 'Greek' training, involving the free education of the mind and body in addition to the schooling of the heart, was an emancipatory program for women's education, and one which demonstrates how the 'modern' may consist of a reworking of earlier cultural modes.[11]

In addition to this package of ideals and aspirations were the goals of classical study as formulated in late nineteenth-century Canada, which differed somewhat from the elite Oxbridge counterpart. Although Greek, and then Latin, were phased out as compulsory subjects for all university students, and Greek was dropped for senior matriculation (Harris 47), Latin remained as a requirement for the B.A., and Greek persisted as a popular option or specialty. That the classics were considered invaluable training for work in the modern languages, and that Latin was required for high school teaching, were points used to argue for the extension of such courses to women at the grammar school level. In addition, the study of Greek and Latin was allied at the end of the century with two important and often daring areas of thought: the higher criticism, and the fledgling study of archaeology; that is, with the new sciences of textual and historical interpretation.[12] Although many students switched to the attractive modern languages option, this was not solely a 'decline' of the classics, for the training became more specialized, varied, and detailed when not compulsory (Harris 137–8). In addition, the vogue of Matthew Arnold in English Canada may have contributed to the continuing elevation of the classics; for they provided that access to the study of ancient deeds and histories from which the 'Hellenized' thinker could draw general principles.

The vernacularized classicism of the Margaret Eaton School was oriented both to the ideals and the pragmatics of classical study, exercised in all of material, methods, and rationale. Such 'Greek' ideals were deeply resonant with the Delsartist beliefs of the principal. While Delsartism was originally formulated, in the mid-nineteenth century, as a theory of movement and voice expression for actors, by the time of a second wave of North American popularity its influence was to be detected in other areas of the arts, notably the modern dance. (Isadora Duncan and the partners of the Denishawn troupe were all trained as Delsartists.) This led, in turn, to other theories of free movement, including eurhythmics. In addition, some writers were intrigued by Delsartism's correlation of metrics and natural breath rhythms, and by its proto-symbolist doctrine of correspondences: 'To each spiritual function responds a function of the body; to each grand function of the body corresponds a spiritual act,' wrote dancer Ted Shawn (Shawn 22). As the physical education instructor at Victoria's Annesley Hall, Scott Raff aimed to develop 'freedom of the body' through morning training in 'swedish apparatus, Delsarte, and aesthetic movements' and evening classes in 'aesthetic movements and the Swedish folk dances followed by a class in Fencing' (Emma Scott Raff to the Board of Management of Annesley Hall [1905?], Director of Physical Education, Reports, VUA, 90.064V, 3/19); her classes, for both Victoria and the MES, stood in distinct contrast to the militia-styled drills of the Strathcona system used elsewhere at Toronto (Lenskyj 218). The literary, expressive, and dramatic training of the Margaret Eaton School was also conducted on Delsartist principles, and Scott Raff continued to rely on the Boston School in choosing teachers and texts.

Even while insisting that 'all culture should carry with it a bread-winning power' ('Canadian Women' 26), Scott Raff maintained the philosophical principles of the program and refused to provide a narrowly vocational training. It appears that the students themselves did not always share their founder's aims. They sometimes cried, 'Prepare us in the shortest possible time to earn our bread!' Scott Raff reported. At one point, 'the world seemed to go mad about Dancing' (Emma Nasmith, address to the directors, n.d., E, series 22, box 6, file 1); while another year, the school was 'besieged by stage-struck students' (Emma Scott Raff, report, Oct. 1907, E, series 22, box 6, file 1). The greatest demand would be for education in physical culture, since the emergent 'Y', camp, and settlement house movements meant that women with these qualifications had the greatest success finding jobs.[13] But the school continued to insist that all students, no matter their intended area, study all curricular components, and the subjects themselves were taught in a system of interdisciplinary cross-reference. In this respect, the curriculum of the school would become a literalization of the perceived relationship between women's 'bodies' and 'texts.' Significantly, a book by Emma Scott Raff, a commencement address later published, was entitled *Of Queens' Gardens*, taking its title from one of the two original lectures in Ruskin's *Sesame and Lilies*, in which Ruskin examined – in his words – 'the majesty of the influence of good books, and of good women' (vi).

This combination of high-mindedness and practicality appealed to young women of the day; and while the number of students attending the school full-time remained relatively stable over the years (building from twelve to an average of approximately twenty-five, but rising to more than forty by the mid-1920s) there was a considerable swelling of part-time enrolment over the same period. By 1925, the school's final year at the North Street location, the part-time enrolment had reached 1,064 course registrations, and both a student residence and a separate physical education annex had been constructed.

This growth occurred in several sectors. First, a series of reciprocal arrangements developed between Victoria College and the school. Scott Raff's overlapping jobs, the college's need for rhetorical and oratorical instruction, and the school's need for more facilities meant there was considerable transfer of people and funds between the two. In return for use of the Annesley Hall gymnasium and some additional monies, the MES provided expressive training for women arts students from Victoria College and to the male divinity students from the associated theological school, while MES students, in the early years, lived in the Annesley residence and availed themselves of the college's arts program. In later years, the school would develop training courses for both Methodist and Anglican deaconesses, schooling them in the critical reading skills needed, so that 'Christian workers can learn to read the Bible intelligently' (letter, Emma Scott Raff to R.Y. Eaton, 29 Nov. 1915, E, series 22, box 6, file 1). In addition, the MES took over some functions of the Toronto Conservatory of Music when it shut down its own school of expression in 1919.

But the greatest area of growth came from the development of part-time, outreach, and extension programs. Scott Raff was insistent that all courses in the school be open to part-time students, or to those who wished to take single course instruction; and while a number of women did pursue this option, many preferred the evening and Saturday classes and discussion groups. The 1925 annual statement, for example, shows 57 students registered full-time at the school (40 in physical education and 17 in literature and expression), but 367 others in the deaconess stream, in day classes ranging from dalcroze eurhythmics and swimming to book discussion groups, and in dramatic arts courses for children (financial statement, 1925, E, series 22, box 6, file 5). In addition, courses in both physical and speech remediation for children and adults were offered. Off-campus and extension work accounted for more of the school's growth; instructors at the school gave talks and helped to establish reading groups for other organizations (Nasmith 271); while 1920 found the school staff giving instruction to four hundred public school teachers at ten different locations (Emma Scott Raff, report, Jan. 1920, E, series 22, box 6, file 1). Such extension activities stretched across southern Ontario. Emma Scott Raff travelled in her dual role as recitationist and school principal, talking in Barrie, for example (letters, Emma Scott Raff to Dora Mavor Moore, 1912, DMMP), and giving a monthly course in Brantford on *The Ring and the Book* (letter, Emma Scott Raff to directors, n.d., E, series 22, box 6, file 1). It appears that students from the school also toured: 'Interpretive dancing is an innovation to Owen Sound,' the student magazine commented (*Mesolae* [1921]: 48). There was sufficient activity that by 1921 Scott Raff's daughter, Dorothy, had become secretary of the extension program.

This aspect of the school's work needs to be considered when judging its orientation and impact. The Margaret Eaton School has usually been dismissed as a finishing school; and while it did open with a 'finishing' program (presumably from financial necessity), Emma Scott Raff was soon able to announce to the directors that 'most of the incoming students registered for the Teachers' and Professional Courses are matriculants, or those having covered Junior or Senior Leaving in Collegiate and College' (letter, Emma Scott Raff to directors, n.d., E, series 22, box 6, file 1). Helen Lenskyj has noted the contradictory impulses of the school: while non-militarist and relatively unrestrictive in its physical education program, the school also subscribed to the ideals of 'true womanhood,' which dovetailed with the patriotic and military ethos of the war years (219). Further, as Lenskyj writes, 'although the existence of a predominantly female teacher training institution was potentially a progressive step ... the school's strong connections with Toronto's upper middle class establishment in its early years guaranteed a high degree of conservatism' (218). In being for the most part populated by the 'daughters of educated men' (in Woolf's term), the school was consistent with higher education of the day; but the outreach and remediation work of the school are evidence of a democratic leaning.[14] Most significantly, an insistence on the training of women for useful, paid work in the public sphere, as early as 1907, made the school unusual for its time. (And its training of women for stage careers aroused some controversy.) Just as the 'philosophy' of the school was mixed in a way typical of the thought of the transition years (and of the newly postcolonial society), so were its 'politics' as complex as those of other cultural and intellectual institutions in Canada at the turn of the century.[15]

While there were changes and expansions over the years, by the time of its first full year in 1908–9, the organization of staff and curriculum was set, and would be followed with some modifications until the mid-1920s. The curriculum was organized according to three fields: dramatic arts and expression, literature and arts topics, and physical education. (The first two were amalgamated in 1921, resulting in a two-stream program.) Scott Raff taught the courses in expression, in addition to her duties as principal, and was assisted in her area by Gertrude Philp for voice culture, reading, and interpretation, and by N. Topley Thomas for 'Theory of Expression' and 'Dramatic Thinking.' The arts subjects were undertaken by Charlotte Ross and Florence Withrow, the first instructing in English and French literature, rhetoric, and composition, the latter undertaking a wide variety of historical and mythological topics. French and German conversation were offered by Madame Goudis and Fraulein Nothnagel; Constance Wreyford was listed as teaching physical education, although she would be replaced by Mary Hamilton the next year. While only Scott Raff, Ross, and Thomas were salaried employees, in fact all of the staff worked long hours and the day (and pay) could vary greatly according to the number of students and the amount of extension work at any given time.[16] Over the years, occasional courses were given by members of the Victoria staff, such as A.H. Reynar and E.J. Pratt, while poet and critic Katherine Hale taught at the school in its first full year. In total, over thirty occasional instructors supplemented the faculty during the years 1907–25 (see Jackson 34–5).

Full-time students had the option of three different courses of study, as described in the calendar:

The Professional Course demands Matriculation at entrance and covers our whole outline of study including 25 class lectures per week, and private tuition in voice culture

General Culture Course – for those who want elocution and platform work as an art, embraces the University English Topics or Matriculation, (an option) Voice Culture, Physical Culture, Deportment and Recitation, with Criticism

The Specialists [sic] *Course* – Arranged for students who want the University English Topics with Voice Culture and Physical Culture for three periods per week during the Collegiate year (*Calendar*, 1908–9)

All students proceeding to certificates from the school took general courses in composition, rhetoric, and literature (largely nineteenth-century poetry, with some Shakespeare, although they would cover many more plays in the dramatic arts program). The introduction of rhetoric and composition to the curriculum, which had been suggested by Burwash, kept alive a mode of study increasingly disfavoured by the eastern universities. The courses became more expressly literary for students adding the 'University English Topics'; and the approach, as near as it can be discerned, was what would have been called in the day 'aesthetic criticism.'[17]

Three periods structure the topics. Shakespeare provided a curricular cornerstone, and was studied through many plays representing all genres; and Spenser and Milton would be added to this Renaissance component for students undertaking advanced study. Some writers from the eighteenth century appear regularly on the curriculum, usually Goldsmith and Pope. The nineteenth century was covered in more detail, with a focus on poetry – the Romantics, Tennyson, Rossetti, and particularly Browning – combined with the study of essays by Macaulay, Carlyle, and Ruskin. As indicated by the title of the course, there is a close and intentional correspondence to the Toronto curriculum of the day. The first-year introductory course at Toronto in 1908 covered poetry from Pope to Tennyson (with a special study of the latter, but more or less omitting the Romantics) and anthology prose selections 'from Lamb to Stevenson inclusive' (*University of Toronto Calendar*, 1908–9: 117). The second year was devoted to Shakespeare and Chaucer, while the third offered Old English, Milton, eighteenth-century topics, and nineteenth-century verse – the Romantics, Browning, Arnold, and D.G. Rossetti. A more concentrated fourth year involved histories of prose style and of the early English drama, a Beowulf course, and a study of eighteenth-century prose fiction and non-fiction (*University of Toronto Calendar*, 1908–9). Fifteen years later, the curriculum had been updated only by the addition of Hardy, a single poem by Yeats, and the Canadian poets from the department's *Representative Poetry* anthology (*University of Toronto Calendar*, 1923–4). While the Toronto curriculum understandably had more scope and specialization, the topics of the MES may be viewed as a microcosmic version.

However, there the similarities end, for the topics were only one portion of the literary education offered by the school, and the other avenues of literary and expressive study allowed a more varied and more modern range of texts. In the dramatic arts course, for example – in which Dora Mavor (later Moore) was first a student and then an instructor – students were given a wide range of plays and a sustained exposure to contemporary writing. This course continued the study of Shakespeare, along with Greek drama and early English drama (including morality plays), but added to this a considerable number of recent, and especially symbolist, works: by Ibsen, Strindberg, Yeats, and Lady Gregory, for example. Children's plays were read, as some graduates would go on to work with that age group; and popular plays and light comedies would later be studied and staged. Textual study was supplemented by practical training, both in classes and through the work of the Associate Players, which specialized in the plays of the Irish Literary Movement and trained a number of men and women later to be active in the development of the little theatre and the Dominion Drama Festival.[18]

The education women received at the MES was augmented by the numerous public lectures held in the school's auditorium, provided by the staff, members of the university faculty, and academics, writers, and performers visiting Toronto. While these were open to the public, they appear to have been closely integrated with the women's course of study, and the year's program would be listed in the annual calendar. In 1908–9, for example, Professors Falconer, Alexander, and Wallace would speak, respectively, on 'Greek Sculpture,' 'Jane Austen,' and 'The Early Church Drama'; and the Hon. Richard Harcourt and *Globe* editor J.A. MacDonald would provide a lecture on Shakespeare and a reading from Browning. School staff also took part, Topley Thomas speaking on *Midsummer Night's Dream* and Scott Raff on the Irish drama; while Richard Burton, a visiting professor from Minnesota, talked on 'Modern Romance.' In addition, in that year students were offered a 'Musicale' and visits by unspecified 'Canadian Poets' (*Calendar*, 1908–9). Scott Raff, as a member of the Heliconian Club's drama committee, was well placed to greet eminent visitors to the city; and a parade of theatrical personages from Forbes-Robertson to Yeats held forth in the Greek Theatre.

Another supplement to the program was provided by the many reading and discussion groups that the school undertook from its inception in 1901, the most successful being weekly discussion groups on Shakespeare and on Browning that were popular with business women and teachers (Nasmith 271). (Scott Raff's 'Tuesday Evening Literary Class' on Browning began in 1910 with ten students and had an attendance of over two hundred a few years later [Jackson 10].) In 1919 a Discussion Club was founded 'for formal debates, informal discussions and oratorical contests' (Howard 16–17), and from this grew the student magazine *Mesolae*, which took the school's acronym as its title. The issues devote attention to aesthetic questions as well as news of the school and discussion of current events.

Perhaps the most novel of the organizations was the Reading Group for the Study of Contemporary Authors, composed of both students and interested professional women under the direction of Charlotte Ross. Each year an author was selected for concentrated study: Ibsen,

Maeterlinck, Meredith, Shaw, Watts-Dunton, Tolstoi, Fiona MacLeod, Samuel Butler, Tagore, and Irish playwrights were some of the group's early topics, while Shaw, Galsworthy, Hardy, Conrad, and the influence of folklore on modern writers were covered in the postwar period. Classes met every second week and the curriculum was ambitious. In the course on Maeterlinck, for example, the discussants would read three or four plays for each session; while the first three weeks of the course on Shaw dealt with 'The Influence of Nietzsche ...,' Shaw's 'Dramatic Ideals,' and the controversial question of 'Bernard Shaw and the Censorship' (program, OISE).

Other topics, stemming from the principal's special interests, were introduced to the curriculum in more informal ways. In the 1918–19 season, for example, Scott Raff gave a series of short histories of the world's great literatures, with readings from Tolstoi, the peripatetic translator Lafcadio Hearn, Hugo, and *The Hung Lou Meng* (*Calendar*, 1919–20). Emma Scott Raff had a particular interest in Canadian literature (an account of the Victoria College 'Lit' shows her delighting her audience 'by her reading from several Canadian poets, giving, among others, selections from Miss Coleman and Mrs. Blewett' [*Acta Victoriana* 32, 3 (1908): 299]), and it appears that Canadian authors regularly gave readings at the school. Scott Raff also lectured on folklore, and in October 1912 the first meeting of a new folklore society was held in the principal's studio (Emma Scott Raff to Dora Mavor Moore, 24 Oct. 1912, DMMP, box 60). One of the school's more eminent visiting instructors was Cecil Sharp, who gave several week-long classes on English folksongs and dancing (flyer, OISE).

While it is difficult to reconstruct the classroom approaches taken, since the school's academic records were destroyed, several texts remain which give some indication of an iconoclastic pedagogy, and which suggest that even the more traditional 'topics' may have been in practice rather divergent from the university's equivalent. A sheaf of teaching notes on 'Greek Movement' shows the attempt to unite literary, dramatic, and expressive study with physical culture, and glosses Scott Raff's puzzling statement that her ideal school would be a 'gymnasium whose end and aim is rhythm' (Emma Scott Raff to R.Y. Eaton, letter, 22 Nov. 1915, E, series 22, box 6, file 1). The teaching notes detail a series of exercises in steps, motions, and postures, and the instructions are interleaved with meditations and quotations from Euripides, Pindar, and Plato. According to the notes, the exercises are performed to poetry of different moods and metrics, since 'moving to words gives the gestures that quality of dramatic significance and the rhythm of speech which is necessary to the interpretations of the choruses of the Greek dramas that are the final climax to all Greek dance' (teaching notes, DMMP). The finale of the course is movement to the chorus of *Iphigenia*, in the Gilbert Murray translation.

More evidence of pedagogic practice is provided by the works of Samuel Curry, in whose Boston School several of the MES instructors trained, and whose press provided the texts and anthologies most commonly employed. In *Browning and the Dramatic Monologue*, for example, Curry makes the case for this ignored genre as a centrally important form, for it awakens 'a perception of the necessary connection between the living voice and literature' in a culture which normally prizes the written over the oral. Study of the monologue, Curry affirmed, would bring 'the most important study of the natural languages into practical relationship with the study of literature' (Curry 256). The method that Curry follows, according to this text, consists of restoring to literary interpretation a sense of the rhetorical and addressive function of the work, for 'the monologue is a study of the effect of mind upon mind, of the adaptation of the ideas of one individual to another, and of the revelation this makes of the characters of speaker and listener' (13). The dramatic monologue is therefore pedagogically illustrative because it is metonymic of literature more generally: 'It gives insight into human character, embodies the poetry of everyday life, and reveals the mystery of the human heart, as possibly no other literary form can do' (259). Curry's principles in large part underpin the choices of authors and texts in the MES curriculum, and explain the central importance of Browning to the study, as well as the selection of dramatic works, chosen on the basis of their voice parts.

The Margaret Eaton School's literary program therefore differed in some substantial ways from the other contemporary curricula. Its 'canon' expanded to include a wider range of contemporary literature, including non-English literature in translation, and found room for oral genres and areas such as folklore and children's literature. It carried on two forms of instruction dropped in the universities, maintaining rhetoric in two guises (through the study of composition, and through the analysis of speakers and effects in the expressive study); and developed a comprehensive oratorical training. Both 'younger sister' and independent woman, aiming for both curricular duplication and innovation, the Margaret Eaton School maintained a continuingly complex relationship to Toronto and to its own financial directors. An increasing debt, which

Margaret Beattie Eaton could no longer assume, added to the city's expropriation of the North Street site for a road-widening project, led to the dissolution of the school as a literary academy and the enforced resignation of Scott Raff in 1925. Charlotte Ross was passed over as her successor in favour of a male candidate; Hart House theatre director Bertram Forsyth oversaw the school for one more year before it became devoted solely to training in physical education. It remained in that form until 1941, when it was finally absorbed by the university, becoming the basis for what is now the School of Physical and Health Education.

This was not the first attempt to join the school to the university. As early as 1915, Scott Raff and Nathanael Burwash had attempted to persuade the Victoria administration to endow a chair for the school, to ensure continuity of staffing and of the expressive program (letter, Emma Scott Raff to R.Y. Eaton, 29 Nov. 1915, E, series 22, box 6, file 1). Of greater potential import were discussions conducted in the early 1920s with Presidents Bowles and Falconer of Victoria College and Toronto, with the intent to incorporate the Margaret Eaton School into the university. According to this plan, the school would form the basis for three new departments, in vocal expression, dramatic arts, and physical education (various letters, E, series 8, box 11, file X8/4.) The idea enjoyed some support in the academic community, including the backing of Sir Henry Newbolt, author of the famous Newbolt Report on national education, who seems to have taken an interest in the school on his visit to Toronto in 1923 (letter, Emma Scott Raff to directors, 2 May 1925, E, series 8, box 8, file X8/4). But the plan eventually failed (as did a proposal in the 1930s to use the school as the basis for a campus women's centre, which, as of this writing, the university still lacks). It is interesting to speculate what the effects of this academic merger might have been, not only on English studies at Toronto, but by extension the rest of the country.

For, while the literary education of the Margaret Eaton School was different in both philosophy and practice from university curricula of the day, keeping alive the traditional arts of oratory and rhetoric and developing a uniquely interdisciplinary approach, its greatest innovation may have been the commitment to education of the individual. For Nathanael Burwash, George Nasmith wrote, the curriculum 'was twenty years ahead of its time because it was concerned with the development of individual personality and not with attempting to force that personality through a routine system which had the tendency to sup-

press individuality as was the practice in many schools of the time'
(Nasmith 270). While 'We Strive for the Good and the Beautiful' was the
school's official motto, its philosophy may more aptly be summed up in
Emma Scott Raff's homely, and oft-repeated, maxim: we take people as
we find them.

Abbreviations

DMMP: Dora Mavor Moore Papers, Thomas Fisher Rare Book Library, Univer-
sity of Toronto
E: T. Eaton Company Records, Archives of Ontario
H: Toronto Heliconian Club Papers, Archives of Ontario
MTPL: Theatre Collection, Central Reference Library, Metropolitan Toronto
Public Library
OISE: Ontario Institute for Studies in Education
VUA: Victoria University Archives

Notes

1 This study tracks the MES until its conversion (in 1926) into a school special-
izing in women's physical and outdoor education. In 1941 the MES was
absorbed into the University of Toronto, forming the basis of what is now the
School of Physical and Health Education.
2 The most thorough accounts of the school are provided by Dorothy Jackson
in *A Brief History of Three Schools* (whose title refers to the three stages of its
development), and by John Byl in a recent dissertation, which concentrates
on the school's physical training programs. Robert Barry Scott's 'A Study of
Amateur Theatre in Toronto: 1900-1930' deals with the theatrical activities of
Emma Scott Raff and with the school's Associate Players. Mary G. Hamilton,
instructor in physical education and later MES principal, has detailed its outdoor education program in *The Call of Algonquin*, and the school figures
briefly in histories of physical education in Canada (see Lenskyj, O'Bryan,
and Van Vliet).
3 I have dealt in more detail with the school's dramatic arts program and activities – as well as the histories of principal Emma Scott Raff and benefactor
Margaret Beattie Eaton – in 'Making the Modern: Twenty-Five Years of the
Margaret Eaton School of Literature and Expression.'
4 The study of rhetoric in Canada was steadily replaced by an 'English' belles-
lettrism (see Hubert and Garrett-Petts); and, while oratorical instruction con-

tinued to flourish in the United States (see Johnson), in English Canada it persisted almost solely as a branch of homiletics.

5 The affiliation with the Methodist Victoria College, however, does provide one link to these earlier schools; and board member and sometime instructor Margaret Procter Burwash had taught at the Wesleyan Female College.

6 Delsartism, a theory of integrated voice and movement named after its French founder François Delsarte, was imported into the United States by the actor-impresario Steele MacKay (with whom Scott Raff's instructor, Samuel Curry, had studied). Originally influential in the theatrical community, by the late nineteenth century it was enjoying a double resurgence: writers, artists, and dancers were engaged by the synthesizations of the system, while criticizing a more popular reception by which 'Delsarte' became an (almost comically) coded menu of movements, gestures, and intonations adopted by recitationists and amateur actors.

   This overlap of semi-mystical thought with literary and artistic endeavour is an important part of English-Canadian intellectual tradition for the transition years, as Michèle Lacombe has demonstrated in the case of theosophy.

7 An interesting chiasmus of personnel and purposes occurs with the 'Report' and the 'Reply.' Charlotte Ross fought for coeducation at Toronto, and later joined the university's senate as its first woman member. George Wrong, chair of the committee which recommended women's segregation, helped to design the history program at the MES. Burwash, who not only was an educational segregationist but was also opposed to the hiring of women teachers in the public school system (Lenskyj 205) was consistently encouraging to both school and staff, and headed its management board until his death.

8 Scott Raff was a founder of the Heliconian Club, the women's counterpart to the Arts and Letters Club, and maintained an active association as both a drama committee member and cultural contributor. The minute books and bulletins show her reading from *The Hour Glass* as early as April 1909 (*Minutes 1909–1919*, H, MU 8096, file 6); speaking on modern drama and reading from St John Ervine's *Jane Clegg* in 1924; and hosting a reception ten years later (*Bulletins*, H, MU 8095). The club used the school's theatre for recitals and tableaux, and met in the principal's studio while raising funds for its own headquarters.

9 The Victoria Women's Residence and Educational Society, chaired by Margaret Burwash, proposed that a Department of Expression be linked to the Annesley Hall residence. This plan was opposed, however, by the women undergraduates, who noted that the expression course was of Scott Raff's own design and not developed by the university authorities; further, the instructor enjoyed no official university standing ('To the Board of

Regents ...,' petition [1901?]). By all accounts, Scott Raff's courses were popular; so the concern seems to have been about parallel education. (This was not shared by the male arts and theological students, who supported the plan ['To Chancellor Burwash ...,' petition (1901?)].) The idea may also have been opposed because work in expression smacked to some of vocational, rather than a larger intellectual, training (letter, A.A. Chown to Margaret Burwash, 1 Aug. 1901, Burwash Papers, VUA, 92.002V, file 135).

10 The Margaret Eaton School was established as a company, overseen by a board of directors, who were also shareholders, although Margaret Beattie Eaton retained all but seven of the two hundred shares. The board was usually composed of Margaret Eaton, Emma Scott Raff, Nathanael Burwash, Margaret Burwash, and four Eaton family members or business associates. The company was legally dissolved 12 March 1950 (E, series 8, box 11, file X8/4).

11 Celeste Schenck has noted that the equation between radical form and politics needs to be queried for modernists, and asks whether 'the seemingly, genteel, conservative poetics of women poets ... might pitch a more radical politics than we had considered possible' (231).

12 C.T. Currelly, founder of the Royal Ontario Museum, noted that all the early archaeologists had trained in classics, and that it was still considered an essential preparation (Currelly 227).

Debates over the higher criticism in Canada are in large measure a feature of the transition years. While German scholars had worked on biblical texts by the late eighteenth century, these ideas would not become widely known in Canada until Confederation. The adjudication of new knowledge and faith, through the medium of the idealism characteristic of English-Canadian intellectual life, occupied theologians and academics in the latter part of the nineteenth century and well into the twentieth (see Grant 79–84).

13 And the students were not above poking fun at the aims of the school. The student magazine *Mesolae* of 1921 parodied a student waiting to enter the room at the annual ball: 'With a quiet dignity which marked us as a student of the Margaret Eaton School of Literature and Expression we expanded our torso, brought the sternum over the basis of support, breathed once for life and once for voice, [and] focused our breath behind our teeth' (40; MTPL, TH 71354).

14 A point of comparison may be useful. While the University of Toronto allowed a handful of teachers to take individual courses as early as 1905, extension education was not begun until 1917 (see Blyth).

15 Indicative is the oscillation of the school's statement of purpose, which appeared annually in the calendar. Originally it concluded by mentioning

the preparation of women for home and family life, but a new sentence was added in the war years, reflecting an increased emphasis on public duty: 'Further, we believe that we can give nothing to our fellowmen but ourselves, and our best self can only be revealed through co-ordination of the physical and spiritual life' (*Calendar*, 1914–15). The calendar sometimes shows the first conclusion, and sometimes the second, during the next ten years.

16 By 1909, when enrolment had stabilized, salaries were set at $1,200 for Scott Raff, $600 for Ross, and $500 (with a percentage of the receipts from private pupils) for Thomas. The history instructor received one dollar per lecture; the others were on part-time wages or received a percentage of class fees (minutes of directors meeting, 8 Nov. 1909, Burwash Papers, VUA, 92.002V, file 135). The question of teacher salaries occurred frequently in Emma Scott Raff's depositions to the school's financial directors. 'In the case of Miss Ross, Miss Thomas and Miss Thrall,' she later wrote, 'we have to guarantee a living wage ... the number of hours is not counted or even considered by them ... they are doing and always have done their best for the school, regardless of pay' (letter, Emma Scott Raff to R.Y. Eaton, 22 Nov. 1915, E, series 22, box 6, file 1).

17 Writing in 1917, John Logan gives a particularly relevant definition of this critical approach and its Canadian application: 'In a young country, such as Canada, the "mothering" of aesthetic taste and standards must be Spartan rather than Athenian, in method and aim. That is to say: in a country where the people are, perforce, primarily concerned with material possessions, and only secondarily with material goods, criticism must be rigorously pragmatic and pedagogic: while, in the first place, it declares this or that to be a bad or a good performance in literature, painting, drama, or music, it must also, in the second place, be constructive by a reasonable justification, according to established standards, of a piece of criticism, and thus hold up the ideal and point the better way both to the artistic craftsman and to the public' (7–8).

18 The approach of the Associate Players is economically described by Dorothy Taylor, who may have had the Players in mind when she described the theatrical scene: 'In the first days of Little Theatres in Canada, the importance of technique was recognized by the earnest workers whose aim it was to bring to the minds of the playgoing public of their community the highest ideals of the drama. They talked eagerly of the superiority of drapes over conventional "scenery"; they hinted at the aesthetic value of the spoken drama as a means of expression; and they chose for production the plays that seemed most assuredly to fulfil the new desire' (42).

Works Cited

Arthur, Eric. *Toronto: No Mean City.* 2d ed. Toronto: U Toronto P, 1978.

Blyth, J.A. *Foundling at Varsity: A History of the Division of University Extension, University of Toronto.* [Toronto]: School of Continuing Studies, U of Toronto, 1976.

Byl, John. 'The Margaret Eaton School, 1901–1942: Women's Education in Elocution, Drama and Physical Education.' Diss. U of New York at Buffalo, 1992.

'Canadian Women in the Public Eye: Mrs. G.G. Nasmith.' *Saturday Night* (11 Sept. 1920): 26.

Currelly, C.T. *I Brought the Ages Home.* Toronto: Ryerson, 1956.

Curry, S.S. *Browning and the Dramatic Monologue: Nature and Interpretation of an Overlooked Form of Literature.* [1908]. Rpt. New York: Haskell House, 1965.

Grant, John Webster. 'Religious and Theological Writings to 1960.' *Literary History of Canada: Canadian Literature in English.* 2d ed. 3 vols. Toronto: U Toronto P, 1976. 2:75–94.

Hamilton, Mary G. *The Call of Algonquin: A Biography of a Summer Camp.* Toronto: Ryerson, 1958.

Harris, Robin S. *A History of Higher Education in Canada 1663–1960.* Toronto: U Toronto P, 1976.

Howard, Lois. 'What Is the Discussion Club?' *Mesolae* (1921): 16–17.

Hubert, Henry, and W.F. Garrett-Petts. 'Foreword: An Historical Narrative of Textual Studies in Canada.' *Textual Studies in Canada / Etudes textuelles au Canada* 1 (1991): 1–30.

Jackson, Dorothy N.R. *A Brief History of Three Schools. The School of Expression. The Margaret Eaton School of Literature and Expression. The Margaret Eaton School. 1901–1941.* N.p.: n.p., [1953?].

Johnson, Nan. *Nineteenth-Century Rhetoric in North America.* Carbondale, Ill.: Southern Illinois P, 1991.

Keys, D.R. ['D.R.K.']. 'τὸ καλοκαγαθόν. The Margaret Eaton School of Literature and Expression.' *University of Toronto Monthly* 7, 5 (March 1907): 124–6.

Lacombe, Michèle. 'Theosophy and the Canadian Idealist Tradition: A Preliminary Exploration.' *Journal of Canadian Studies / Revue d'études canadiennes* 17, 2 (Summer/été 1982): 100–18.

LaPierre, Jo. 'The Academic Life of Canadian Coeds, 1880–1900.' *Historical Studies in Education / Revue d'histoire de l'éducation* 1, 1 (Spring/printemps 1989): 225–45.

Lenskyj, Helen. 'The Role of Physical Education in the Socialization of Girls in Ontario, 1890–1930.' Diss. U of Toronto 1983.

Logan, John. *Aesthetic Criticism in Canada: Its Aims, Methods and Status. Being a*

Short Propaedeutic to the Appreciation of the Fine Arts and the Writing of Criticism, on Literature, Painting and Dramatic and Musical Performance. Toronto: McClelland, Goodchild and Stewart, 1917.

Murray, Heather. 'Making the Modern: Twenty-Five Years of the Margaret Eaton School of Literature and Expression.' *Essays in Theatre / Etudes théâtrales* 10, 1 (Nov. 1991): 39–57.

Nasmith, George. *Timothy Eaton.* Toronto: McClelland and Stewart, 1923.

O'Bryan, Maureen H. 'Physical Education – a Study of Professional Education in Ontario Universities.' Diss. U of Toronto 1973.

Peacock, Sandra J. *Jane Harrison: The Mask and the Self.* New Haven: Yale UP, 1988.

Prentice, Alison. 'Scholarly Passion: Two Persons Who Caught It.' *Women Who Taught: Perspectives on the History of Women and Teaching.* Ed. Alison Prentice and Marjorie R. Theobald. Toronto: U Toronto P, 1991. 258–83.

Raff, Emma Scott. *Of Queens' Gardens.* [Toronto]: n.p., [1914?]. [OISE]

'Reply of the Alumnae.' *University of Toronto Monthly* 9, 8 (June 1909): 289–91.

'Report of the Committee Appointed to Enquire in Regard to a Possible College for Women.' [Chair G. Wrong.] *University of Toronto Monthly* 9, 8 (June 1909): 286–9.

Ruskin, John. 'Preface to the Small Edition of 1882.' *Sesame and Lilies.* Sunnyside, Kent: George Allen, 1882. v–xi.

Schenck, Celeste M. 'Exiled by Genre: Modernism, Canonicity, and the Politics of Exclusion.' *Women's Writing in Exile.* Ed. Mary Lynn Broe and Angela Ingram. Chapel Hill, N.C.: U North Carolina P, 1989. 225–50.

Scott, Robert Barry. 'A Study of Amateur Theatre in Toronto: 1900–1930.' Diss. U of New Brunswick, 1966.

Shawn, Ted. *Every Little Movement: A Book about François Delsarte, the Man and His Philosophy, His Science of Applied Aesthetics, the Application of This Science to the Art of the Dance, and the Influence of Delsarte on American Dance.* 2d ed. Brooklyn, NY: Dance Horizons, Inc., 1963.

Taylor, Dorothy. 'What about Little Theatres?' *Canadian Forum* 9, 98 (Nov. 1928): 42–3.

University of Toronto Calendar for the Year 1908–1909. [Toronto]: The University Press, [1908].

Van Vliet, M.L. *Physical Education in Canada.* Scarborough, Ont.: Prentice-Hall, 1965.

Woolf, Virginia. 'On Not Knowing Greek.' *Collected Essays.* 4 vols. London: Hogarth P, 1966. 1:1–13.

– *A Room of One's Own.* London: Hogarth P, 1929.

– *Three Guineas.* London: Hogarth P, 1938.

4

Resistance and Reception: Backgrounds to Theory in English Canada

I believe that all vital teaching of English, with culture and enlightened citizenship for its object, must be conveyed directly through the literature of the language ... It is, of course, of the utmost importance that our pupils should be made acquainted with those few rules of syntax and analysis which are to be regarded as fundamental. But when all is said, it yet remains true of most of the English instruction of the day that it takes the pupil into the Valley of Dry Bones and sets him diligently to the task of bringing one bone unto another; but of the breath of the wind of heaven which is at last to quicken his work he finds no one to tell him anything. (Roberts 488)

Charles G.D. Roberts's essay 'The Teaching of English' appeared in the progressive New York journal the *Christian Union* in April 1888, accompanying the mournful editorial announcement of the death of Matthew Arnold. Roberts, then a junior professor of English (and French and political economy – even, at times, logic) at King's College in Windsor, Nova Scotia, pleads for a distinctively 'literary' rather than rhetorical teaching; and, further, for the reading of living authors, in a plan for English studies which is proudly and explicitly Arnoldian. Roberts also makes an implicit case for the inherent worth of English study, and one need look no further for a reason than the bizarre but then common allocation of his teaching duties. Combining philosophic rationale, pedagogic practicality, and institutional canniness, Roberts provides an early example of what is to become a distinctive if minor genre in literary studies, in Canada as elsewhere: the visionary or revisionary programmatic polemic.

The history of 'theory' in English Canada, of its reception and the resistance to it, is as long as the history of the discipline itself; but this is a history with which most of us are barely familiar.[1] Thus, when it has seemed necessary to analyse what has and has not been the effect of theory in the 1970s, '80s, and '90s, we have relied upon analytical and historical materials developed in and for England and the United States.[2] These are sometimes helpful and sometimes inapplicable, but in either case cannot substitute for an indigenous institutional analysis.

In attempting to account for the variegated fate of theory in the English-Canadian academy today, this chapter surveys some influential accounts of the 'resistance to theory,' to determine their usefulness to the Canadian situation. From this I conclude that two forms of work have particular promise. First, it would be useful to outline the development of critical paradigms for the English-Canadian academy, with attention to national and local differences. (Here 'paradigms' is defined in the most simple sense, as patterns or templates of disciplinary definition and method.) Second, it is necessary to analyse the relationship between the discipline of English and its institutions – that is, to relate critical and pedagogic structures to school, society, and state. (Such analysis also needs to examine literary study in its extra- or even contra-institutional settings.)[3] But both these examinations require history and data currently lacking. I hope to contribute to thinking on the first of these topics by sketching the development of paradigms for English studies in English Canada (and by providing, in the discursive footnotes, some resource material). The multivarious 'moment' of Charles G.D. Roberts prefigures the structure of English studies one hundred years later in its complexity of models and motives, and it is against this distinctively English-Canadian structure – with its dominant, residual, and emergent critical forms – that the contemporary resistance to theory, and the reception of it, can be read.[4] This chapter attempts to provide, then, the backgrounds to 'theory' in English Canada; but the history of those resistances and receptions, incorporations and innovations, remains to be read, and written – and made.

Since theory is often seen by its practitioners as having intrinsic merit, the continuing resistance to it requires explanation.[5] Further, even where theory has received an acceptance of sorts, for the most part traditional disciplinary organization and assumptions have remained intact; thus the 'resistance' to theory in Canada is less a case of critical blindness or neglect, and more a case of curricular superaddition. (A familiar example would be the grafting of a theory course, or a 'theorized' course, onto a program otherwise resolutely conservative.) The uneasy fit of 'theory' to 'field' and 'institution' has occasioned a turn to the examination of field and institution themselves, as the texts that theory must read.

Because there is scant history and data about criticism and its institutions for Canada, there has been a tendency to turn to analyses developed elsewhere. Recent work offers three types of explanation for the phenomenon known as 'resistance to theory.'[6]

Argument number one is the argument from politics. Here theory is seen as inherently left and the academy (or its official representatives) as inherently conservative or even rightist. Thus the debate about theory becomes mapped onto national political issues; in turn, national political concerns are seen to be played out, microcosmically but mimetically, in the academy.

Argument number two looks to what may, for convenience, be termed 'paradigms.' A methodology or set of assumptions is seen as the 'normal science' which theory cannot displace. For example, in the United States, New Criticism is seen to prevent theory; in England, it is a residual Leavisism. Such resistance to theory may be configured, more broadly, as a resistance of semiology to rhetoric (de Man 'Semiology') or as a resistance to any non-interpretive literary scholarship (Culler). In his 'Presidential Address,' J. Hillis Miller sees in the U.S. academy a turn to a crudely 'historical' or cultural work; and warns that theory's own 'triumph' may be in direct proportion to the degree to which it is becoming detheorized, generalized, and certain.

Argument number three, which follows, explains such resistances as part of a historical pattern. Gerald Graff, for example, countering a tendency to contrast current disciplinary upheaval to an imagined consensual past, outlines a history of contending paradigms for the U.S. academy (Graff 1987; Graff and Warner 1989). For Graff, English is by definition conflictual and resistant.

How adequately do these three accounts explain the resistance to theory? And how applicable are they to the situation in English Canada?

The first argument, from politics, operates powerfully in the United States precisely because it equates institutional and national politics. This explanation seems most useful for describing a certain 'structure of feeling' of theory practitioners, and a situation in which 'theory' defines less one's work than one's institutional self-positioning. While Canadian proponents tend to view theory as progressive, 'theory' has not functioned as an exclusive carrier of political claims. (This is possibly because an unbroken legacy of progressive voices in the Canadian university, and a more recent orientation to English Marxist work, have kept alive the question of social utility.) However, the fact that theory is seen as a 'foreign' transplant raises nationalist concerns; similar problems are generated by the awkward fit of theory to the national literatures; and this is often expressed as a concern about the language of theory, with theory viewed as arcane, mandarin, or impractical. Finally, a continuing current of progressivism within the discipline, both in its writers and scholars, means that simple left-right divisions are never easy to maintain; or, for that matter, to discern, since the Canadian academy has not (so far) been subject to the direct right-wing attacks made on U.S. and English universities.

Argument number two, resistance by paradigm, has been the most influential. Such explanations, however, tend to reify the term to be opposed (such as New Criticism) and to collapse the debates in that term's history. Further, such accounts cannot offer a satisfactory analysis of how this dominance is maintained, for to say that the paradigm has become a 'normal science' is to beg the question. Again, the English 're-reading' work has much to offer, as it attempts through historical and documentary analysis to outline the mechanisms of paradigm maintenance – of a residual Leavisite legacy, for example. In Canada, however, it is difficult to discern a dominant paradigm against which the 'new' must inevitably battle; and certainly theoretical resistance cannnot be explained solely in terms of New Criticism or Leavisism. Too, different forms of theoretical work have achieved varying degrees of acceptance or credence. (To offer one example: while 'New French Feminism' elsewhere appeared incommensurable with an 'Anglo-American' approach, here it quickly sparked the critical and creative work of both Québécois and English-Canadian women writers.)

Argument number three defines resistance as an endemic feature of English. Framed by Graff as a history of duelling paradigms, this explanation cannot account for materials and points of view that are excluded from the series of debates. Further, Graff's disciplinary dialectic cannot account for the pluralized, or at least variant, state of English studies in Canada; a study which, as I am suggesting, may be more profitably viewed as a sedimentation of different 'layers' of critical development. But Graff's work convincingly demonstrates the need to examine the operations of theories within their institutional settings.

In sum, the strengths and omissions of these explanations for the 'resistance to theory' suggest two promising areas for work in English Canada – that is, the detailing of disciplinary paradigms and the analysis of their institutionalization. The first can take direction both from recent archival and analytic work on disciplinary history (Baldick, Doyle, Eagleton, Gossman, Graff, and Graff and Warner; and Fee, Harris, Hubert, Johnson, and Morgan for Canada); and from theoretical work on disciplinarity itself, such as Derrida's work on the 'state' (in both senses) of philosophy and Samuel Weber's disclosure of the enclosures and exclusions of disciplinary categories. Institutional analysis is also needed to place English study in relation to universities and the state, and to interpret the ins and outs of the discipline in terms of these relations. (This work is needed both for theoretical 'advance' and for effective defence of a beleaguered humanities study.) Again, the 're-reading' work of daily documents and practices is instructive. But this is a difficult analysis to undertake, since lack of disciplinary self-reflexivity makes the ordinary at times invisible; and the increasing size of the university, and the development of a separate academic managerial class, mean that fewer of us will have direct dealings with the administrative and governmental face.

The next part of this analysis will attempt to contribute to the first of these two suggested areas, by sketching the vectors and factors of disciplinary paradigms in English Canada. While the analysis is not historical, it follows a rough chronology intended to be suggestive.

During his tenure at King's College, Roberts was placed at a particular intersection of heritages and influences. Roberts's classical training was under George Parkin, a man with a particular gift for bringing classics and contemporary literature into dialogue. Roberts, as the son of a minister, engaged in debates over the 'higher' biblical criticism, which challenged the bedrock of religious authority by adding historical to hermeneutic questions. He was attuned – as were the Maritime provinces of his day – to intellectual life in England and Europe and the Eastern seaboard.[7] (We need only read the works of the 'Confederation' poet Roberts in *The Yellow Book*, or learn that 'maple leaf' poet Bliss Carman was a first North American proponent of the symbolists, to see this attunement as more than a colonial yearning.)[8] There is also about Roberts a particular sense of *modernité*: his fascination with Wilde's aestheticism, with the bohemian, with the paranormal, with poetic experimentation. Roberts's notion of the 'literary,' then, was thoroughly up-to-date; he was a tireless booster as well of a nascent Canadian writing of which he was to become so representative a figure. His correspondence with Carman might sound oddly familiar to a junior academic today, with complaints about the entrenched study of linguistics, philology, and the dreaded Anglo-Saxon, in letters detailing the saga of their unsuccessful attempts to gain jobs in American and Canadian universities, which sought only the Johns Hopkins or Oxbridge educated (see Boone; and Gundy). Roberts's vision of literature teaching is brought into conflict with traditional study in his essay of 1888. References to Arnold permit him to organize this mixture of traditions and modernisms into a coherent program – a program which was never enacted, but which marks a formative moment of English studies in Canada.

From the earliest years of the discipline, several basic patterns of distribution and organization may be discerned, and they continue to function as structural principles. As Henry Hubert has suggested in *Harmonious Perfection*, the history of English studies throughout the nineteenth century is a story of contention between Scottish-based rhetorical utilitarianism and British belles-lettrism; a tale of low church and high church, liberal and tory, rhetoric and aesthetics. While several early and influential dissenting reformists made strong philosophical and practical cases for the social value of rhetorical study – in Thomas McCulloch's *The Nature and Uses of a Liberal Education* and the Pictou Academy, or Egerton Ryerson's *Inaugural Address* and Victoria College – this was not to persist as the dominant direction in higher education. As Nan Johnson has discovered, British belles-lettristic theory – including an examination of classical precedents and the inculcation of 'Taste' – characterized the curriculum until the end of the nineteenth century and in some cases even beyond, in contrast to the American development of a primarily pragmatic approach. While a more 'practical' study continued at the primary and secondary levels and in low-church colleges (or colleges modelled on them), and was later to be introduced at western institutions concerned about the skills of applicants, rhetorical study was displaced in the eastern and central universities.[9] The alignment of British-model education with the Anglican elite of the Maritimes and Canada West is one reason for this development; another is that belles-lettristic and later aesthetic literary study was readily accommodated to the idealism which was the prevalent, almost determinant, intellectual direction of the nineteenth century in Canada (see McKillop; and Shortt).[10] But it should also be noted that rationales for literature and aesthetic study were able to succeed to the degree that they could incorporate, or at least address, the agenda of education for individual and national improvement laid down by those practically minded educational founders.

Thus the institutionalization of literary study is not a matter of the academy alone. While in the late nineteenth century and the early twentieth the universities were more independent than they now are (there was no elaborate superstructure of university-government relations),[11] they were, in the public eye and their own, more closely attuned to the public system of education overall, with university professors characteristically producing public lectures, programs for humanities studies, and even lower-school curricula and texts.[12] This is more than a top-down directing of education (although it was that, too); it is also an important source of disciplinary self-definition in Canada. The late development of graduate studies and resultant lack of expectation of scholarly productivity caused an orientation to teaching that remains strong, even in institutions now isolated from the school systems and internally stratified.

The above characterized the discipline in its early years, and its basic (and continuing) structural features. A program of education for citizenry provided an early rationale for liberal arts study, and a specifically vocational education was late to develop; literature study was institutionalized through demonstrations of its value for this purpose.[13] The legacy of the European Romantics (and particularly their focus on national literatures) could be accommodated to this home-grown program, as is apparent in the writings of early reviewers and critics (see Fee). 'Most striking about the early efforts,' writes Len Findlay, 'is the shrewdness and clarity with which they established the topics that have remained at the centre of Canadian theoretical debate: the possibility and desirability of a distinctive Canadian literature and the nature of literature's contribution to the national life' (1227).

The predisposition to English educational ideas, and the indigenous development of a program for national education and its social utility, laid the groundwork for an interested reception of the ideas of Matthew Arnold, especially with his 1884 speaking tour (see Opala). That these ideas did not always travel under the name of 'Arnold' is a sign both of a ready assimilation and of an irreverent appropriation for domestic purposes. Recent concentration on the centrality of Arnold to state and colonial education (Baldick, Doyle) can easily obscure the ways in which his ideas were seized by nationalist and progressive literary forces here. For example, as has been noted in chapter 2, not only Roberts but also 'Fidelis' (Agnes Maule Machar) advocated an Arnoldian study; while, in a neat turn, the 'nativist' fighters for a Canadian appointment in English at Toronto could accuse the conservative forces of not knowing their

Arnold. This adoption was not unique to Canada, but there seems to have been a particularly ready fit of Arnold's ideas to the national education program here. In turn, Arnoldianism provided a compelling series of rationales that allowed English to move into the centre of humanities study in Canada and to retain that position for many years (Jasen 'Arnoldian'; Jasen 'English Canadian'). (That Canada's universities are public institutions meant that the potential applicability was sensed at all levels.) Arnoldianism, it might be said, provided a solid bridge between the demands of colonial education and the belles-lettrism and idealism of an evolving study.

The discipline in English Canada went on to develop in a markedly distinctive way. Early critical work was eclectic, and most often intended for public consumption. This 'amateurism' of study remained a feature until, perhaps, the end of the Second World War, kept in place in large measure by the restriction to undergraduate teaching and the lack of an infrastructure – grants, journals, libraries, professional associations – that make sustained activity possible (see MacLure). (And some notions of the inherent 'gentlemanliness' of English still remain.) Concern over the professionalization of literary study through increasing specialization, either of teaching or inquiry, has worried English-Canadian academicians for some decades now (at the same time as it has provided powerful disciplinary self-justifications). But this acceptance of interdisciplinarity in the early years of the discipline merits examination.[14]

David Galbraith has remarked that departments of English seem to be able to drift only in one of two directions – to history or to philosophy.[15] The Canadian choice is emblematized by the fact that Toronto, Queen's, and Western had dual chairs in English and history until 1894, 1910, and 1920 respectively (Klinck 329–30) and that Toronto maintained a joint program until 1936, at which point it chose independence rather than membership in the then new honours course in social and philosophical studies (see Harris). Some early tendencies to develop an aesthetic criticism were overshadowed by what was to become a dominant and unique disciplinary directive – the placing of literary texts in relation to history and intellectual history.[16] It is a development which begins with the wide-ranging work of Sir Daniel Wilson, which is developed by such scholars as Malcolm Wallace, and which is institutionalized in the person and policies of A.S.P. Woodhouse. As early as 1889, the curricular relationship of historical to aesthetic approaches is adjudicated, with W.J. Alexander's inaugural address, *The Study of Literature*. This disposition to historical study is strengthened by the embeddedness of early Canadian literary work in a context of historical study: as Carl Klinck notes, 'literary history ... had made a start, albeit a slow one, under conditions similar to, and influenced by, contemporary research in general Canadian history' (327). And, as Northrop Frye has pointed out, this historical orientation is to underpin later work which seems on the surface dramatically different. Harold Innis, he reminds us, began with historical studies of the economics of fish and furs; while Frye took as a point of departure the 'history of ideas' work characterized by Woodhouse. ('It seeemed to me that these "ideas" were really elements or units in what Tillyard calls a world picture ...' [33].) This historical orientation, specific to English Canada, may be seen to provide a third and perhaps dominant level of the disciplinary strata, as well as a distinctive identity to the work done in this country.[17]

However, while English-Canadian criticism was developing in strength and definition (a progression detailed in Millar MacLure's survey), by the late 1940s it was becoming clear that a stronger support would be needed if Canadians were to take a place in the scholarly world; this becomes apparent in the surveys undertaken by Brebner and by Kirkconnell and Woodhouse. The founding of the Canada Council from the 1951 Massey Report is a turning-point here; as is the 1957 establishment of the Association of University Teachers of English (later ACUTE and then ACCUTE), which in its early form devoted considerable attention to professional and pedagogic matters (see Garson). (It enters, of course, later into the narrative of 'theory' as one of the main forums for the formulation and debate of the topic.) The postwar establishment of graduate education and expansion of universities and hiring accelerated these processes of development and stratification, and initiated a more complex relationship between university and government. One feature of the discipline at this time was its centrality to humanities study, coming in part from the Ryersonian educational agenda and in part from the figures drawn from English (Woodhouse to Priestley to Whalley to Frye) who have been able public defenders of humanist study. This helped English to maintain its footing even during post–Second World War calls for practical education for national prosperity. How English gained, and then lost, this position provides matter for rueful reflection.

If the years between the wars are marked by general developments for the discipline, the post–Second World War period is characterized by local differences and specializations. This differentiation was accelerated with the rise of new universities and the expansion of existent ones and the consequent hiring. The legacy of this time is what may be considered the distinctive 'flavour' of different departments: some more Leavisite than others; some New Critical; some devoted to textual or editorial work, in differences institutional and individual. (For example, New Critical perspectives could find a ready home at some institutions – especially those hiring, and sometimes from the United States, in the '60s – while its relationship to other departments was famously embattled.)[18] It is normally to this top level of paradigm development that we pay attention when thinking about departmental politics and disciplinary resistances.

While the pros and cons of both New Criticism and Leavisism fuelled debates in the university quarterlies, other forms of critical work were forming in a distinctively Canadian context; each, in some sense, prepared the ground for theory. Three varieties of new work may be discerned – the communications theory of Harold Innis and Marshall McLuhan (and, at points, Dennis Lee); the synthesizing work of Northrop Frye; and the taxonomic thematics of a developing 'Canlit' criticism. Distinctive as these forms may be, they had some common consequences for 'theory.' Each offered, from different perspectives, a challenge to discriminations and choices based solely on 'aesthetic' criteria, and posed questions not directed to interpretive ends. Each validated approaches based on social or national (that is, extra-literary) considerations.[19] All pushed the walls of an already elastic disciplinary boundary; all kept alive the notion of English's 'inner' interdisciplinariness.

The moment of the entry of 'theory' to the academy was thus as richly complex as the moment of the formulation of English studies: a dominant critical mode by which aesthetic questions are referred to historical considerations; a residual pedagogic mandate forged in democratic concerns and rhetorical study; an emergent theoretical and proto-theoretical work. And it is to be hoped that an equally complex admixture some quarter-century later – its critical impulses generated within and without the English-Canadian community – will provide the tensions and extensions that keep theory self-'resistant' in the way de Man has configured ('Resistance').

This chronology takes English studies up to the point of entry of 'theory,' and here it deliberately stops, for the purpose is not to provide a history of theory in English Canada, nor of the debates surrounding it, but rather to display 'theory' against the existent terrain of the discipline in English Canada.[20] What lessons might be learned from the above?

First, the continuing close connection of English in Canada with pub-lic education, and attention to pedagogic principle, means that theory's 'teachability' demands reflection and demonstration. These are ques-tions which cannot be sidestepped.

Second, and related, it may be possible to make connections between theoretical activity and more traditional disciplinary directions; for example, the early formulation of rhetorical study as a precondition for informed and active citizenship. A redescription and redefinition of the project, from the teaching of 'theory' to the teaching of 'reading,' might be in order.

Third, it might be fruitful to see to how great an extent the idea of 'theory' as social thinking and cultural work can be aligned with a strong existent sense of public responsibility, and a predisposition for contextual work. That would be to ally 'theory' firmly to both past and current defences of humanities study in this country.

Fourth, perhaps too much attention has been paid to the 'top' level of disciplinary manifestation (New Critical or Leavisite orientations) and too little to the historical orientation of the discipline. The 'resistance' to theory in Canada may not be a case of resistance to 'theory' at all, but resistance to theory-as-philosophy. To how great a degree has the popu-lar equation of 'theory' with 'deconstruction' re-mobilized sentiment in favour of the historical?

Fifth, it is, I believe, a mistake to see 'English' as inherently conserva-tive. It may be wise – and good for 'theory' itself – to connect theory to an inherent and indigenous strain of academic progressivism.

Sixth, turning 'theory' onto our own daily practices and documents will help us to better locate the arguments and rationales to be devel-oped at the national and local level.

And last, appeals to the heritage and immutability of the way things are ought to be countered by reference to past change and always present diversity.

Notes

1 One of many available examples is the issue of *University of Toronto Quarterly* (58, 4 [Summer 1989]) on the topic of 'professionalism.' It was interesting to note that the writers who are English professors made their arguments almost solely with reference to English and U.S. intellectual history. This says less about the orientation of the writers themselves than it does about

the difficulties of casting arguments with reference to the discipline in English Canada, given the absence of material on the subject.

2 Historical material would include disciplinary histories by Baldick, Doyle, Eagleton, and Gossman (in England), and Graff, most influentially, in the United States. Analytic material used in Canada includes English 're-reading' work (Batsleer et al., Brooker and Humm et al., Widdowson et al., and the journal *Literature/Teaching/Politics*); and U.S. debates on professionalism, left criticism, and disciplinarity, for example. It is also worth noting that a number of these analyses focus on the development of English at Oxbridge; by which time English in Canada had been firmly established for at least fifty years.

3 In my opinion, there is a tendency in some 're-reading' work to see literary study as inherently or intrinsically linked to state social reproduction; this predisposition is caused, in part, by the focus on Oxbridge. Understanding the place of literary study in populist and progressive education will help to give a more complex picture of the discipline and its potential.

4 It is Raymond Williams's idea that emergent and residual, as well as dominant, cultures may be present in any given formation.

5 It is difficult to develop an across-the-board explanation. There are marked differences between types of theoretical work, as well as variations in the degree of acceptance they have received. The place (or lack thereof) of feminist literary theory and postcolonial theory, to give two examples, is clearly overdetermined.

It should also be noted that this examination is specific to English. The situation of theory in departments of comparative literature, for example, is very different.

Last, on the term 'resistance': here I am less concerned with the question of why 'theory' as a separate subject area is or is not taught, and more with the limited effect of the theoretical challenge to canon, curriculum, and pedagogy.

6 This paper omits two very popular but 'untheoretical' accounts. An argument from personality, which sees 'resistance' as stemming from powerful personal figures (Walter Jackson Bate, by synecdoche) is less applicable to a Canadian situation, where figures, either 'pro' or 'con,' lack comparable clout. This argument may describe departmental-level politics but cannot give a general account. A second argument, from perceived national characteristics, sees resistance as coming from an innate American anti-intellectualism or inculcated British commonsensicality. This has all the limits of any stereotype; it seems to function best as a gesture of exasperation. But – to give the argument momentary credence – it does not apply here if, as

Margaret Atwood suggests, English Canadians have a 'synthetic habit of mind' (illustrated by Innis, McLuhan, Frye, and, one would add, Atwood herself). 'Give the same pattern to a model American, a model English and a model Canadian critic: the American will say "This is how it works"; the Englishman "How good, how true to Life" (or, "How boring, tasteless and trite"); the Canadian will say "This is where it fits into the entire universe"' (Atwood 62–3). Surely theory should have found a ready home here.

7 On intellectual culture in the Maritime provinces of the day, see Malcolm Ross.

8 Carman's *Behind the Arras*, for example, shows traces of his earlier translations of Verlaine (M. Miller 151); more influentially, he and Richard Hovey used their journal the *Chap Book* (probably the first little magazine in the United States) to introduce the symbolists to North America.

9 An interesting example of a twentieth-century (1927–8) incorporation of rhetoric/composition instruction into the curriculum is provided by the University of Alberta (see Broadus). The emphasis on composition in the later-founded universities helps to account for the concentration of creative writing programs in the western universities.

10 The life and career of James Cappon of Queen's provides a good case study of the overlap of idealist philosophy and a nascent English study; see Shortt's 'James Cappon: The Ideal in Culture.'

11 Axelrod provides an interesting history of university-government relations for the province of Ontario.

12 In Ontario, in particular, the intrication of university professors with secondary education in English was significant. George Paxton Young, a professor of moral philosophy, was also at times a school inspector (see Morgan); most notably, W.J. Alexander prepared curricula and such teaching texts as the many editions of *Select Poems* and *Shorter Poems*. Various members of the faculty of Toronto and other universities (such as O.J. Stevenson of Guelph and James Cappon of Queen's) were also involved with pedagogic development and texts; this was made possible, in part, by the 1886 formation of the Modern Language Association of Ontario, which dealt with education at all levels. Even in provinces where there was little or no direct influence, early scholarly work characteristically took the form of public lecturing and speeches and publication for non-academic audiences.

13 While my concern here is with critical developments, it should be noted that this 'public' face to education allowed two important forms of representation. In Canada as elsewhere, women were enthusiastic early entrants to the discipline (see Neatby, and 'Women Students in Modern Languages'); and there has always been a high proportion of creative writers among depart-

mental staff (an important component of the progressive politics of the discipline – see mastheads of the *Canadian Forum* – and of nationalist debates). Both groups are part of the 'hidden history' of the discipline.

14 G.G. Sedgewick's 1928 talk 'The Unity of the Humanities,' delivered to an early conference of English professors, is an interesting example of this interdisciplinary impulse.

15 In conversation.

16 On aesthetic criticism, see J.D. Logan's 1917 *Aesthetic Criticism in Canada*.

17 Graff cites Douglas Bush's 1948 MLA presidential address, calling for historically based study, as a major critical departure in the American academy. In her review of Graff and Harris, Groening points out that the Toronto-trained Bush was simply advocating what was already standard practice in Canada.

18 For an instance of New Criticism in Canada, see Marchand's biography of McLuhan. For the memoirs of a Canadian Leavisite, see Keith.

19 In formulating his criticism of Frye's 'verbal universe' (91–6), Terry Eagleton appears unaware of Frye's pedagogic writings – and of the social gospel movement.

20 For recent critical and theoretical surveys, see Cameron, Fee, Findlay, and Rajan.

Works Cited

Alexander, W.J. *The Study of Literature: Inaugural Lecture Delivered in the Convocation Hall, October 12th 1889.* Toronto: Rowsell and Hutchison, 1889.

Atwood, Margaret. 'Eleven Years of *Alphabet.*' *Canadian Literature* 49 (Summer 1971): 60–4.

Axelrod, Paul. *Scholars and Dollars: Politics, Economics, and the Universities of Ontario 1945–1980.* Toronto: U Toronto P, 1982.

Baldick, Chris. *The Social Mission of English Criticism, 1848–1932.* Oxford: Clarendon P, 1983.

Batsleer, Janet, et al., eds. *Rewriting English: Cultural Politics of Gender and Class.* London: Methuen, 1985.

Boone Laurel. *The Collected Letters of Charles G.D. Roberts.* Fredericton, N.B.: Goose Lane Editions, 1989.

Brebner, John Bartlet. *Scholarship for Canada: The Function of Graduate Studies.* Ottawa: Canadian Social Science Research Council, 1945.

Broadus, E.K. 'A Plan for Dealing with Weakness in English.' *National Conference of Canadian Universities Proceedings* (1927): 95–9.

Brooker, Peter, and Peter Humm, eds. *Dialogue and Difference: English into the Nineties.* London: Routledge, 1989.

Cameron, Barry. 'Theory and Criticism: Trends in Canadian Literature.' *Literary History of Canada: Canadian Literature in English*. Ed. W.H. New. 3d ed. 4 vols. Toronto: U Toronto P, 1990. 4:108–32.

Culler, Jonathan. 'Beyond Interpretation.' *The Pursuit of Signs: Semiotics, Literature, Deconstruction*. Ithaca, N.Y.: Cornell UP, 1981. 3–17.

de Man, Paul. 'The Resistance to Theory.' *The Resistance to Theory*. Minneapolis: U Minnesota P, 1986. 3–20.

– 'Semiology and Rhetoric.' *Allegories of Reading*. New Haven: Yale UP, 1979. 3–20.

Derrida, Jacques. 'Ou commence et comment finit un corps enseignant.' *Politiques de la philosophie*. Ed. Dominique Grisoni. Paris: Bernard Grasset, 1976. 55–98.

Doyle, Brian. *English and Englishness*. London: Routledge, 1989.

Eagleton, Terry. *Literary Theory: An Introduction*. Minneapolis: U Minnesota P, 1983. 17–53.

Fee, Margery. 'Criticism,' in 'Literature in English: Theory and Criticism.' *The Canadian Encyclopedia*. 2d ed. 4 vols. Edmonton: Hurtig, 1988. 2:1227–8.

– 'English-Canadian Criticism, 1890–1950: Defining and Establishing a National Literature.' Diss. U of Toronto 1981.

'Fidelis' [Agnes Maule Machar]. 'The True Principles of Teaching English.' *Canada Educational Monthly and 'School Magazine'* 11, 2 (Feb. 1889): 46–8.

Findlay, Leonard M. 'Literature in English: Theory and Criticism.' *The Canadian Encyclopedia*. 2d ed. 4 vols. Edmonton: Hurtig, 1988. 2:1227.

Frye, Northrop. ' Across the River and Out of the Trees.' *Divisions on a Ground: Essays on Canadian Culture*. Ed. and introd. James Polk. Toronto: Anansi, 1982. 26–40.

Garson, Marjorie. *ACUTE: The First Twenty-Five Years, 1957–1982: A Brief History of the Association of Canadian University Teachers of English*. N.p.: [the Association], [1982].

Gossman, Lionel. 'Literature and Education.' *New Literary History* 13, 2 (Winter 1982): 341–71.

Graff, Gerald. *Professing Literature: An Institutional History*. Chicago: U Chicago P, 1987.

– and Michael Warner, eds. *The Origins of Literary Studies in America: A Documentary Anthology*. London: Routledge, 1989.

Groening, Laura. 'Modernizing Academia: An American and a Canadian Vision.' *Dalhousie Review* 67, 4 (Winter 1987–8): 511–22.

Gundy, H. Pearson, ed. *Letters of Bliss Carman*. Kingston and Montreal: McGill-Queen's UP, 1981.

Harris, Robin. *English Studies at Toronto: A History*. Toronto: U Toronto P, 1988.

Hubert, Henry. *Harmonious Perfection: The Development of English Studies in Nineteenth-Century Anglo-Canadian Colleges*. East Lansing, Mich.: Michigan State UP, 1994.

Jasen, Pat. 'Arnoldian Humanism, English Studies, and the Canadian University.' *Queen's Quarterly* 95, 3 (Autumn 1988): 550–66.

– 'The English Canadian Liberal Arts Curriculum: An Intellectual History, 1880–1950.' Diss. U of Manitoba 1987.

Johnson, Nan. 'Rhetoric and Belles Lettres in the Canadian Academy: An Historical Analysis.' *College English* 50, 8 (Dec. 1988): 861–73.

Keith, W.J. 'The Wood and the Trees: A Personal Response.' *University of Toronto Quarterly* 58, 4 (Summer 1989): 469–74.

Kirkconnell, Watson, and A.S.P. Woodhouse. *The Humanities in Canada*. Ottawa: Humanities Research Council of Canada, 1947.

Klinck, C.F. 'Bookmen and Scholars.' *Aspects of Nineteenth-Century Ontario*. Ed. F. Armstrong. Toronto: U Toronto P, 1974. 327–33.

Logan, J.D. *Aesthetic Criticism in Canada: Its Aims, Methods and Status. Being a Short Propaedeutic to the Appreciation of the Fine Arts and the Writing of Criticism, on Literature, Painting and Dramatic and Musical Performance*. Toronto: McClelland, Goodchild and Stewart, 1917.

McCulloch, Thomas (Rev.). *The Nature and Uses of a Liberal Education Illustrated: Being the Lecture Delivered at the Opening of the Building, Erected for the Accommodation of the Classes of the Pictou Academical Institution*. Halifax: A.H. Holland, Printer, 1819.

McKillop, A.B. *Contours of Canadian Thought*. Toronto: U Toronto P, 1987.

MacLure, Millar. 'Literary Scholarship.' *Literary History of Canada: Canadian Literature in English*. Ed. Carl F. Klinck. 2d ed. 3 vols. Toronto: U Toronto P, 1976. 2:53–74.

Marchand, Philip. *Marshall McLuhan: The Medium and the Messenger*. Toronto: Random House, 1989.

Miller, J. Hillis. 'Presidential Address 1986: The Triumph of Theory, the Resistance to Reading, and the Question of the Material Base.' *PMLA* 102, 3 (May 1987): 281–91.

Miller, Muriel. *Bliss Carman: Quest and Revolt*. St John's, Nfld.: Jefferson P, 1985.

Morgan, Robert James. 'English Studies as Cultural Production in Ontario 1860–1929.' Diss. U of Toronto 1987.

Neatby, Hilda. *Queen's University. Vol. I. 1841–1917*. Ed. Frederick W. Gibson and Roger Graham. Montreal: Queen's UP, 1978.

Opala, Beatrice Barbara. 'Matthew Arnold in Canada.' M.A. thesis, McGill U, 1968.

Rajan, Balachandra. 'Scholarship and Criticism.' *Literary History of Canada: Cana-*

dian Literature in English. Ed. W.H. New. 3d ed. 4 vols. Toronto: U Toronto P, 1990. 4:133–58.

Roberts, Charles G.D. 'The Teaching of English.' *Christian Union* 37, 16 (19 April 1888): 488–9.

Ross, Malcolm. '"A Strange Aesthetic Ferment."' *Canadian Literature* 68/69 (Spring/Summer 1976): 13–25.

Ryerson, Egerton (Rev.). *Inaugural Address on the Nature and Advantages of an English and Liberal Education.* Toronto: By Order of the Board of Trustees and Visitors, 1842.

Sedgewick, G.G. 'The Unity of the Humanities.' *Dalhousie Review* 8 (1928–9): 357–67.

Shortt, S.E.D. 'James Cappon: The Ideal in Culture.' *The Search for an Ideal: Six Canadian Intellectuals and Their Convictions in an Age of Transition, 1890–1930.* Toronto: U Toronto P, 1976. 59–75.

'Symposium: The Professionalization of Intellectuals.' *University of Toronto Quarterly* 58, 4 (Summer 1989): 439–512.

Weber, Samuel. *Demarcating the Disciplines: Philosophy, Literature, Art.* Minneapolis: U Minnesota P, 1986.

Widdowson, Peter, ed. *Re-Reading English.* London: Methuen, 1982.

Williams, Raymond. 'Base and Superstructure in Marxist Cultural Theory.' *Problems in Materialism and Culture.* London: Verso, 1980. 31–49.

'Women Students in Modern Languages.' *Modern Language Instruction in Canada.* 2 vols. [Publications of the American and Canadian Committees on Modern Languages, vol. 6.] Toronto: U Toronto P, 1928. 1:468–74.

PART II: INSTITUTION

5

Women in English

In a room where I teach, at St Hilda's College, the sun pours in on warm autumn days through the stained glass windows donated to the college some years ago. St Hilda is depicted in blues and greens and reds in her characteristic attitudes and with scenes from a life at the time eminent and consequential, but now little known and unstudied. In the window on the left, she extends a book, on which are written the words 'Hilda' and 'Caedmon,' to the kneeling cowherd who, Bede informs us, was suddenly blessed with the original gift of vernacular religious verse. In the second window, she is on her knees before a Christ crucified; in the third, seated, she gives instruction to a group of small people – perhaps children – crowded around her. These are iconic scenes from the life of St Hilda: abbess of Hereteu, founder of the renowned monastic community of Streanaeshalch, counsel to kings, maker of bishops, delegate to the Council of Whitby, known for her learning, piety, and charity. But these windows also depict her in the common postures and positions of women in their relation to learning and letters: as receiver of knowledge, as inspiration, as teacher (if only to the small), and as the midwife of English poetry.

The first of these windows (designed by Yvonne Williams) was donated to the college by the accomplished Mossie May (Waddington) Kirkwood, and dedicated to the memory of her sister, the artist Valerie Dell Adams.[1] Prior to becoming an assistant professor at Trinity College and then its dean of women, Kirkwood was a long-time sessional appointee in the Department of English at University College, before that department would allow regular appointments to women, and even then, she was required in the 1930s to report to the president of the university how she spent her salary (Ford 59). All the more interesting, then, is this subtly humorous revisioning of the Caedmon tale. For here Hilda, as she offers the book to Caedmon, usurps the place of the 'man' (*sum mon*) who, in Bede's account, appeared to Caedmon in the night and bade him sing. Blessed Hilda, herself the director of a two-sex monastic community, might be struck by the location of these windows, in the more modest buildings of the women's residence, set apart from the college of which it is the poor sister. (Clearly, in Virginia Woolf's memorable phrase, we are still paying into 'Arthur's Education Fund.') Equally important to this scene is the group of students sitting around the seminar table. Honours English majors, many of them, and lovers of literature all, they are for the most part, and sometimes overwhelmingly, women.[2]

Much recent work has been devoted to women authors and the relation of women to literature and to language. A number of lines of inquiry have contributed to this flourishing and important area. Lesser known or unknown women authors are discovered and their better known contemporaries are reclaimed and reread. The very categories of 'literature' – of aesthetic quality and generic merit – by which women have traditionally been excluded, have themselves been assessed and found wanting. New writing is encouraged and eagerly received; feminist critical work places the writer in her social circumstances and the reader in her active relationship. The figure of woman in canonical literatures – as stereotype, image, inspiration – is critiqued and symptomatically read, and the question of 'women's language' is explored empirically, theoretically, polemically. The double task, of making a place for women's literature and feminist study in the existent academy, and of developing parallel programs, is still under way. So much work has been done that the question is now often raised of whether feminist literary study is becoming synonymous with feminism – at least in the academy – and of the possible consequences of this. The sort of thinking and institutional alignments formed by feminist critical work have been invaluable, however, for combatting ever narrowing programmatic notions of 'literacy,' whether cultural or otherwise. And the arguments made for canonical widening are extended to other cultural, ethnic, and national inclusions in the academy itself. While the relationship of feminist literary theory to feminism more generally may need to be rethought, and while, as always, the question of *which* women are represented remains, the vigour and commitment of these endeavours can scarcely be in doubt, and feminist literary workers remain an important voice for pluralism in the academy.

Less attention, however, has been devoted to the relationship of women to the institutions of academic and literary study; here I will make a case for such analysis, and will survey in the text and notes some of the available resources.[3] This chapter begins by considering English as a so-called 'feminine' discipline. A glance at the enthusiastic entry of women into 'English' at the turn of the century may provide some useful parallels to the position of women in the academy today. This particular position is related to what might be seen as one of the most pronounced and particular 'gender pyramids' of all the disciplines. The consequences of this distribution in English are many, not the least of which is the fact that when we are talking about 'English,' we are really talking about the education or social formation of young women, who are the majority of students. The paper concludes by suggesting some factors in a 'discipline-specific' analysis of the position of women in English.

Certainly, women are depicted in literature and literary study in discriminatory or diminished ways. But it is not just a question of negative stereotypes, for woman is everywhere figured in canonical literature in positive terms. The woman of European literature is sphinx and muse, question and answer, star and flower. The Native woman in the Euro-Canadian-authored literature of North America is wisdom and silence, nature and knowledge, land – and 'lost' land. Woman is heart, hand, head, backbone, womb – in short, everything except her (whole) self. Metaphorically transformed, synecdochically dismembered, metonymically shunted along, woman in the all-knowing discourse of the Literary is completely ... figured out.

But while 'woman' is the very condition for the existence of poetry, English departments sometimes seem to prefer to get along without women altogether. (This has allowed the rise of an entire literary sub-genre – the feminist-authored English department murder mystery.)[4] How, then, does the all-important in English literature become the more-or-less extraneous in English studies?

Peter Stallybrass and Allon White have postulated in *The Politics and Poetics of Transgression* that hierarchy is fundamental to sense-making in European cultures: the 'high' rejects the 'low' while depending upon it materially (for its productive and, one might add, reproductive capability) and symbolically (as carrier of the forbidden and therefore fantasized). From this, 'the low-Other is despised and denied at the level of political organization and social being whilst it is instrumentally constitutive of the shared imaginary repertoires of the dominant culture'

(5–6). In this way, to use White and Stallybrass's formulation, what is socially peripheral is symbolically central and vice versa – and the tendency to confuse the two, or to suggest that symbolic valuation ever compensates for social marginalization, must be countered with the recognition that the symbolically central are central to a system not of their own making or control. Since literature is one crucial way by which women are 'valued' – in all the senses of that word – then feminist text-reading practices are necessary to cut across the grain of the ostensible. There is also something to be learned by examining the placement of women within (and without) language and literary study; for here we have the anomalous situation of a discipline that has often been described as 'feminine' (whether approvingly or disapprovingly) and which has been seen as especially suited to women's abilities. There have been notable women scholars and critics; the discipline still attracts women students especially; much important feminist work has been done through literary and linguistic theory; and English departments have frequently accommodated women's studies – as many less 'conservative' departments have not. In fact, English as a discipline developed in tandem with the entry of women to colleges and universities, in many cases its study being restricted to women, or women to it.[5]

Women have been seen since the early eighteenth century as especially suited by talent and inclination to language study.[6] This idea of 'fit' and 'fittedness' is central to the nineteenth-century development of 'English,' as such writers as Brian Doyle have demonstrated. Just as women are seen as 'fit' for its study – and, later, women's perceived nurturing gifts will make us seem especially 'fit' to teach it – so English is seen to 'fit' people for life, and in two ways. First, it equips them with necessary skills and even virtues. (The university institutionalization of literary study in England has its moment in the origin of the civil service examinations.) The second 'fitting' function of English studies was best expressed by Matthew Arnold. Literary study is thought to promote social harmony by reducing and reconciling competing interests. Thus the importance of English in the education of workers, women, children, and those of the colonized who are expected to form an administrative or service class (as opposed, for example, to Black people in the slave states, where the criminalization of literacy was part of a program of absolute disenfranchisement).[7]

In England, the expansionist project of economic imperialism and the integrationist project of cultural socialization are deeply interdependent in the foundation of English studies; and, in the post–First World War period, English became seen as the foundation of national study. In the U.S. academy, as Richard Ohmann has suggested, the rise of language and literacy study has a genesis in the consolidation of monopoly capitalism; while in the Canadian academy, a 'democratized' Arnoldianism mapped readily onto an existent belles-lettrism and a Ryersonian rationale for national development through rhetorical training. In all cases, 'English' as a discipline has a role – although, it must be emphasized, a far from hegemonic role – in the creation of and placement of a national citizenry. And women were there from the beginning.

The role of women in English has been best researched for England, but it is illustrative of the parallel development of women's education and English studies itself.[8] Just as literature functioned as the 'poor man's classics' in worker education and extension programs, so it became women's 'Greats' in the university. The years before the First World War, when the study of English was sometimes referred to as 'pink sunsets' (and the homophobic implications are clear), was also the time of the rise of the woman scholar. This moment has been described by Virginia Woolf in *Three Guineas* and, especially, in *A Room of One's Own*; we find it too in the career of Vera Brittain, who in her writings – and, I like to think, in her very name – described the multiple aspirations of women who loved literature early in this century.

In *The Rise of English Studies* Palmer lists the ratios of women to men candidates for the honours examination in the early Oxford years. From the beginning, women outnumbered men by at least two to one (10 women to 4 men in 1897; 12 to 5 in 1898, for example). The proportion then increased to three, sometimes even four, to one in the first decade of the new century (Palmer 116). The overall popularity of the subject is indicated by the 152 men and 118 women listed in the normal honours course in the Michaelmas term of 1919, and the 17 men and 2 women reading for the B.Litt. in that year (149). By the early 1920s, however, the numbers of men and women candidates had become approximately equal, with 52 women and 50 men sitting examinations (148).

While Palmer's statistics are revealing, and prove that English was a women's discipline for some time, most disciplinary historians omit women altogether from their accounts of the early years, or begin their histories once the men have arrived. Stephen Potter in *The Muse in Chains*, for example, notes only the four men of 1894 and sympathizes 'with the feelings of these students, with what must have been an intolerable sense of isolation,' at the same time remarking that 'there were twice as many names on the women's honours list ...' (Potter 203). In the

U.S. academy, as Gerald Graff notes, 'it seems to have been a virtual commonplace of this period that college students were impervious to humanistic education' – a commonplace Graff himself seems to accept, although as he had noted in his own preceding paragraph, women were filling such courses in the large universities of the Middle West (107).

The influx of women into the modern languages at University College, Toronto, provides an interesting Canadian example. While women were affiliated with the college as early as the 1870s, this took the form of parallel, and usually privately arranged, tutorial instruction; they were excluded from examinations, awards, and in most cases the lectures themselves.[9] While some adventurous students attempted to circumvent these restrictions – Eliza May Balmer, it is rumoured, suffered a nervous collapse after forcing her way into lectures, while one of the daughters of *Globe and Mail* publisher George Brown eavesdropped on Daniel Wilson's classes – the issue was brought to a crisis when a number of women won modern language matriculation scholarships, which they were unable to use.[10] The case of Alice Cummings, winner of the modern language entrance scholarship for 1879, was taken to the university senate by her school, Hamilton Collegiate Institute (Squair 4); when Daniel Wilson succeeded in blocking change at the university level, the Toronto Women's Literary Club, by means of a long petition campaign and skilful lobbying, forced the provincial parliament to overrule.[11] (The Club then took on new challenges, reconstituting itself as the Canadian Woman's Suffrage Association, the first national suffrage group in the country.) The literary women of University College also went on to many achievements, including the founding of a journal – interestingly named, first *Sesame*, then *The Rebel* – which was later to become the base for the *Canadian Forum*. When a 1928 working group of the American and Canadian Committees on Modern Languages examined the phenomenon of 'Women Students in Modern Languages,' they noted that the university honours English program was half women as early as 1889. This led the report writers to speculate as follows:

There may be something in the fact that the expansion of modern studies happened about the same time as the arrival of university women; or again the women may have seized on language and literature as the branches of learning in which their early experiments would meet with less masculine competition, their advent thus causing rather than coinciding with the expansion in language study. Or it may be that there are economic reasons; language teaching in the high schools is largely in the hands of women, a fact which would evidently affect university enrolment, but again might equally be a result of it. It is further alleged that when the feminine population of a given university course approaches 50% the men rapidly disappear. ('Women Students' 471)

The difficulty of the report writers in assigning cause and effect is evidence of the deep intrication of women in the subject matter.

While English was a fledgling discipline, existing 'parasitically,' in Palmer's terms (116), it was considered fit for women; but the entrenchment of the discipline is also the story of its masculinization.[12] Jo McMurtry notes for the U.S. academy the double-edged problem posed by the numbers of women students, when she writes:

In short, while women helped to put English on the map by providing bodies to fill the classroom, they became an implicit liability when it came to demonstrating how hard the new subject was ... The solution was a two-pronged one. English must be shown to be fiendishly difficult ... And the rigorous standards would then reflect back favourably upon any women students in the classes. (McMurtry 13)

English was not to remain a women's discipline for long. Terry Eagleton has pithily described a 'rise' of English studies which was also the growth of its institutionalization and professionalization: 'In the early 1920s it was desperately unclear why English was worth studying at all; by the early 1930s it had become a question of why it was worth wasting your time on anything else' (Eagleton 31). To this one must add, again referring to such women as Woolf and Brittain, that this desperate unclarity must have been men's alone, and what Eagleton is describing is really the discipline's masculinization.[13] This was a twofold process, involving an encoding of the moral purpose of literary study along Leavisite lines, and an eventual enhancement of its scientificity *via* New Criticism. The place of women was to become progressively defined through the discipline's complex evolutions, devolutions, demarcations, and self-descriptions.

In his history of the professionalization of English study in the United States, Gerald Graff sees a series of competing paradigms. At first glance, Graff's history would seem to lack interest from a feminist perspective, as his saga of disciplinary dualisms cannot account for the many voices – often women's voices – unheard, or only faintly heard, in the academic forum. But Graff's history usefully demonstrates the development of the series of binaries in which women have been deeded the lower or castaway terms. The original entry of women into English was through negative definition, as women were placed there in lieu of classics (for which they were not trained) or subjects of practical or political utility (for which they would have no use). Women reading English were often excluded from public lectures; or, when they attended them, were not awarded degrees for their study. When degrees were granted (often, initially, to certify women for teaching posts), those positions were confined to lower educational levels.

A rapidly branching series of disciplinary bifurcations has also sorted women out. In the split between teaching and scholarship, women were seen as qualified only for the former role. When women persisted as scholars, they were considered fit for traditional forms of scholarly work but not for the 'newer' forms of attentive and scrupulous close-reading. (Thus, for example, the historical prominence of women – although often underpaid and untenured women – at my own university, where editorial work has been, and remains, respected.) The teaching/research divide is by now institutionalized in a number of ways: colleges versus universities, composition versus literature teaching, and from this – especially in the U.S. academy – comes a deeply entrenched division into 'part-timers' and full-time employees; the untenured and tenured; those with over-full teaching loads and those with reduced loads; the under- and fully waged.[14]

The high profile of women's studies in the academy, and recent attempts to hire women, would give the impression that this situation is now alleviated. It would appear, however, that strains on the system, whether from expanded constituencies, budget cutbacks, or programmatic pressure, will force this gap. The humanities, as a whole, are increasingly disenfranchised in terms of funding in comparison to the sciences and 'high tech' disciplines, both because they are seen as having less social or economic utility and because they are less able to generate private funding. This especially affects women, who still work and study predominantly in the humanities – just as cutbacks in student funding, though they may be 'across the board,' especially affect women since they have less earning power and are more likely to be returning students or bearing responsibility for child care.[15] In times of financial adversity, universities increasingly favour the 'financial flexibility' offered by pools of part-time employees; while the de-unionization of the United States renders employees increasingly vulnerable. While there appears to have been a distinct improvement in the percentage of new hirings of women in Canadian English departments, this must be balanced against the net loss of women sometimes incurred when senior women faculty retire and are not replaced. Here I am concentrating only on women as students and academic employees – but would note, as well, the damage sustained by women-centred programs (such as women's studies programs), in addition to women-centred campus services. Once again, the impact is especially pronounced on disciplines such as English, in which the proportion of women is high.

At the base of the gender pyramid of 'English' are the students – young women, in the majority. English, it could be said, *is* the instruction of young women; and thus, when we are talking about 'English,' we are talking about their social formation. And when we are talking about the placement and experience of any woman student in English studies, we are talking about a situation which is highly overdetermined. Yet this is a situation which has received, to date, only partial analysis.

Feminist critiques of literary education have taken several lines, although they have been most sustained in their examination of schooling at the lower levels. Attacks on sexism, and stereotyping of people and family forms, particularly as found in textbooks and readers and teaching materials, were an important and early form of feminist literary analysis, with examples too numerous to be mentioned; such analysis influenced, in part, the feminist response to materials used in university and college courses. (Kate Millett's attack on D.H Lawrence, long a favourite of fiction survey courses, would be one example of the extension of such analysis.) A more general critique has looked at English as a form of humanities/'humanist' education, seeing English as a powerful mechanism for socializing women into appropriate gender roles. Gill Frith's 'Little Women, Good Wives: Is English Good for Girls?' (a piece written, polemically, for girl students), Elaine Showalter's 'Women and the Literary Curriculum,' and Sandra Gilbert's 'The Education of Henrietta Adams' are examples of work aimed at different levels of the educational strata. As Gilbert amusingly writes of the education of this fictional, yet familiar, English student:

As Oedipus, she had interrogated, and yet acquiesced in, the fatality that causes a man to kill his father and marry his mother; as Pip, she had learned never to trust a fatal *femme* like Estella Havisham but rather to lower her expectations and make her own way in the world; as Huck Finn, she had lit out for the territories, escaping both the false gentility and the constricting domesticity of a slave-owning society ruled by fussy ladies like Aunt Polly; as J. Alfred Prufrock, she had worried about 'the over-whelming question' toward which flighty women who 'come and go/talking of Michelangelo' might lead her; as Nick Carraway, she had admired the Faustian intensity of Jay Gatsby and deplored the selfish aplomb of Daisy Buchanan. (5–6)

The later attack on the canon rests on such foundations.

Other analyses are concerned less with specific works than with the presuppositions of their study. Carolyn Steedman's *The Tidy House*, an extraordinary analysis of writing instruction and of a domestic novella written by a group of little girls, shows both how 'English' forms girls and how they form English – creatively, resistantly, for their own purposes. bell hooks's 'Black and Female: Reflections on Graduate School' is an incisive indictment of a racism in literary education that extends beyond eurocentrism of material and method to the derogatory treatment of Black students. Such analyses suggest that reform of English study cannot be undertaken without analysis of the determinant institutions. First, although it is often difficult to see the relationship of humanities education to the state – far easier to find such connections in directly vocational, technological, or 'streamed' systems – humanities study is a mechanism for reproduction not only of a citizenry generally, but of the sex/gender system and its divisions of labour more especially.[16] Second, while it is (again) easier to see how such formation operates at the lower educational levels, we cannot assume that it stops at the university and college levels – only that its workings are different.

The position of women in English, as both teachers and students, remains in the 1990s much as it has been in the past, and this can be contextualized in the situation of universities and colleges generally.[17] There have been variable and generally disappointing levels of change in post-secondary institutions. Many measures are developed piecemeal, and policies which do evolve meet uneven implementation. Women faculty, staff, and students work in institutions where language, learning, and the allocation of labour are still gender-specific, although institutions tend to assert that people of colour and women enjoy equal access to their facilities, and that aberrations from this are individual and rectifiable acts of 'discrimination.' Statistics and anecdotes pointing to the improved position of women and other groups in some sectors must be read against the evidence of a relatively resistant background.

While incidents of anti-feminist backlash in the Canadian academy have received recent attention, a more generalized (and cut-back driven) 'backsliding' may be of greater consequence. Small-scale changes such as occasional hiring decisions can function as exceptions which justify the rule; paper policies allow institutional complacency; there is a longing for business as usual, or a sense that the 'woman question' is sufficiently answered. For women in the academy, this translates into a contestation for already gained ground – and a continuing struggle without well-articulated and substantiated institutional support.

How, then, to account for the persistence of systemic discrimination in the face of hard work by some, fine resolutions by others, and good will on the part of many? Two possible explanations come to mind. First, universities and colleges are unable to develop policies in which broad redefinitions of 'work' are required, as would be the case for policies that would affect all women workers in the institution or that would span work across various disciplines. Examination of the general notion of academic work, and of the 'normal science' of different disciplines, would be useful here. Second, a seemingly 'vertical' gap between policy and implementation might better be read 'horizontally,' as variance at the department level (variance, it should be added, which at times works in women's favour, when a department's own policies better the institutional norm). Collection and analysis of information about the position of women, by discipline and department, are needed if we are to account for complexities of response and find specific remedies.

But it is necessary to think, as well, of the more subjective factors, whether of a discipline-specific 'normal science' or of larger-scale academic paradigms which are reinforced in discipline-specific ways. While systemic discrimination is held in place by many and more material factors (and while there is, of course, discrimination in the university more overt than that experienced by women academics and teachers) there is still something to be learned from examination of traditional notions of scholarship and decorum.

Less attention has been paid to these more 'abstract' aspects of academic work since it is often the case that only 'hard' data will be accepted by administrations and government bodies as evidence of the need for change. But such 'subjective' discriminations exist as more than the stuff of rich anecdotal lore – they support injustice, make change difficult, and permit only weak correctives. A foundational, but still timely, Canadian study provides a useful approach. In 'An Analysis of Ideological Structures and How Women Are Excluded: Considerations for Academic Women,' sociologist Dorothy Smith shows how, historically and in the present, 'women have been largely excluded from the work of producing forms of thought and the images and symbols in which thought is expressed and ordered' (354). (Here 'ideology' indicates not a set of political beliefs, but the ordering and sanctioning of heuristic and social relations.) Women (where admitted at all) have been confined to the lower ranks, and allocated only restricted participation in professional faculties. Underpinning this placement is the notion that women are suited to be teachers and transmitters of knowledge, but not its originators or regulators. Thus women are excluded from 'gatekeeping' social and institutional functions; in scholarly matters, women and their work are seen as lying always outside fields and disciplines whose definitions are circular and self-perpetuating.

The situation that Smith described in 1975 remains the same today. Women are found predominantly as sessionals, part-timers, and in other limited term and non-tenurable positions as the 'last hired, first fired' of the academic world, and existent academic paradigms sanction this state of affairs. Smith notes that women are seen to lack necessary authority – she quotes Mary Ellman, that 'the male body lends credence to assertions, while the female takes it away' – and that this 'perception' receives discipline-specific reinforcement in sociology, for example, where women are an express object of sociological study and thus disqualified as sources of authoritative knowledge. One could see, from this, how other disciplines reinforce such notions in their own way: for example, the de-authorization of women academics sanctioned by their scarcity in engineering and, conversely, by their predominance in nursing; by the invisibility of women in history and their omnipresence as the 'matter' of medicine. This *a priori* relegation of women's roles prohibits women's actual scholarly contributions from modifying an assumed core area of inquiry or changing its boundaries.

Smith's category of 'authority' could be broken down into component characteristics in which women are often found lacking; and, again, these 'lacks' will have a discipline-specific definition. Women's careers, for economic or biological reasons, frequently do not fit the *profile* of the standard professional trajectory, with such possible variances as late career entry, part-time study, interruptions for child rearing, and different patterns of research and publication. Further, women may be perceived as too 'young' or inexperienced; or, conversely, seen as 'old' by departments hunting for 'new blood.'[18] Women, in their behaviour and in their work, may be seen to lack *impersonality* and *objectivity*, two intricated 'standards' of both scholarship and decorum. New demands for *applicability* in research and scholarship can exclude feminist work, which is exploratory, often speculative, and undertaken at this time mostly in the humanities and social sciences, in which women are primarily employed. Feminist work may violate accepted divisions into *field*, seeming to belong only obliquely to a traditional discipline, and perhaps published in journals lying outside it altogether. Last, women by their 'nature' do not fit the very notion of *fittedness* itself.

The same sorts of unstated assumptions may discriminate against women students who, again, do not fit the 'profile' of the excellent student; or, if perceived as excellent, may still be seen as unfitted for higher study.[19] Women in the academy are often part-time or returning students, or are carrying child-care and income-earning responsibilities; factors which should operate as evidence of their commitment, but are seen as indicating a lack of high seriousness. Women tend to speak less in seminar groups; and when they do, their contributions are unlikely to be incorporated into the main lines of the discussion.[20] Achievement is attributed to plodding hard work or, by contrast, to individual sensitivity, but less to intellectual capacity or endeavour. The sorts of disciplinary paradigms mentioned above can also operate against women students; again, women are not seen themselves as 'knowers' when their discipline postulates them as that-which-is-to-be-known – mystery, hysteric, deviant. Last, women simply do not 'look' like knowers when the professoriate is predominantly male (and white), as it almost invariably is. The impact of this sort of impressionism, especially in the humanities, should not be underrated.

This becomes worked out in the 'soft' discipline of English in some particular ways. Women students and scholars are confined by a canon and curriculum which, given the transcendent 'humanism' of the enterprise, and a belief in self-evident greatness, remain relatively unaltered. I have tried to suggest above that material factors – including the need to have cheap labourers in the academy – pervade what are often taken to be 'intellectual' decisions. But for the moment, it may be instructive to see what disciplinary assumptions and paradigms and folklore in English help to hold this situation in place.

Integration is the Arnoldian notion of cultural wholeness and a social wholeness, achieved in part through literary study; too, it is the New Critical valuation of the fully achieved art object. This assumes an unquestioned community of concern and interest, and dismisses specific interests as vested or immature. On these criteria, for example, feminist literary or scholarly work may be devalued as partial or aesthetically incomplete.

Imitation refers to the intrinsic pedagogic method of English studies –

age-old, but reinvigorated by the mimetic psychologism of I.A. Richards – which inevitably prizes more than mental characteristics or text-reading practices and which makes the study of English central to processes of social reproduction. Women have been excluded from the patriarchal line of scholarly transmission and seen as less intrinsically suited to the task of aware and balanced reading; excluded, in fact, because the text to approximate is really the mind of the professor.

This shades into *impressionism*, which gestures to the general academic willingness to judge appearances and fittedness, but refers more specifically to the love/hate relationship English has to its own theoretical and epistemological status, and our tendency to equate formal characteristics with the structures of knowledge. This leads, often, to a falling-back on the 'standard' of the implicitly or consensually known. In particular, this may cause the classification of self-reflexive or critical pursuits, such as feminist inquiry, as fundamentally extra-disciplinary.

By *idealism* I do not disparage the ethical aspirations of literary scholars and students and the sense of moral purpose that drives the discipline, but rather the conceptual ossification which is an occupational hazard.

And the *isolation* of post-secondary English severs the university from the larger society and other educational systems. This rends scholarship from pedagogy, which reinforces a gender stratification of women as students and lower-level instructors, men as professors and higher-level administrators. And it allows us to think of English solely as a haven in a heartless world – or, even, in a heartless university – when it is, in fact, important to education for power-through-symbolic-control in our culture, and as more than a 'humanizing' face for technological study.

Which is not, of course, to say that the 'humanist' aspirations of English study should be discounted or lost. All of the above characteristics begin with *i* to remind us of their status as 'ideology.' But if we think of 'ideology,' again, as the ordering of most basic social and knowledge relations, then we can see why English is an important and contended terrain. Certainly, it was so for the women who came, with aspirations and ideals, to English study in its early years; and so it remains, for those of us in the discipline today.

Notes

1 I am grateful to former dean of women Elizabeth Rowlinson for the history of the windows.

2 According to Dagg and P. Thompson, 69 per cent of English literature under-graduates in Canada are women (29), and the 1986 and 1991 census results reveal that women compose approximately 66 per cent of the graduates in English language and literature (Statistics Canada, *Major Fields of Study,* table 1).

3 At the outset, it should be mentioned that the MLA has commissioned and sponsored a number of important books on women in the academy. See De Sole and Hoffmann; Reuben and Hoffmann; Stringer and I. Thompson; Tinsley, Reuben, and Crothers; and I. Thompson and Roberts. The strength, and weakness, of these works is that they have generality and broad applicability – they could be speaking as well about the position of women in any department.

   PMLA and *College English* publish periodic asssessments of the status of women in the profession. The most recent MLA overview of women in modern languages is provided by Huber.

   Some important studies are provided by George (in debate with Ong) on literary study as combative study, and by Stimpson on the placements of women in the academy. Walsh talks about the masculinization of graduate literary study in English Canada; Stoneman details attempts to incorporate feminist perspectives into a graduate program. Collected essays by Florence Howe and Adrienne Rich are deeply rooted in their respective ranges of practical experience.

   While there are many collections on the topic of feminism and the academy, the volume edited by A. Thompson and Wilcox – *Teaching Women: Feminism and English Studies* – is discipline-specific, and examines both institutional and pedagogic issues.

4 For example, the works of 'Amanda Cross' (Carolyn Heilbrun), most pertinently *Death in a Tenured Position*. See also J.S. Borthwick, Susan Kenney, Valerie Miner, and Edith Skrom, for example.

5 At Queen's University, to take one example, English was the first class offered in the newly opened college for women in 1869; and in the next year, rhetoric and logic, English, and natural history were approved by the senate for their study (Neatby 133).

6 This perceived suitability of women to literary and language study was central to late-nineteenth-century discussions of women's higher education. For example, in 'The Education of Women and the Poetic Senses,' T.M. Macintyre (principal of the Brantford Ladies College) considered that, while men and women have the same mental equipment, their sensations and emotional nature differ; women's 'predominance of soul' means that language, literature, and history study should predominate in their university educa-

tion. J.M. Dawson, one of the most forceful Canadian proponents of women's educational enfranchisment, advocated a well-rounded education for women (including professional training), but felt women had a special aptitude for languages.

7 An examination of the more recent role of literacy and literature education in class formation is provided by Batsleer et al. in *Rewriting English*, a work in which they envisage a reformed English studies.

8 The early history of women in English exists in scattered places. Gerald Graff and Michael Warner's *The Origins of Literary Studies in America* presents fascinating excerpts from Vida Dutton Scudder's biography and from Martha Carey Thomas's letters and journals. See also Scudder's *On Journey* and Theresa Corcoran's book on Scudder, which, while it concentrates on her career as a political activist, provides a full bibliography. See also the collection of Thomas's writings edited by Marjorie Dobkin, and the sections on Thomas in Bernard, and in McMurtry. Gail Griffin's 'Alma Mater' details her discovery of an inspiring female predecessor.

   For England, see Doyle (1982; 1989), Eagleton, and Gossman. Susan Leonardi's *Dangerous by Degrees*, on the Somerville novelists, examines the place of literary women at Oxford before and after the First World War.

   One early Somerville graduate was Wilhelmina Gordon, who finished with first class honours in 1908 and returned to Canada, achieving the status of assistant professor in the Queen's department after teaching there for sixteen years (see Dewar). Kathleen Coburn's autobiographical *In Pursuit of Coleridge*, covering a later period, recounts the career of this Canadian scholar-adventurer.

9 Both Victoria and Trinity granted women students full status several years before University College.

10 These courageous women deserve a few more words. According to Anne Rochon Ford, the story of Balmer's breakdown is apocryphal. (That it was widely believed and transmitted for decades says much about the anxieties of women students in the early years.) Balmer won the modern language scholarships three years running (1882, 1883, 1884), tied for the General Proficiency Scholarship in her final year (Squair 4), and went on to a long teaching career at Harbord Collegiate.

   Daniel Wilson, a close personal friend of the Brown family, bet one of the daughters that he would let her attend his lectures when she reached his height. She outgrew him, and was allowed to sit in his office with the door open to the adjoining lecture room (Ford 11–12). This could be either Catharine Edith Brown or Margaret Nelson Brown; both were in the modern languages, and the latter won the gold medal in that subject for 1885.

11 Sarah Anne Curzon, a member of the literary society, wrote a comedy on the topic two years before admission was finally granted. In 'The Sweet Girl Graduate,' Kate, an aspiring student, attends classes in drag and wins all the U.C. medals. (I am grateful to Ann Wilson for telling me about this play.)

A sustained examination of the struggle for entry is provided by Nancy Thompson.

12 Stimpson notes how women are most welcome into 'empty fields,' which then become increasingly populated by men (175).

13 Two moving statements of the aspirations of women are provided by scholars who themselves were the product of English study in these early years. See Gardner; and Tuve.

14 The consequences for women faculty are detailed in a number of anecdotal accounts. See, especially, Joan Abramsom; and Nan Moglin. The situation and 'structure of feeling' of women in English is the topic of a number of novels: see French, Godwin, Hite, Russ, among others.

15 For a thorough cataloguing of these factors in a Canadian province, see Bueckert et al., 'The Impact of Restraint ...'

16 Here Michèle Barrett's *Women's Oppression Today* remains a pivotal study. See, especially, chapters 3 and 4.

17 *MisEducation*, by Dagg and P. Thompson, is a thorough tally of systemic discrimination against women in Canada's universities.

18 Mary Wilson Carpenter provides an incisive analysis of the operations of sex-ageism in literary studies.

19 How women English students are assessed and graded is the subject of a study by Chris Weedon.

20 See Krupnick on the place of women in seminar groups.

Works Cited

Abramson, Joan. *The Invisible Woman*. San Francisco: Jossey-Bass, 1975.

Baldick, Chris. *The Social Mission of English Criticism, 1848–1932*. Oxford: Clarendon P, 1983.

Barrett, Michèle. *Women's Oppression Today: Problems in Marxist Feminist Analysis*. London: Verso, 1980.

Batsleer, Janet, et al., eds. *Rewriting English: Cultural Politics of Gender and Class*. London: Methuen, 1985.

Bernard, Jessie. *Academic Women*. University Park, Penn.: Pennsylvania State UP, 1964.

Borthwick, J.S. *The Student Body*. New York: St Martin's P, 1986.

Brittain, Vera. *Testament of Youth: An Autobiographical Study of the Years 1900–1925*. New York: Macmillan, 1938.

Bueckert, L., L. Renaud, and M.L. Stewart. 'The Impact of "Restraint" on Women's Participation in B.C. Colleges and Institutes, 1983–1985.' [Sponsored by the Canadian Research Institute for the Advancement of Women / Institut canadien de recherches sur les femmes.] Burnaby, B.C.: Women's Studies Program, Simon Fraser U, n.d.

Carpenter, Mary Wilson. 'Eco, Oedipus, and the "View" of the University.' *Diacritics* 20, 1 (Spring 1990): 77–85.

Coburn, Kathleen. *In Pursuit of Coleridge*. Toronto: Clarke Irwin, 1977.

Corcoran, Theresa, S.C. *Vida Dutton Scudder*. Boston: Twayne, 1982.

Cross, Amanda. *Death in a Tenured Position*. New York: Ballantine, 1981.

Curzon, Sarah Anne. 'The Sweet Girl Graduate: A Comedy in Five Acts.' *Women Pioneers*. Vol. 2 of *Canada's Lost Plays*. Ed. Anton Wagner. Toronto: Canadian Theatre Review Publications, 1979. 140–54.

Dagg, Anne Innis, and Patricia J. Thompson. *MisEducation: Women and Canadian Universities*. Toronto: Ontario Institute for Studies in Education, 1988.

Dawson, John William. *Educated Women: An Address Delivered before the Delta Sigma Society of McGill University, December 1889*. Montreal [?]: private circulation, 1889. [CIHM 03665]

De Sole, Gloria, and Leonore Hoffmann, eds. *Rocking the Boat: Academic Women and Academic Processes*. New York: Modern Languages Association, 1981.

Dewar, David G. 'Wilhelmina Gordon.' *Queen's Profiles*. Kingston, Ont.: Office of Endowment and Public Relations of Queen's University, 1951. 85–8.

Dobkin, Marjorie Housepian, ed. *The Making of a Feminist: Early Journals and Letters of M. Carey Thomas*. N.p.: Kent State UP, 1979.

Doyle, Brian. *English and Englishness*. London: Routledge, 1989.

– 'The Hidden History of English Studies.' *Re-Reading English*. Ed. Peter Widdowson. London: Methuen, 1982. 17–31.

Eagleton, Terry. 'The Rise of English.' *Literary Theory: An Introduction*. Minneapolis: U Minnesota P, 1983. 17–53.

Ford, Anne Rochon. *A Path Not Strewn with Roses: One Hundred Years of Women at the University of Toronto 1884–1984*. Toronto: U Toronto P, 1985.

French, Marilyn. *The Women's Room*. New York: Summit, 1977.

Frith, Gillian. 'Little Women, Good Wives: Is English Good for Girls?' *Feminism for Girls: An Adventure Story*. Ed. Angela McRobbie and Trisha McCabe. London: Routledge and Kegan Paul, 1981. 27–49.

Gardner, Helen. *Literary Studies: An Inaugural Lecture Delivered before the University of Oxford*. Oxford: Clarendon P, 1967.

George, Diana Hume. 'The Miltonic Ideal: A Paradigm for the Structure of

Relations between Men and Women in Academia.' *College English* 40, 8 (April 1979): 864–70.

– '"Stumbling on Melons": Sexual Dialectics and Discrimination in English Departments.' *English Literature: Opening Up the Canon.* Ed. Leslie A. Fiedler and Houston A. Baker, Jr. Baltimore: Johns Hopkins UP, 1981. 107–36.

Gilbert, Sandra M. 'The Education of Henrietta Adams.' *Profession 84* (1984): 5–9.

Godwin, Gail. *The Odd Woman.* New York: Knopf, 1974.

Gossman, Lionel. 'Literature and Education.' *New Literary History* 13, 2 (Winter 1982): 341–71.

Graff, Gerald. *Professing Literature: An Institutional History.* Chicago: U Chicago P, 1987.

– and Michael Warner, eds. *The Origins of Literary Studies in America: A Documentary Anthology.* New York: Routledge, 1989.

Griffin, Gail. 'Alma Mater.' *Profession 90* (1990): 37–42.

Hite, Molly. *Class Porn.* Freedom, Calif.: Crossing P, 1987.

hooks, bell. 'Black and Female: Reflections on Graduate School.' *Talking Back: Thinking Feminist / Thinking Black.* Toronto: Between the Lines, 1988. 55–61.

Howe, Florence. *Myths of Coeducation: Selected Essays 1964–1983.* Bloomington, Ind.: Indiana UP, 1984.

Huber, Bettina J. 'Women in the Modern Languages, 1970–90.' *Profession 90* (1990): 58–73.

Kenney, Susan. *Graves in Academe.* New York: Viking/Penguin, 1985.

Krupnick, Catherine G. 'Women and Men in the Classroom: Inequality and Its Remedies.' *On Teaching and Learning: The Journal of the Harvard Danforth Center* (May 1985): 18–25.

Leonardi, Susan J. *Dangerous by Degrees: Women at Oxford and the Somerville College Novelists.* New Brunswick, N.J.: Rutgers UP, 1989.

Macintrye, T.M. 'The Education of Women and the Poetic Senses.' *Canada Education Monthly and 'School Magazine'* 9, 12 (1887): 377–84.

McMurtry, Jo. *English Language, English Literature: The Creation of an Academic Discipline.* Hamden, Conn.: Archon Books, 1985.

Millett, Kate. *Sexual Politics.* Garden City, N.Y.: Doubleday, 1970.

Miner, Valerie. *Murder in the English Department.* Freedom, Calif.: Crossing P, 1982.

Moglin, Nan Bauer. 'The Demoralization Paper; or, Janet Mandelbaum, Jane Clifford, Anna Giardino, Zelda Campbell, Mira Ward, and Myself: The Fate of Six English Teachers.' *College English* 44, 6 (Oct. 1982): 575–82.

Neatby, Hilda. *Queen's University. Vol. I 1841–1917.* Ed. Frederick W. Gibson and Roger Graham. Montreal: McGill-Queen's UP, 1978.

Ohmann, Richard. 'Literacy, Technology, and Monopoly Capitalism.' *College English* 47, 7 (1985): 675–89.

Ong, Walter J. 'Agonistic Structures in Academia: Past to Present.' *Daedalus* 103 (1974): 229–38.

– 'Agonistic Structures in Academia: Past to Present.' [Expanded version.] *Interchange* [Ontario Institute for Studies in Education] 5, 4 (1974): 1–12.

Palmer, David. *The Rise of English Studies: An Account of the Study of English Language and Literature* ... London: Oxford UP, 1965.

Potter, Stephen. *The Muse in Chains: A Study in Education.* London: Cape, 1937.

Reuben, Elaine, and Leonore Hoffmann, eds. *'Unladylike and Unprofessional': Academic Women and Academic Unions.* New York: Modern Languages Association, 1975.

Rich, Adrienne. *On Lies, Secrets and Silence: Selected Prose 1966-1978.* New York: Norton, 1979.

Russ, Joanna. *On Strike against God: A Lesbian Love Story.* Freedom, Calif.: Crossing P, 1985.

Scudder, Vida Dutton. *On Journey.* New York: E.P. Dutton, 1937.

Showalter, Elaine. 'Women and the Literary Curriculum.' *College English* 32, 8 (May 1971): 855–61.

Skrom, Edith. *The Mark Twain Murders.* New York: Dell, 1989.

Smith, Dorothy. 'An Analysis of Ideological Structures and How Women Are Excluded: Considerations for Academic Women.' *Canadian Review of Sociology and Anthropology* 12, 4 (1975): 353–69.

Squair, John. *I. Admission of Women to the University of Toronto and University College. II. Rectification of a Passage in 'Alumni Associations in the University of Toronto' (1922).* Toronto: U Toronto P, 1926.

Stallybrass, Peter, and Allon White. *The Politics and Poetics of Transgression.* London: Methuen, 1986.

Statistics Canada. *Major Fields of Study of Postsecondary Graduates / Principaux Domaines d'études des diplômés postsecondaires.* Ottawa: Industry, Science and Technology, 1993. 1991 Census of Canada. Catalogue no. 93-329.

Steedman, Carolyn. *The Tidy House: Little Girls Writing.* London: Virago, 1982.

Stimpson, Catharine. 'Ad/d Feminam: Women, Literature and Society.' *Literature and Society.* Ed. Edward Said. Baltimore: Johns Hopkins UP, 1980. 174–92.

Stoneman, Patsy. 'Powerhouse or Ivory Tower? Feminism and Postgraduate English.' *Teaching Women: Feminism and English Studies.* Ed. Ann Thompson and Helen Wilcox. Manchester: Manchester UP, 1989. 96–112.

Stringer, Patricia A., and Irene Thompson, eds. *Stepping off the Pedestal: Academic Women in the South.* New York: Modern Languages Association, 1982.

Thompson, Ann, and Helen Wilcox, eds. *Teaching Women: Feminism and English Studies*. Manchester: Manchester UP, 1989.

Thompson, Irene, and Audrey Roberts, eds. *The Road Retaken: Women Reenter the Academy*. New York : Modern Languages Association, 1985.

Thompson, Nancy Ramsay. 'The Controversy over the Admission of Women to University College, University of Toronto.' Thesis U of Toronto 1974.

Tinsley, Adrian, Elaine Reuben, and Diane Crothers, eds. *Academic Women: Sex Discrimination and the Law*. New York: Modern Languages Association, 1975.

Tuve, Rosemund. 'AAUW Fellows and Their Survival.' *Essays by Rosemund Tuve: Spenser, Herbert, Milton*. Ed. Thomas P. Roche, Jr. Princeton, N.J.: Princeton UP, 1970. 15–27.

Walsh, Anne. 'A Theory-Narrative in Five Movements / The Maps Are Drawn by a Living Choir: Contexts for the Practice of a Feminist Metatheory of Literary History.' *Interchange* [Ontario Institute for Studies in Education] 17, 1 (Spring 1986): 1–22.

Weedon, Chris. 'Engendering Stereotypes.' *Literature/Teaching/Politics* 1 (1982): 37–49.

'Women Students in Modern Languages.' *Modern Language Instruction in Canada*. 2 vols. [Publications of the American and Canadian Committees on Modern Languages, Vol. 6.] Toronto: U Toronto P, 1928. 1:468–74.

Woolf, Virginia. *A Room of One's Own*. London: Hogarth P, 1929.

– *Three Guineas*. London: Hogarth P, 1938.

6

Close Reading, Closed Writing

So pervasive and persistent is the 'close reading' as an assignment at the university level that it is tempting to consider it as a synecdoche for the English essay. Certainly, there are many types of literature assignments – the research piece, character study, and so forth – in even the most conservative or restricted programs. But there is something integral about this one. The close reading is basic to the pedagogic practice we tend to value most highly, the detailed discussion that takes place in the seminar session. It occurs as an assignment in a number of guises and a variety of contexts, most particularly in the essay and in the examination sight passage. In a discipline that timetables 'mastery' of material first, and theoretical inquiry later, if at all, it is often the closest we come in the classroom to the deliberate, or even incidental, inculcation of skills or explanation of methodology, the closest we come to articulating what a reading practice is or might be and the reasons for it.

Because it is so common that it is taken for granted, so institutionalized that it is invisible, so central to our concerns that it provides a most basic test, the close reading assignment functions as an index to English in the academy. What is said and not said about it, how it is placed and displaced, hold clues to how we view work in English studies and the construction of those studies as discipline and profession, inquiry and institution. Without trying to postulate an all-purpose disciplinary model, it might be suggested that in English Canada there is a particularly interesting mix of paradigms that predominate in Britain and the United States respectively. Each is a latent content where the other is manifest, however. The 'greats' or 'author and society' questions typical of British examinations, for example, require at base a New Critical–style close reading (Longhurst 152), even as New Critical approaches in the United States academy are often justified through Leavisian appeals, although they may not go by that name. Both have in common a notion of the mimeticism of literary study, of a reflective relationship of reader to author and work, which is found, and perhaps founded, in the writings of I.A. Richards. While the close reading with its concomitant assumptions has come under fire from all quarters, it persists in our practices, and especially pedagogic ones. Here the concern is less to criticize the close reading than to analyse this institutionalization and intractability.

'The close-reading theme,' writes Edgar V. Roberts in the third (1973) edition of his perennially popular *Writing Themes about Literature*, 'can be either very general or very technical, depending on the skills you have acquired when you undertake to write it. Mainly, however, the aim of the assignment is to give you a chance to exercise your general perceptions and knowledge as a reader' (89). It further permits concentration in keeping with a student's 'abilities and interests': 'you may have acquired some interest and knowledge of political science and wish to concentrate on the political implications of a passage in Shakespeare's *Richard II*' (89–90). A 'certain awareness of *style* and *prosody*' is required, but the theme 'will only touch on these elements indirectly.' Instead, writes Roberts, 'you are to focus attention on everything in the passage or work assigned' (90). Leaving aside the oxymoronic direction to 'focus ... on everything,' and this further contradiction with the statement that the 'theme can take the form of your abilities and interests,' it may be noted that these instructions are typical of those given in essay writing and literary handbooks and in such familiar assignments as the following:

1 Choose one passage and show how some of the features work together to provide the meaning ... Your essay should focus closely on the selected passage, but should show how an understanding of its meaning relies on an understanding of its relation to the themes and structures of the poem as a whole ... [examination question]
2 Write a short essay on the following passage ... [examination question]
3 Choose one of the following poems and analyse it in the manner we have discussed in class ... Who is the speaker and what is his situation? What are the main parts of the poem and what does each contribute to the whole? What do the various figures of speech and images contribute ...? [essay topic]

4 Give a 'reading' of this poem ... [essay topic, assigned orally]
5 Discuss, in as much detail as possible, the subject(s) and theme(s) of
   the attached poem ... Analyse the elements of cohesion in the poem at
   all levels – graphology, phonology, lexis (and imagery), and grammar
   ... Comment on any other points of interest or curiosity not covered in
   the above. [test]
6 Over the course of this term, we have examined the many ways in
   which poetry makes meaning ... Using these categories and concepts,
   give a reading of this poem, avoiding too rigid 'interpretation' and
   allowing the poem its full complexity ... Bring to bear all the working
   tools and techniques we have developed throughout the term. [take-
   home examination]

The six sample assignments, collected from several institutions, cover a
range of situations and approaches. The first topic refers to a lengthier
poem already discussed in class, while the second is a standard 'sight
passage' question, although lacking the helpful hints of the first topic.
The third is typical of the essay questions given in the early stages of a
practical criticism seminar, in which students are asked to cover only
one or a restricted number of features. An exercise, it provides practice
for a later, fuller, analysis.

The fourth assignment is sometimes called an 'explication' question,
although a serially structured French *explication* would not in fact suitably demonstrate 'working together.' However, it is a typical assignment in its requirements and informality. Roberts gives a clue as to why
specific instructions are unnecessary:

To assist you in developing good reading techniques, your instructor will probably spend much classroom time in explaining and discussing with you various
poems, novels, plays and stories. As you experience this classroom guidance,
you should develop the ability to read well without guidance. The theme asking
you to perform a close reading of a passage is an important means by which
your instructor can verify your progress as a reader. (89)

That students do need guidance is a point Roberts makes in the book's
preface, 'To the Instructor,' where he bemoans students' lack of familiarity with such basics as structure and point of view:

Under these conditions the instructors either waste valuable time explaining
theme assignments or else continue to receive inadequate student writing about

literature. This book is offered as a solution. Its aim is to free instructors from the drudgery and lost time of making assignments and to help students by explaining and illustrating many approaches to literary technique in order to provide a sound basis for analysis. (xv–xvi)

What are we to make of the disjunctions between these addresses to student and teacher? On the one hand, the student is the beneficiary of 'much classroom time' and 'classroom guidance' and now is ready to take the test for a solo licence. On the other hand, students are 'handicapped,' to use Roberts's word, by knowing neither terms nor their applications, and in order to correct this the instructor must 'waste valuable time explaining theme assignments.' And further contradictions ensue. In the quotation addressed to the student, there is a tacit assumption that 'the ability to read well without guidance' is the same as the ability to write well without guidance, since an essay functions as the 'means by which your instructor can verify your progress as a reader,' and a smooth transition from reading to talking to writing is envisaged. In the preface to the instructor, however, there is no sense of an integration between classroom practice and the testing of the individual, nor of a connection between independent reading and written expression. Rather, there is a stark contrast between 'valuable time' spent on literature and 'wasted' on the discussion of assignments. The pronominally free-floating status of 'wasted time' blurs the question of whose time this is. On Roberts's terms, the close reading is central to both student work ('exercise your general perceptions and knowledge as a reader') and teacher work ('means by which your instructor can verify'). The distinction, then, is that while the student is to be involved with the *process* of essay writing and is to find this 'exercise' profitable and the time well spent, the instructor's concern is with the finished *product* and, further, only a product of a certain quality. Catherine Belsey notes the suppression of 'process' in both literary criticism in the expressive-realist mode (in which works are either a 'natural reflection' or 'spontaneous expression') and in the distribution system under capitalism (in which commodities are displayed in their finished form, removed from the factories of their production) (126). The close reading assignment involves a similar mystification in the field of education.

In Roberts's handbook, instructors (even in the preface devoted to them) are addressed in the third person: the student is interpellated directly as 'you.' In the contrasts between the address to the student and the instructor, in the pointing of 'receive assignments' in the direction of the teacher, and in the final aim to free instructors from the 'drudgery and lost time of making assignments,' it appears that the interests of student and teacher are at variance. What is valuable for one is profitless for the other; furthermore, two very different scales of value emerge. The ambiguity of 'making assignments' signals an anxiety over this divergence. Is 'making' an assignment the same as designing one (surely an important part of instructor work) or explaining one ('drudgery and lost time') or the same as the homophonically shadowed 'marking assignments'? In such branchings are the splits between instructor and student, literature and composition, professionalism and labour, inscribed. It is with the 'crisis' in literacy, the demand for composition courses, and the desire of some university instructors to remain professors of literature rather than writing, that future editions of Roberts's handbook will be more directly involved.

The assumption from Roberts's book and from topics 2 and 4 above, that students should already know how to handle assignments, is countered to some degree in all other essay and examination topics, as it surely is in the actual practice of many teachers. The fifth and sixth topics especially are each attempts to assist students with this notoriously difficult assignment and to shift to some extent its premises. In the fifth, the instructor is encouraging the use of sociolinguistic terminology. If 'cohesion' has maintained its stability as a linguistic term and not become a synonym for interrelatedness, then it marks an approach through which the text may be situated in discourse rather than treated as an aesthetic totality. The sixth, with its pronominal plurals, its exhortative tone, its battling lexis of regulation and independence, reveals a whole complex of teacherly feelings – in this case, my own. While the assignment places the students, it also delineates the literature teacher's structure of experience, of hope and disappointment, effort and recuperation, understanding and bafflement. All the above assignments speak of and from this, in their own ways.

It is a New Critical commonplace that the poem is so richly complex that no other form is sufficiently subtle to do it justice. Small wonder, then, that students experience difficulties with this assignment. Students give various reasons for this dilemma: that it is 'hard to do it by oneself'; that it is 'hard to do it all at once.' In this way they acknowledge the difficulties of generating in isolation the material that is produced in classroom discussions and of 'pulling it all together' once one has it. Even when students can accomplish the first task (frequently described as 'knowing what to look for'), the second part, usually referred to by both teachers and students as 'organization,' continues to provide problems.

The close reading assignment seems to violate rules of essay writing which students may have learned with effort and used with success. A clear thesis statement is reductionist or heretically paraphrastic, while a methodological development of argument with clear sub-statements may make the paper seem unintegrated, unable to achieve 'focus on everything.' Some students are daunted by the amount of material to be handled. Editing contradicts the spirit of the assignment; but apparently logical arrangements (line-by-line or category-by-category) are taboo. (Here the formalism or pseudo-scientism of the New Critical enterprise is at war with its 'literary' status.) Questions remain – whether biographical information may be used to introduce or contextualize the reading, for example. Even when the assignment is clearly understood, it may still appear an unreasonable set of demands. As one student inimitably expressed it: 'In order to understand this very complicated poem, each sentence must be broken down, word-for-word, and in turn each word must be related to another. The poem then becomes a whole and it can then be understood.' This student comes close to paraphrase, or parody, of the method of Jerome Beaty and William Matchett's *Poetry from Statement to Meaning*. Like Stephen Leacock's comic hero, who jumped on his horse and rode madly off in all directions, students begin a task which seems not really achievable. And in their sense of this they are, I believe, correct: the close reading is not achievable, nor is it meant to be. And if students experience difficulties with it, this is because, as I hope to show, it is an assignment designed in such a way that they should. This 'problem' in student work may thus be read as a disciplinary 'problematic.'

What sort of assistance are students actually given with this notoriously difficult assignment? It seems indicative that the principal essay writing guides devote very little time to it, despite its centrality and the particular problems it poses. Sylvan Barnet's *A Short Guide to Writing about Literature* (1979) distinguishes three principal kinds of criticism – explication, analysis, and review, defining explication as

a line-by-line or episode-by-episode commentary on what is going on in a text ... It takes some skill to work one's way along without saying, 'In line one ..., in the second line ...' [I]t is not a paraphrase ... but a commentary revealing your sense of the meaning of the work. To this end it calls attention, as it proceeds, to the implications of words, the function of rhymes, the shifts in point of view, the development of contrasts and any other contributions to the meaning. (9–10)

Barnet's 'explication' shares with the close reading the goal of showing 'the relation of the parts' by 'calling attention to implications.' But line-by-line progression is at odds with the demands of the close reading proper. The explication is a close reading rid of the problem of organiza-tion – a dilemma that will uncannily recur. The two-page section on the explication is prefaced by a recommendation that students put aside extra-textual knowledge in order to 'confine' attention to the poem (10). The seven-page treatment of the analysis paper, by contrast, provides advice on collecting and organizing material, and a number of 'princi-ples' for its handling are deduced. Presumably, then, the explication requires that no material be generated, since it is already there in the 'meaning of the work,' and the student's 'sense' of this meaning and the poem's 'contributions' to it. Students are reassured that 'organization of such an essay is rarely a problem' (88).

The explanation of organization, however, is; and here, as in other handbooks, the fall-back position is instruction by example. Two stu-dent papers are provided, one for 'tone' (headed as a sample explica-tion) and another for 'rhythm' (listed in the index though not in the table of contents as an explication). And sample readings by Mark Van Doren and Donald Hall integrate the elements of poetry which have been treated serially in Barnet's text.

Clearly, organization of the close reading is a case of integration rather than order. It is not solved by the directive to proceed line-by-line or to copy achieved readings any more than the question of subjectivity is addressed by the suggestion that the writer have 'opinions' but talk 'more about the work than himself or herself' (18) – any more, for that matter, than the problem of extra-textual evidence (or history) is solved by telling students to ignore it. These cruxes will recur in other essay writing guides, as they do throughout the discipline; so will the problem of teaching something which seems to defy analysis. (The latter is partic-ularly evident in the rhetorics I am treating which are, like many com-position texts used in North America, fundamentally Aristotelian.) The alternative, then, is to teach by sample and suggestion.

This is the course followed by Roberts. In the first four editions of *Writing Themes about Literature*, 'the method is to go from precept to example,' with general discussion of the 'problems raised by a sample theme that illustrates the problems in a theme-length form.' Some stu-dents may wish to 'follow the patterns closely,' while others 'will adapt the discussions and samples to their own needs' (1973, xvi). Roberts explains the effectivity of this sample-model instruction:

The samples have been conceived and written in the belief that the word *imitation* does not need to be preceded by words like *slavish* or *mere*. Much poor composition results from uncertainty about what is expected in the way of imitation. While the student seeks a *form* in which to express himself, he dissipates his energies and does not devote enough attention to a careful study of the literary text that has been assigned. If the student can learn from the discussion of a technical problem and can compare this discussion with a sample theme, he will set his mind working in the right channels and produce superior themes. (xvi–xvii)

The chapters are arranged 'in an order of increasing difficulty and technicality' (xviii) of assignments, in which 'The Theme on a Close Reading' comes seventh of the sixteen 'theme' chapters. In all editions of *Writing Themes about Literature*, introductory attention is given to the steps in the development of an essay. The student is instructed to develop a central or controlling idea, to make a list of topic sentences, and to form a thesis statement that bridges them and around which 'the entire theme is to be organized' (8). This advice holds for the close reading as well. In the introduction, 'you should make plain your central idea,' the student is reminded. Roberts adds that 'in a theme involving a close reading it is sometimes difficult to arrive at a central idea, but if your theme is to be good, you must produce some guiding point that makes sense out of your reading' (92–3). Next, 'your plan in the body of the theme is to combine the results of your close reading with the central idea you have asserted' (93). As for a conclusion, the student must 'be sure that you touch once more upon your central idea before you end the paper' (94). The plan of the 'analytical sentence outline' is seen to be universally applicable.

   In the 1983 fifth edition of Roberts's work, however, much is changed. The preliminary information on structuring an essay has its own section entitled 'The Process of Writing Themes about Literature'; and the text and its vocabulary ('process,' 'brainstorming') bear the marks of recent composition theory and the 'new rhetoric.' The chapter called 'Two Themes Based on a Close Reading' has been moved from the seventh to the fourteenth place in this hierarchy of difficulty. These two seemingly radical changes in fact cap a series of shifts across the editions of *Writing Themes about Literature*. Since the first edition, the close reading has travelled from third to seventh to eighth to fourteenth place in order of difficulty. Accompanying this are oscillations in address to the teacher (as, variously, 'we,' 'you,' 'they,' 'we instructors,' and 'we instructors of composition'); varying recommendations for placement of the text (in composition courses, literature courses, or literature-and-composition courses); and altered notions of its function inside or outside the class (as text or supplement, as an aid to the instructor, or as a self-help *vade mecum*). The modification to the treatment of the close reading essay is attributable in part to these changes in the constitution and constituency of composition courses and the general consciousness-raising caused by new developments in rhetorical and composition theory. But it also seems produced by an anxiety over the text's own terms of reference and teaching tactics. The close reading assignment appears to become progressively unsuited to the book's underpinning 'thesis' model of composition (a model which writing teachers increasingly disfavour), and it exposes the inadequacy of the learning-by-imitation model which one would have thought most suited to it.

The second (1986) edition of Kelley Griffith, Jr's, *Writing Essays about Literature* also shows the marks of new theoretical movements. It talks of 'interpretive communities' and of a multiple audience for student work, composed of instructor and peers. The shift of stress to a communication model of essay writing does not, however, effect fundamental changes in the way student work is envisaged. Rather, this work is placed within a liberal-pluralist world of freely competing interests, in which ideas rise and fall on the basis of their merit.

The controlling premise of *Writing Essays about Literature* is that all essays are at base argumentative. This, and the book's focus on organization and the generation of topics, preclude it from treating the close reading as a special subject. But the general treatment of the literature essay shows that close reading assumptions permeate other assignments. Since 'good literature pleases by reflecting and giving order to life and by redefining our own place in the real world' (1), the literature scholar can have it all ways at once. Works are faithfully mimetic (they reflect) and at the same time offer an alternative social vision (they redefine). The work pleases and instructs, pleases by instructing; as with Richards, a certain sensory gratification comes from the re-establishment of equilibrium or order. And nothing could speak more softly of the quiet socializing function of literature and literary study than this unobtrusive reversal of Aristotle's formula. The English essay is not 'purely emotional persuasion, like advertisements or propaganda.' Instead, 'you write arguments because you care about the free exchange of ideas.' A *New York Times* essay by the novelist John Irving is seen as initiating a chain reaction: 'You can write a response to him, and he or someone else can write a response to you, and so on and so forth until

everyone agrees or drops the topic' (11). Given Griffith's atomistic interpretive universe, fission and entropy are the only alternatives.

The notion of the free exchange of ideas raises the problem of validity
in interpretation – a question which the subjectivism-within-objectivism
of the close reading puts most sharply. Even if a piece in the *New York
Times* and a first-year student paper were situated equally, had the same
chance to convince and persuade, still some interpretations are more
equal than others. But while this dilemma may occupy entire issues of
scholarly journals, it is easily resolved in the classroom. Although 'no single view ... can be the all-encompassing or final view,' although 'cultures
change, people change, and as a result perception changes'; still, 'this
does not mean that all interpretations of a work are equally valid.' (The
justification for this interpretive hierarchy is an interesting example, in
which the child's enjoyment of a book such as *Alice in Wonderland* is con-
trasted to an adult pleasure to which are added 'entirely new under-
standings.' Since the transitional position between childhood and
adulthood is occupied by the very students to whom Griffith's book is
addressed, questioning the movement from plurality to validity would
be tantamount, as it is construed here, to indicating an unwillingness to
develop mature understanding, to put away childish things.)

This crisis of validity is then equally an issue of subjectivity and citizenry, shown here through Griffith's splitting of the essay genre into
argumentative, informational, and personal types. The premise of an
'interpretive community' to which all may belong serves here – as it
does, I would add, throughout the work of Stanley Fish – to obscure the
boundaries of such communities and the way in which admission to
them is regulated. It assumes that there are different communities to
which one may have access and whose collective viewpoints will freely
compete. But the seminar group is not an interpretive community on the
level of an editorial board or a group of conference discussants: 'you'
does not actually engage in debate with John Irving or even, really, with
the professor. And the close reading essay is not a piece of criticism but
is rather a test of admission, a trial.

Theories of literature are not simply the stuff of scholarly debate. In
fact, the most pervasive notions are those which are not or cannot be
articulated and which are not methodically or evenly applied. They are
the 'normal science,' the deep background of assumptions and authorities against which new ideas may blend or seem 'ugly,' in Gertrude
Stein's term. And these notions of textual value and literary authority
spill over into our conception of English and the teaching of it. Much

recent work has focused on the unspoken or unacknowledged assumptions of New and Leavisite criticisms. It is possible to think of the characteristic conjuncture of them as providing a disciplinary or professional, rather than a merely scholarly, paradigm. This conjuncture provides the moral, purposive, and practical mean of English studies and, more importantly, the epistemology, the network of what can be thought and said. Under this criticism, the individual and self-contained art work is accorded highest value, and we may reasonably expect that other things will be valued to the extent that they approximate its characteristics.

The working assumption of New Criticism, then, whether as a reading or teaching method or as an assignment, is that poems are self-contained 'worlds,' aesthetic totalities distinguished by complex inter-relationships between the parts, these parts forming a whole greater than their sum. And a further assumption is that a 'practice' consisting of classroom discussion will be sufficient to overcome barriers to understanding, for these are English yet trans-cultural icons and ultimately accessible to us. The close reading assignment recapitulates these assumptions, and students are asked to write a paper which is to be, in significant ways, like the poem they are writing about – balanced, complex, complete, unreductionist, organic. So deep are the principles at work here that they are rarely articulated expressly; their traces can be seen only in the instructor's choice of works and evaluative vocabulary – the 'integration' of one poem, the 'failure' of another. It is not surprising that performance on the close reading paper is used as the mark of 'good' or 'promising' students – that is, students who have decoded the discipline. The close reading assignment, perhaps more than any other, seems to require evaluation on formal criteria and, perhaps, to permit evaluation on impressionistic grounds. It therefore fulfils a strongly normalizing function. The fact that it is the least explicable assignment makes it integral to English studies, as does the assumption of learning through mimesis. This valuation of the fully achieved art object (essays like poems) and its effectivity (essays from poems) operates persuasively in English studies. If the close reading piece is supposedly like a poem under New Critical criteria, so is the seminar group itself – balanced, complex, synergistic, diversified, and cooperative systems of interrelationship within an autonomous body removed from a historical or social context. A poem, as John Crowe Ransom defines it, sets up 'a small version of our natural world in its original dignity,' but it is also 'like a democratic state ... which realizes the ends of a state without sacrificing the personal character of its citizens' (quoted in Fekete 193). In Cleanth Brooks's definition, it is unity achieved through subordination to 'a total and governing attitude' (quoted in Fekete 93).

The 'total and governing attitude' is of course provided not by the students themselves but by the (effaced) authority of the instructor. The New Critical notion of the text as a pre-existent given upon which *post-facto* critical operations are performed reinforces a pedagogic system in which the answer is already known. The workings of this system are blurred by the give and take, the free play, of the seminar group; its marks are readable in the final examination paper. The idea of pre-existent text underlines the design of the standard curriculum, in which students study material or works first and then may have an upper-level theory seminar. From this comes, in Tony Davies's words, 'the systemic ambiguity of the undergraduate position itself,' between a 'seemingly natural, immediate response and elaborated "method"' (33). The fight we wage to save the small group seminar, given administrative pressures for more 'productive' large classes and lectures, obscures the fact that the seminar group, like the close reading assignment, is not a given (or a given good), but rather has a history and a disciplinary and institutional fit (Hartman; Ohmann), and fulfils disciplinary and professional mandates. In examining this, the intent is not criticize the assignment or the instructors who use it, but to try to account for the general sense that it is a useful form of work, or at least one for which there are no apparent substitutes. For many people, the close reading carries not only what is central to the discipline (interpretation) but what is best about it; and it bears, like the idealized seminar group, traces of its reformist pedagogic project. These features help to account for the persistence of the close reading assignment and its current placement.

The close reading remains although many of its premises have been questioned. The isolation of the text, and the inevitable ahistoricism of New and Leavisite criticisms, have received much attention. Here I will concentrate on the mimeticism of the close reading by looking at the close reading as a persistent and more-than-theoretical paradigm. This mimeticism is at the heart of the moral justification of literary study and the professional regulation of it.

Any rational enterprise, as Stephen Toulmin points out, has two faces or fronts. 'We can think of it as a discipline, comprising a communal tradition of procedures and techniques for dealing with theoretical or practical problems; or we can think of it as a profession, comprising the organized set of institutions, roles, and men whose task it is to apply and improve those procedures and techniques' (142). But, of course, not all participants in any inquiry have a consonant notion of the discipline or a like standing in the profession, or in fact necessarily any standing at all. (The term 'men,' here as everywhere else, signposts this fact.) The assumption of identity, like the assumption of the poem as an object rather than a speech act, obscures the processes by which what is different is made same – or kept dissimilar.

To Toulmin's delineations of 'discipline' and 'profession,' then, must be added the connotations to which Foucault has alerted us (*Discipline; History*). A discipline, according to the dictionary, is a 'department of learning or knowledge.' It is also the 'orderly conduct and action which result from training' and 'order maintained and observed among pupils or other persons under control of command.' In its ecclesiastical sense, discipline is 'the exercise of the power of censure, admonition, excommunication, and other penal measures' (*OED*). The categories of 'professor' or 'professional' have come adrift through the sustained amateurism of the first through much of the history of literary study. But both are rooted in the notion of the 'profession' as an act of open declaration, acknowledgment, or avowal. As a transitive and intransitive, with passive, active, and reflexive modes, the verb 'profess' works many ways: one may profess, or profess something, or be oneself professed, admitted (*OED*). The slide in 'discipline' from knowledge to order to control and the notion of a 'profession' as both personal testament and token of community entry indicate the interworkings of these two terms.

This complex of disciplinary and professional mandates complete with religious and regulative inflections is found fully formed in I.A. Richards's *Practical Criticism* and provides a justification both for the close reading (or sight reading) and the field of English studies itself. Richards, whose training was in moral philosophy, had long been concerned with a perceived social disintegration and ideational erosion – caused, as he had come to see it in the late '20s, by the rise of mass culture. His practical criticism experiment was not originally intended to provide a mode of literary analysis, but rather was set up as a 'fieldwork in comparative ideology' to examine the breakdown of shared knowledge and the conceptual overloading of individuals (6). Students were given poems from which identifying marks had been removed; their readings are developed, in *Practical Criticism*, into a typology of readerly error, categorized by inability to distinguish sense, tone, feeling, and intention. Richards intended to introduce system and rigour to an early academic criticism which was at that point belles-lettristic.

In the more philosophical sections which follow, Richards speculates on the necessity of establishing equipoise in the minds of individuals, the cultural value of such balance, and the way it could be achieved by the study of interpretation. Buddhism, Taoism, and a particularly Wordsworthian nostalgia work together here in what is, as much as anything, a story of creation and the fall: 'We may take self-completion as our starting point.' On Richards's analysis, however, the perfect mind nowhere exists 'due to man's innate constitution and to the accidents to which he is exposed' (285). As compensation for this 'default,' we are given knowledge, the 'greater complexity and finer differentiation of responses,' which enable us to both adjust to 'a partly uncongenial environment' and to relieve the 'internal strains' caused by it. 'And a re-ordering of [the organism's] impulses so as to reduce their interferences with one another to a minimum would be the most successful – and the most "natural" – direction which this tendency would take' (286–7).

It is not surprising to find a myth of phylogeny recapitulating the myths of ontogeny and ontology here. A special concern of *Practical Criticism* is that the 'original endowment' (224) of the child is so soon supplanted by 'ill-appropriate, stereotyped reactions.' This is caused by a *'withdrawal from experience'* (Richards's emphasis), which can come about in many ways. It may be caused physically, 'as when a London child grows up without ever seeing the country or the sea'; or morally, through deprivation by a parent of the 'expansive' adventures of childhood. A child, 'too easily persuaded,' may develop parasitically; and an intellectual impoverishment occurs when insufficient experience 'is theoretically elaborated into a system that hides the real world from us' (246). Given this situation, the only possible corrective is 'a closer contact with reality, either directly, through experience of actual things, or more mediately through other minds which are in closer contact' (251). While it is necessary to expose, as Terry Eagleton does, the ramifications of the belief that 'you can vicariously fulfill someone's desire for a fuller life by handing them *Pride and Prejudice'* (27) – still, a more straightforward and wishful statement of the social mission of English studies would be difficult to find. From this contact with reality would come, according to Richards, a 're-ordering':

a partial self-completion, temporary and provisional upon the external world remaining for the individual much what it had been in the past. And by such self-completion the superior man *would* 'effect a union of the external and the internal.' Being more at one within itself the mind thereby becomes more appropriately responsive to the outer world. (287)

Nor could we find a clearer statement of the particular, nascent New Critical methods of this mission. If the world will remain 'much what it had been in the past,' is this a statement of the ineffectuality of criticism or an affirmation of its power to move us, in Ransom's phrase, to 'our natural world in its original dignity'? This would be (to quote Leavis quoting T.S. Eliot) a world in which the natural rhythms of life, the footsteps and hoof-beats now drowned by the roar of engines and modern urban life, could be heard (McCallum 157).

The meditative moment of Richards is thus the moment of Leavis and of *Scrutiny*. But it is, as well, the moment of contemporary literary studies, in which students are seen as deafened by rock music, baffled by videos, and disturbed by the ever-increasing chances of their annihilation. It is this latter, of course, that betrays our impetus to 'equipoise,' to a personal 'union of the external and the internal,' and demands as nothing else can a criticism under which the world is not left as it had been 'in the past.'

Literature teaching, Geoffrey Hartman has remarked, may be the last evangelical profession – a statement which applies equally to its protestants as to the members of the established church. And if the above seems to present English at its most moral, this is, again, not to contrast a benevolent discipline to a malevolent profession, but to show that the indistinguishability of them is in fact the real state of affairs. It is this disciplinary directive that permits the postulation of the 'superior man' and of the 'minds' which are in 'closer contact' with reality; just as the organization of power through professionalism means that no one person is, identifiably, that 'superior man.' Instead – and in a mode which the writings of Balibar, Bourdieu, and Foucault have been devoted to exploring – power is a matter of the constitution of a professional, or social, subject, a process to which 'humanities' study is central, although often seen as peripheral or even oppositional. Just as the essay is assessed for formal characteristics drawn from the perceived features of poems, so the student is judged on criteria provided by the 'mind' of the ideal or *imago* professor (or 'magister implicatus,' in James Sosnoski's term). And just as the value of the student's personality can be measured, on Richards's scheme, by the degree to which this work demonstrates 'attention to the self validating virtues of great poetry' (Baldick

152), so the teacher and 'his' processes of reading become the actual object of study, through a 'dramatic occupation' of the position of authority supposedly held by the text under consideration (Hertz 66). But while the integrity and independence of the poem have come recently under question, this professional model and professional modelling remain for the most part unexamined.

If the underlying mimeticism of English studies is so strong as to leave questioned reading practices in place, and professional placement practices unquestioned, is there a way of breaking the mirror? We might begin by taking the texts of both the literary and disciplinary as available to a reanimated rhetorical reading. W.K. Wimsatt writes in the introduction to *The Verbal Icon* that 'the poem conceived as a thing in between the poet and the audience is, of course, an abstraction. The poem is an act ... But if we are to lay hold of the poetic act to comprehend and evaluate it, and if it has to pass currency as a critical object, it must be hypostatized' (xvii). The verbal icon, then, is a fiction; and to de-hypostatize the poem (the essay, the profession), we need to restore the poem (the essay, the profession) to a place in discourse. Current theoretical work has done much to reinstate the intentional 'fallacy' of writerly labour and the affective 'fallacy' of readerly production, thus restoring this 'currency' to social circulation. But we must reanimate the 'critical object' itself by reading rhetorically, and in the fullest sense of that term. Tropes and structures do not necessarily reflect, aid, or assist content; nor do all features of a text 'work together' (as my own readings above were intended to show). To read the intervention of figure, sound, and style into logic, grammar, and content, and to develop this as a pedagogic practice, would seem to be the next and most important step in critical literary studies pedagogy, and it might take up where 'theory' teaching has left off. At the least, it would free close reading from the close reading.

Works Cited

Baldick, Chris. *The Social Mission of English Criticism, 1848–1932*. Oxford: Clarendon P, 1983.

Balibar, Renée. *Les Français fictifs: le rapport des styles littéraires au français national*. Paris: Hachette, 1974.

Barnet, Sylvan. *A Short Guide to Writing about Literature*, 4th ed. Boston: Little, 1979.

Beaty, Jerome, and William H. Matchett. *Poetry from Statement to Meaning*. New York: Oxford UP, 1965.

Belsey, Catherine. *Critical Practice*. London: Methuen, 1980.

Bourdieu, Pierre, and Jean-Claude Passeron. *Reproduction in Education, Society and Culture*. Trans. Richard Nice. London: Sage, 1977.

Davies, Tony. 'Common Sense and Critical Practice.' *Re-Reading English*. Ed. Peter Widdowson. London: Methuen, 1982. 32–43.

Eagleton, Terry. *Literary Theory: An Introduction*. Minneapolis: U of Minnesota P, 1983.

Fekete, John. *The Critical Twilight: Explorations in the Ideology of Anglo-American Literary Theory from Eliot to McLuhan*. London: Routledge, 1977.

Fish, Stanley. *Is There a Text in This Class?: The Authority of Interpretive Communities*. Cambridge, Mass.: Harvard UP, 1980.

Foucault, Michel. *Discipline and Punish*. Trans. Alan Sheridan. London: Penguin, 1975.

– *The History of Sexuality, Vol. 1. An Introduction*. Trans. Robert Hurkey. New York: Pantheon, 1978.

Griffith, Kelley, Jr. *Writing Essays about Literature: A Guide and Style Sheet*. 2d ed. New York: Harcourt, 1986.

Hartman, Geoffrey H. *Criticism in the Wilderness: The Study of Literature Today*. New Haven: Yale UP, 1980.

Hertz, Neil. 'Two Extravagent Teachings.' *Yale French Studies* 63 (1982): 59–71.

Longhurst, Derek. '"Not for All Time, but for an Age": An Approach to Shakespeare Studies.' *Re-Reading English*. Ed. Peter Widdowson. London: Methuen, 1982. 150–63.

McCallum, Pamela. *Literature and Method: Towards a Critique of I.A. Richards, T.S. Eliot and F.R. Leavis*. Dublin: Gill, 1983.

Ohmann, Richard. *English in America: A Radical View of the Profession*. New York: Oxford UP, 1976.

Richards, I.A. *Practical Criticism: A Study of Literary Judgement*. Rev. ed. London: Kegan Paul, 1930.

Roberts, Edgar V. *Writing Themes about Literature*. 1st ed. (1964); 2d ed. (1969); 3d ed. (1973); 4th ed. (1979); 5th ed. (1983). Englewood Cliffs, N.J.: Prentice.

Sosnoski, James. 'Literary Study as a Field for Inquiry.' *Boundary* 2 13, 2–3 (Winter/Spring 1985): 91–104.

Toulmin, Stephen. *Human Understanding: The Collective Use and Evolution of Concepts*. Princeton: Princeton UP, 1972.

Wimsatt, William. *The Verbal Icon*. Lexington: U of Kentucky P, 1954.

7

From Canon to Curriculum

The death of George Grant is mourned by many, and for many reasons. His demand that ethical issues be kept in the foreground of national life, his sustained attention to the most difficult moral and political questions, and his refusal to relinquish a distinctly Canadian social vision even as the hope of its realization dims – all these are aspects of George Grant's life and work which are inspirational even to those in disagreement with him. The loss of an indigenous educational theorist is particularly critical if it will cause us to rely more than we already do on issues and theories formulated in a U.S. context.

Grant's 'The University Curriculum' appeared twenty-five years ago in the collection *Technology and Empire*. On Grant's analysis, curriculum is the 'essence' of any university and determines its character. But despite individual variations of specialization and subject area, despite innovations and anachronisms, all university curricula in Canada serve the 'primary purpose' of Canadian culture: the need to 'keep technology dynamic within the context of the state capitalist structure' (113). Curriculum does this by facilitating the production of the personnel such a society requires. Here Grant's analysis closely resembles the social reproduction theory of Pierre Bourdieu, for example, where what is 'reproduced' by the educational system is not only members of the citizenry but fundamental economic and political relations. (Grant sees a further form of reproduction at work as well, in which an institutional response to seemingly 'North American' cultural change becomes a way of internalizing an American technological-imperial program.) As technological 'means' become increasingly the educational 'ends,' a vacuum of values is created; and it is this vacuum which is Grant's primary area of concern. His essay, 'The University Curriculum,' is structured by an unspoken play on the relationship between 'empiricism' and 'empire.'

For the present purpose, however, I will focus on Grant's analysis of a further form of reproduction at work in educational systems: the tendency of the educational system and its component parts to reproduce themselves. (While Bourdieu, at least in the earlier work, views this sort of reproduction as inevitable, Grant, it would appear, does not. For Grant, this is another consequence of the fit of educational aims to technological imperatives and is not intrinsic to the enterprise.) Grant pictures our situation as a 'tight circle' which inhibits both critique and change:

... our present forms of existence have sapped the ability to think about standards of excellence and yet at the same time have imposed on us a standard in terms of which the human good is monolithically asserted. Thus, the university curriculum, by the very studies it incorporates, guarantees that there should be no serious criticism of itself or of the society it is shaped to serve. We are unable seriously to judge the university without judging its essence; but since we are educated in terms of that curriculum it is guaranteed that most of us will judge it good. (131)

Grant is not deploring political paralysis, nor – given the date of this essay in the late 1960s – is he denying the existence of on-campus debate and confrontation. (He cites as exemplary the report of the University of Toronto review committee chaired by C.B. Macpherson.) Rather, what is described is a circle which is as much epistemological as it is political – that is, the impossibility of rethinking educational projects on their own terms, of developing an academic self-reflexivity. For Grant, it is the reintroduction of the past and of memory that will break this 'tight circle of the modern fate': Grant's pedagogic project, then, is to reinstate a lost spirit of discovery, a search for the principles of a 'human excellence' which has yet to be achieved. In Grant's closing words, it

cannot be appropriated by those who think of it as sustained simply in the human will, but only by those who have glimpsed that it is sustained by all that is. Although that sustainment cannot be adequately thought by us because of the fragmentation and complexity of our historical inheritance, this is still no reason not to open ourselves to all those occasions in which the reality of that sustaining makes itself present to us. (133)

The situation to which Grant addresses himself is in many respects similar to ours today; and it would be easy, but erroneous, to cite Grant's predicament and program in the interests of a neo-conservative educational agenda. It is important to emphasize the definitional distinctions he makes, and to see how the problems he details remain in need of both resolution and solution (as the considerable abstraction of the essay's conclusion, quoted above, would indicate). First, Grant's introduction of the 'past' to break the means-ends circle of techno-modernity is not a recommendation for the reintroduction of buried cultural treasure to the curriculum. The truth is not assumed to be inherent in any work, and no particular text is mentioned. The intent is not to establish certain knowledge, but to interrupt the cycle of the already known. Second, and following from this, Grant does not work towards the stabilization of 'culture,' whether that is seen as an inheritance from the past or a current consensus or construct. Instead, it is the considerable degree of homogeneity – of nation, education, and 'technique' – which is seen to be the problem. Third, the turn to the past is part of an attempt to develop a critique of curriculum with respect to the concerns of the curriculum, by raising on that level questions of 'value' – even, one might say, of the value of value. And last, the educational project is conceived as part of a thoroughgoing social restructuring, in which the demands of a technological hegemony are replaced by the needs of the body politic. In this respect, Grant's is a 'conservative' cultural project, but can only be called such under a series of definitions of the liberal, the conservative, and the social (and socialist) which are specific to this country. We cannot use these words without indebtedness to George Grant's radical rethinking of the terms and their relations. And educational debate is enriched by the questions he has raised.

Similar considerations occupy us today in our working life in the universities, at symposia and meetings. What is to be taught and by what method? Who is to be represented and why? These questions generate further questions about the social purpose of literary study, the discipline, and disciplinarity itself. Small wonder that these debates are complex, and (what might be euphemistically termed) energetic, involving high degrees of commitment and involvement on the part of their participants. And yet such debates are frequently lacking in focus, even purpose. This may stem in part from a notorious lack of disciplinary self-analysis. Also, we are often unused to considering the institutional and economic and legislative determinants of programs until we have to come to terms with them directly or feel them pressing upon us. In addition, since occasions for collegial exchange and free-floating speculation have become rarer with the intensification of classroom and administrative workloads, discussions of particular topics (for example, hiring or calendar change) become forums for wide-ranging discussions which, while they definitely have bearing on the matter and are intrinsically worthwhile, may at times seem surplus to the task at hand and be labelled counter-productive.

But there is another difficulty which may be perceived in collegial discussions about curriculum. Plainly put, it is that many of us do not think very much about curriculum (and certainly, at the post-secondary level, have not been trained to do so) and lack the basic vocabulary to conduct such discussions. Of particular concern – and it is my concern here – there is a tendency to conflate 'curriculum' with other levels of the pedagogic strata. Of course, 'curriculum' itself is not readily defined either descriptively or prescriptively (and what follows will detail some of the wide array of opinions on the topic). In particular, there is a tendency to conflate 'canon' and 'curriculum,' to speak of them as though they were the same, or as though the settling of the first could lead to the resolution of the second. While the canon debate being examined here is specific to English study, the curricular questions raised by the debate appear to me to have a broader consequence and interest.

The canon debate has been extensive, contentious, and long-lived in English, and somewhat less so in other areas of literary study. There are a number of reasons which could be suggested for the occasion of this debate and its centrality. The subject matter of English itself has permitted the teaching of an increasingly wide variety of literatures – Canadian literature, for example. The elastic departmental boundary of English has allowed a number of cultural constituencies to find a first institutional base there, as is often the case with women's studies, or Afro-American studies in the United States. These additions – which call for a redefinition of what 'English' is in the first place – have made spaces in the curriculum which then have permitted the entry of theorized study. 'Theory' is an area of endeavour which, in turn, poses basic questions about aesthetic and cultural value and its determination. Frequently, these accommodations have not been easily made – in many cases, they have not been made at all – but even where departments remain unaltered our sense of the literary and the range of authors we now seriously consider have been fundamentally changed over the last ten years.

The canon debate has brought with it, as well, some hard critical questions. It is crucial not to underestimate the complexities or the political importance of the continuing debates about the canon. Even when, for strategic reasons, we make strong cases for the merit or importance of an unacknowledged author or under-represented literature, those questions remain. But it is useful to ask about the consequences of the continued conduct of this debate on the level of canon. First, the superaddition of works, authors, and courses has left English programs fundamentally unaltered, albeit expanded. Second, the basic units of curricular and critical organization – 'works,' 'authors,' 'periods' – remain in place. In fact, the canon debate may have reinforced a tendency to text-centricity on the part of English departments, and thus strengthened rather than weakened reliance on the individual text as the basic repository of meaning and value. Third – a more speculative point – this dependency upon texts and the defence of the moral and social purpose of their study (at the expense, sometimes, of the defence of reading and interpretational skill) have maintained a notion of literary mimeticism readily appropriated to the interests of more restricted and illiberal humanities agendas which recommend 'great' works and our unproblematic profit from them.

The temptation to confine educational discussion to the question of content is now almost overwhelming, since both the canon debate and discussions of 'cultural literacy' have kept debates content-oriented. It is interesting to note that although the cultural literacy debate was originally about whether or not education should be based on content at all, it soon came to focus on the specifics of the content being advocated. While E.D. Hirsch's selections of key words and concepts could and should be read as the 'hidden agenda' of the cultural literacy program, nonetheless the question of the teaching of skills fell by the wayside.

Cultural Literacy begins with concern not simply over the 'failure' of education in the United States but over the fact that the system serves some badly and some well. Hirsch sees this discrimination as a case of unequal access to basic information, caused by the dominant educational paradigm of the last decade, which emphasizes skills or critical thinking. For Hirsch, literacy requires both coding and decoding skills and the information to make sense of what is read. No one can succeed without access to this repertory of basic cultural facts and concepts and key words. Their possession is what Hirsch refers to as cultural literacy.

It is important to clarify what Hirsch does and does not mean by these basic units of cultural literacy, samples of which are presented in the much-contended list which forms an appendix to the book and in the lists subsequently published. These are key words of which the cultur-

ally literate will have some recognition, although they may be hard
pressed to give an exact or correct definition. It would seem an exagger-
ation to call these cultural currency; they might better be termed loose
change. This is far from the 'masterwork' approach of Allan Bloom, for
example. These are not entire texts; it is not assumed that prescribed
texts (master or otherwise) will be read; and many of the examples are
drawn from popular culture and day-to-day life. In the second introduction to *Cultural Literacy*, Hirsch is at pains to dissociate his work from
those who would use it as the pretext for a 'Western civilization'
agenda. (Follow-up articles are 'Cultural Literacy Does Not Mean a List
of Works' and '"Cultural Literacy" Doesn't Mean "Core Curriculum."')

Hirsch, however, does not work towards the widest possible representation in the interests of a culture or cultures. Rather – and Hirsch is
explicit on this point and the analogy is his – the teaching of cultural literacy is intended to fix a national culture in the same way that the regulation of grammar and vocabulary is meant to fix a national language.
This national culture is not to be a compilation of cultures, any more
than a national language is a synthesis of dialects. The success, as Hirsch
sees it, of national languages is in turn used as a rationale for devising a
national culture. These points are essential rather than incidental to his
arguments, and the implications of Hirsch's reasoning emerge forcibly
in his condemnation of 'well-intended bilingualism' as a threat not only
to universal literacy but to national unity itself (93). Hirsch is able to
conceive of multiculturalism only as *inter-* rather than *intra-*national.

Criticisms of Hirsch have been made on two grounds. The first cen-
tres on his fixing of a national culture which, his critics argue, could
only be accomplished through the social disenfranchisement of many.
(And even if one accepted that a plural culture could or should be stabilized, his theory would seem to have little to offer to Canada, a society
already officially self-defined as not only multicultural but multinational.) Hirsch has also been criticized for his inability to recommend a
program or implementation for his ideas, instead offering only a series
of negative definitions (as in the article titles mentioned above). These
two failures are inextricably linked, and in a way that is instructive for
rethinking curriculum. First, it appears that there can be no short-cuts
through questions of educational access, representation, and social justice; the very questions which Hirsch intends to settle of course uncannily recur. However we might plan in the light of 'internal' disciplinary
and institutional mandates, the final test of the worth of the curriculum
will always be its responsiveness and responsibility to the society in

which we live, a society conceived in the fullest and most generous sense. Second, a content-driven educational model is ineffectual in providing curriculum or curricular change; selection of material and works must come in the latter stages of curriculum design.

By separating 'canon' and 'curriculum,' I do not intend to imply that we stop discussing the canon, or that representation – what people and ways and ideas are voiced and depicted – is not as crucial, as worth struggling for, as it has ever been. But it may be useful to see if these issues and questions can be raised – as George Grant suggests – at the level of curriculum itself. To initiate this, here are a number of possible ways of thinking about curriculum, drawn in an eclectic and selective way from recent work in curriculum theory. The first six centre on factors intrinsic to a program; the next six place curriculum in its relation to extrinsic factors. The last conceives of curriculum as activity.[1]

First is the idea of curriculum as an aggregate of courses or of a program's offerings. This is perhaps our most common use, and the market-place use, as when we speak of the curriculum of a department, equating it with the syllabus or calendar.

The second popular definition of curriculum lies closest to the etymological base (the Latin *currere*, to run) and conceives of curriculum not as courses but as the course of study of an individual student. It thus is both lesser and greater than the curriculum of the first definition, since a student normally takes only a fraction of the program's offerings; yet curriculum defined in this way also includes tests and examinations and other pedagogic elements not included when we define curriculum in the first sense. This awkward fit of the 'curriculum' of what we offer and the 'curriculum' of the individual student is a basic issue of pedagogic debate. The lack of homology can be celebrated (curriculum should offer maximum choice and individuation) or deplored (curriculum should offer a common 'core' or vocabulary, either of material, skills, or concepts).

Closely related to the above, although perhaps less known above the primary and secondary levels, is the notion of curriculum as a cognitive or conceptual path (or even moral or political path, depending on the type of education), in which the anticipated emotional or intellectual development of the student provides the structure of the program. (The Montessori method is a familiar example.) Development is taken into account somewhat in our divisions into years and the provision of pre-entry courses, although for the most part at the post-secondary level such gradations are made more expressly according to the difficulty of course content.

The fourth and fifth ways of envisaging curriculum may be seen as two paradigms whose alternating dominance provides the history of modern education.

Curriculum as content sees curriculum as organized by information, material, or coverage (whether that, in turn, is seen as breadth or core). A Great Books program would function as an extreme case of a content-based curriculum, in which by definition the content is foundational, and aims, methods, skills, and cultural commonality are assumed to be generated from the reading of these works.

Curriculum as the development of skills is an alternate paradigm, whether the skills to be developed are those of citizenship (as they were for Egerton Ryerson or John Dewey), of literacy, or of thinking. It is against this educational 'formalism,' in his terms, that Hirsch has been developing the information-intensive program that he hopes will turn the tide, as it were, of contemporary education.

While we might see these two impulses as an alternating current, clearly neither exists alone; and, in fact, the one is often seen as a means to the other. For example, the study of English at the undergraduate and graduate level might appear 'content-driven'; that is, it is primarily *about* English literature. That would not be the way F.R. Leavis envisaged it, since he and other members of the *Scrutiny* project saw English as the education *par excellence* for life. And certainly many people in the university now take as a primary project the teaching of a skill – reading – although this is done with an expanded sense of rhetorical repertoire and a distinct hope of reading's cultural utility.

The interdependency of many intrinsic factors occasions a sixth definition, with Paul Hirst's influential description of curriculum as a combination of content, aims, and methods: in Hirst's words, 'a programme of activities designed so that pupils will attain by learning certain specifiable ends or objectives' (2). Curriculum-by-objectives has both its supporters and detractors, but two useful points may be drawn from Hirst's approach. First, objectives need prior formulation, and the selection of materials and methods follows from this; neither material nor method is an aim in itself. Second, Hirst's definition suggests we might devote more sustained attention to the question of method, whether we define this as pedagogic approach or theoretical orientation. This is an aspect of curricular design that tends to be slighted at the post-secondary level. A Hirstian synthetic approach is theoretically sophisticated but at the same time describes the way we often conceive of curriculum in practice. Theme-based, modular, or problem-based instructional units are all deliberate attempts to synthesize curricular factors and to use this synthesis as the base for curricular organization.

What I call 'extrinsic' approaches, by contrast, place curriculum in relation to other structures, whether heuristic or social.[2]

A seventh definition situates curriculum as the formation of departmental or program identity. Here the curriculum is both the distinguishing feature of a department or program, and a contribution to the institution's mandates. The institution provides more than a series of regulations to which we must respond; it provides the basic categorizations (program, department) within which that work must take place, with consequences that the anthropologist Clifford Geertz has assessed. If the term 'institution' is taken to mean more than our own institutional setting, and to refer to educational and academic institutions in a more general way, then it is possible to see (as Samuel Weber has done, for example) how the institution forms scholarly work, if only through maintenance of the 'scholarly.' At this point, social and heuristic structures begin to blur together.

An eighth definition conceives of curriculum in its relationship to a field or discipline; that is, curriculum as the boundary of what is in and out of a given discipline or field. This is a complex relationship for a number of reasons. First, there is no necessary fit between work in a field and what is taught in a classroom in many disciplines. (If there were, every English department in North America would have a course on Zora Neale Hurston.) In fact – and 'theory' is a good example here – there are sometimes debates about whether important scholarly material is teachable at all, especially at the undergraduate level. Further, the notion of curriculum as boundary may need to be differently conceived by humanities departments, which are by definition cross-disciplinary. Curriculum here may function less to police boundaries than to break them. An area with a certain amount of inherent interdisciplinariness, like English, poses a similar puzzle.

The 'knowledge' to which a curriculum relates may be conceived not as a particular field or specialty, but as the knowledge of a nation or culture or people. Here is a ninth formulation of curriculum, which provides continuing debate both educational and political. (It tends, in fact, to be the primary way by which education is discussed in the political realm.) Two questions are important here. First, when we say 'culture,' what culture are we speaking of, and whose? Second, what is the relationship of the curriculum to the culture or cultures? Both questions may be answered from what one might call a left or a right position. We could conceive of Canada as intrinsically multinational or multicultural and say that curriculum should reflect this through its choice of items and perspectives. Or we could say that the United States, for example, has a distinctively 'American' culture extending from founding principles and that education should explain and preserve this. (The Newbolt Report's restructuring of the English educational system after the First World War, around notions of a distinctive British national character, would be one example of the full implementation of such an educational agenda.) Whatever position is taken here, the relationship between culture and curriculum is seen to be mimetic.

A tenth formulation sees curriculum not in a reflective relation to culture but as a form of socially organized knowledge. While these may at first glance seem to be the same, there are significant differences. A theory of 'socially organized knowledge' accounts for stratifications and uneven distributions of knowledge, and sees curriculum as itself an active agent in that social organization of knowledge. The approach to 'curriculum as socially organized knowledge' is often based on the foundational thinking of Michael Young. Such work suggests that the relationship between social structures and (seemingly) heuristic structures demands serious attention. Basil Bernstein has worked on the specifics of this, with his distinction between 'classification' and 'frame,' the first referring to pre-existent categorizations of knowledge, the latter to the degree of control students and teachers can maintain over organization and pacing.

Taken in a certain direction, the theory of socially organized knowledge culminates in social reproduction theory, as in the earlier work of both Pierre Bourdieu and Michael Apple, for example.[3] Here curriculum is seen to reproduce not the knowledges of a culture but its economic and class relations. The strength of reproduction theory is that it allows us to think of schooling not just in the sense of material taught but in the sense of material relations. The weakness is in the way it repeats the mimeticism of the 'culture' theory, assuming an unbroken chain of structural replications from the state down to the classroom. From our own experiences, we know that teachers and students can be questioning, critical, and resistant, and there must be a way of accounting for this.

Michael Apple's later work, and the work of American theorist Henry Giroux, are examples of what could be called the 'spaces' theory since there does not seem to be any other name. It denies that social or power relations of any kind can be hegemonic; rather, there are 'gaps' between levels and perhaps a weakening of forces the further down the chain one goes. Thus, at the level of the classroom there is real room for difference, and curriculum could then be conceived as counter-cultural (in the most utopian formulation) or, better, as an agent for individual empowerment and social change. One should note, too, that all the above models have seen education as a one-way street; variously, transmission from teacher to student, cultural inheritance, or social reproduction. Only at this point can we begin to see curriculum as what Henry Giroux calls a curricular dialectic, in which the experience and backgrounds of teachers *and* students are brought into dialogue. Here we maximize curriculum by expanding received notions of legitimate knowledge. This is the basis of a feminist pedagogy, of course, but it might well be the starting place for other kinds of curricular transformation.

A thirteenth notion, and one which is my own, lets us think of curriculum, not as a thing or an entity, but rather as an activity. It is something that we do. It is, furthermore, the area of private/public intersection where, as teachers, our personal, often isolated, classroom practices are brought into conjunction with the work of our colleagues. Because it allows us to operate creatively, critically, and collectively, curriculum seems to be the educational level where constructive change is most possible and our efforts are best expended.[4] And I add: should we not include students and their contributions in these processes of rethinking and reassessment?

These thirteen ways will perhaps give a sense of the resources we have when we begin curriculum renewal. While they may appear to compound the complex of practical and theoretical questions that any group has to consider, in fact we would probably find that our own thinking on curriculum contains most of these thirteen ways to some degree.

While in 'theory' it may be wise to discuss works and content towards the end of the curricular design project, in practice it would be almost impossible to do so. By this point in the debate, 'canon' is less a reference to authors or books than a shorthand for a cluster of questions, concerns, and positionings. Just as seemingly curricular debates in fact tend to be canonical contentions, so canonical disputes are often extra-canonical and, therefore, are seen to have a certain priority or necessity. There are, however, continuing difficulties with this state of affairs. In the first place, there is no 'canon' – only 'canons' – scholarly canons, pedagogic canons, regionally and institutionally variable canons. Canonical debates need to be sharpened for particular times and circumstances. Second, canonical debate is a narrow band on which to conduct a critique of both continuing practices and lack of representation of real people and perspectives in today's academy; sexism in secondary material and perspectives and discrimination in hiring are two areas which lie outside the bounds of canon. And third – canon is a heuristic categorization. It is not a method by which curricula or departments are organized; thus the relationship of canon to curriculum is not one of application, but translation.

How would this function in relationship to any – typical, mythical – English department? There is a curious fact to be mentioned about our mythical department. It has a singular history and its own institutional and national setting. It has its own needs and mandates and constituencies, its particular quarrels and challenges, and aspirations and standards of which it is proud. Its practices and procedures are worked out over decades through the sustained – and often heated – colloquy of imaginative individuals. How can it possibly be, then, that the product of years of discussion and criticism and labour is an English program that looks pretty much like every other English program on the face of the planet?

One could suggest that in fact English programs are not really designed through processes of curricular definition – whether of objectives, content, methods, or any combination of these – although such processes, indeed, take place. Instead, programs seem to be formed through a sort of disciplinary reproduction. Further, what appears to be reproduced is not so much the content – although there is a high degree of repetition in selection – but rather the organization of that material.[5] This organization of material in turn allows the maintenance of what is considered as knowledge in English and thus the maintenance of 'English' itself. While the organization of material and boundaries functions in a way that is discipline-specific, to identify it as a mode of socially organized knowledge allows us to ask the sorts of questions posed by George Grant, of the relation of this curriculum to other modes of social organization and the 'social' itself. Such questions then become important to, rather than extraneous to, a review of curriculum and its construction.

There are considerable difficulties in initiating this sort of curriculum inquiry, whether one uses Hirst's definition or Young's definition or some other combination. English has traditionally found the formulation of objectives difficult to do, although this comes not from a weak sense of social purpose – English teachers being in the main a committed group with convictions about the importance of their work – but from a weak sense of disciplinarity and epistemological field. The definition of method is also compounded, no matter how we view that term. If we mean 'method' as 'teaching method,' we begin from a point where there is scant common vocabulary for the discussion of pedagogic practices and little general knowledge of their history. (The maintained privacy of the classroom and the rarity of team teaching may reflect a disciplinary suspicion of collaborative scholarly work, which in turn stems from a sense that textual understanding and teaching are both best achieved by the exercise of personal qualities.) If we conceive 'method' as 'methodology,' its discussion is made difficult by a persistent anti-theoretical streak to the discipline, and by the fact that current theoretical inquiry is both conceptually complex and pedagogically underdeveloped. And if 'method' refers to a set or variety of rhetorical and analytical reading and interpretive skills which we wish students to acquire, we will rarely find this formulated as one of the systematically enacted objectives of an English program, although we might ask what it is we actually do, if we do not do this.

An examination of curriculum under Young's definition of curriculum as socially organized knowledge would be hindered by a persistent ivory-towerism, and the endemic refusal to situate literary study in its institutional determinants. (Paradoxically, the anti-humanist bias of the contemporary academy makes this attitude easier to maintain, since 'English' is fond of seeing itself as the counter-culture of the university or the home of its lost values.) An anti-reflexive tendency, and a lack of research on the topic of disciplinary history, are further barriers to be overcome.

At the same time, however, these barriers may be seen not as blocks to curricular innovation but as further reasons to undertake it. As I have tried to suggest, curriculum is an area where there is a considerable body of well-evolved and interesting work. Further, as scholarly work in English studies becomes increasingly specialized and increasingly divergent, it is pedagogy which may best provide an area of common conversation and shared concern. Thus examination of curriculum could help to initiate what are (in my opinion) necessary processes of departmental and disciplinary liaison-building. In addition, curriculum discussions will require the development of a stronger analysis of institutional placement, a better sense of subject and pedagogic history, and a clearer articulation of methodological and theoretical projects. It may also be useful to place literary study in higher education as part of a continuum with literary study at lower educational levels. One could add that in the development of an effective and critical pedagogy, curriculum may well be the most fruitful area of concentration, as the level where institutional determination and departmental collectivity meet individual practice and the classroom. And last, a conscious consideration of curriculum may help us to gain a point of purchase on the tight and tightening circle against which George Grant has warned.

Notes

1 Omitted from the above definitions are considerations of the historical development of the English curriculum. There is a growing body of work which takes institutional, disciplinary, and pedagogic development as its topic. The most thorough studies are by Baldick (for England) and Graff (for the United States). See also Brooker and Humm, Doyle, Eagleton, and Gossman. Ian Michael's recent and comprehensive *The Teaching of English* is devoted primarily to grammar school education, but provides interesting material on the development of English as a subject area and its pedagogies. Two works oriented towards U.S. college-level curricula are by Applebee and McMurtry.

2 In addition to the works cited in the text, there is other interesting thought on curriculum in its heuristic and institutional relations. On the question of English as a field, see Sosnoski. On general consideration of the intersection of 'information' and 'institution,' and the consequences of division into discipline and department, see the special issues of *Boundary 2* and the works of Samuel Weber (in addition to Geertz).

3 In addition to the work of Bourdieu and Giroux on curriculum and social reproduction, see Renée Balibar's 'National Language, Education, Literature.' Richard Ohmann's polemical *English in America* is still timely; see also the more recent *The Politics of Letters*, especially the section 'Literacy, Technology and Monopoly Capitalism.'

Recent work in critical legal studies on the topic of professional formation has much to offer. See Kennedy and Shaffer.

4 Henry Giroux suggests that 'curriculum' is the level where efforts are best expended.

5 Canonical challenges are often seen as occasioning apocalyptic choices: Toni Morrison *or* William Shakespeare. However, most English department curricula are characterized by extensive repetition of works which most of us would consider substitutable. (As one student remarked to me: 'Why do we study *Sons and Lovers* over and over again?') It is eye-opening to list the

works actually taught in a given program, to see how few there are, how great is the degree of duplication, and (sometimes) how disappointingly unimaginative the selections can be.

Works Cited

Apple, Michael. *Ideology and Curriculum*. London: Routledge and Kegan Paul, 1979.
– *Teachers and Texts: A Political Economy of Class and Gender Relations in Education*. New York and London: Routledge and Kegan Paul, 1986.
Applebee, Arthur N. *Tradition and Reform in the Teaching of English*. Urbana, Ill.: National Council of Teachers of English, 1974.
Baldick, Chris. *The Social Mission of English Criticism, 1848–1932*. Oxford: Clarendon P, 1983.
Balibar, Renée. 'National Language, Education, Literature.' *Literature, Politics and Theory: Papers from the Essex Conference*. Ed. Francis Barker et al. London: Methuen, 1986. 126–47.
Bernstein, Basil. *Class, Codes and Control*. Vol. 3. Boston and London: Routledge and Kegan Paul, 1977.
Boundary 2 [special issues: 'On Humanism and the University'] 12, 3 (1984); 13, 2/3 (1985).
Bourdieu, Pierre. *Outline of a Theory of Practice*. Trans. Richard Nice. Cambridge: Cambridge UP, 1977.
– and Jean-Claude Passeron. *Reproduction in Education, Society, and Culture*. Trans. Richard Nice. London: Sage, 1977.
Brooker, Peter, and Peter Humm. *Dialogue and Difference: English into the Nineties*. London: Routledge, 1989.
Doyle, Brian. *English and Englishness*. London: Routledge, 1989.
– 'The Hidden History of English Studies.' *Re-Reading English*. Ed. Peter Widdowson. London: Methuen, 1982. 17–31.
Eagleton, Terry. 'The Rise of English.' *Literary Theory: An Introduction*. Minneapolis: U Minnesota P, 1983. 17–53.
Geertz, Clifford. 'Blurred Genres.' *Local Knowledge: Further Essays in Interpretive Anthropology*. New York: Basic Books, 1983. 19–35.
Giroux, Henry A. *Ideology, Culture, and the Process of Schooling*. Philadelphia: Temple UP, 1981.
– *Theory and Resistance in Education*. South Hadley, Mass.: Begin and Garvey, 1983.
Gossman, Lionel. 'Literature and Education.' *New Literary History* 13, 2 (1982): 341–71.

Graff, Gerald. *Professing Literature: An Institutional History*. Chicago: U Chicago P, 1987.

Grant, George. 'The University Curriculum.' *Technology and Empire: Perspectives on North America*. Toronto: House of Anansi, 1969. 111–33.

Hirsch, E.D. 'Cultural Literacy Does Not Mean a List of Works.' *ADE Bulletin* 84 (1986):1–3.

– '"Cultural Literacy" Doesn't Mean "Core Curriculum."' *English Journal* 74 (1985): 47–50.

– *Cultural Literacy: What Every American Needs to Know*. With Joseph Kett and James Trefil. Boston: Houghton Mifflin, 1987.

Hirst, Paul H. *Knowledge and the Curriculum: A Collection of Philosophical Papers*. London: Routledge and Kegan Paul, 1974.

Kennedy, Duncan. *Legal Education and the Production of Hierarchies*. Cambridge, Mass.: Afar P, 1983.

McMurtry, Jo. *English Language, English Literature: The Creation of an Academic Discipline*. Hamden, Conn.: Archon Books, 1985.

Michael, Ian. *The Teaching of English: From the Sixteenth Century to 1870*. Cambridge: Cambridge UP, 1987.

Ohmann, Richard. *English in America: A Radical View of the Profession*. New York: Oxford UP, 1976.

– 'Literacy, Technology and Monopoly Capitalism.' *College English* 47, 7 (1985): 675–89.

– *The Politics of Letters*. Middletown, Conn.: Wesleyan UP, 1987.

Shaffer, Thomas L. 'Moral Implications and Effects of Legal Education: Or, Brother Justinian Goes to Law School.' *Journal of Legal Education* 34, 2 (1984): 190–204.

Sosnoski, James. 'Literary Study as a Field for Inquiry.' *Boundary 2* 13, 2/3 (1985): 91–104.

Weber, Samuel. 'Ambivalence, the Humanities, and the Study of Literature.' *Diacritics* 15, 2 (1985): 11–25.

–, ed. *Demarcating the Disciplines: Philosophy, Literature, Art*. Glyph Textual Studies, Vol. 1. Minneapolis: U Minnesota P, 1986.

– *Institution and Interpretation*. Theory and History of Literature Series, Vol. 31. Minneapolis: U Minnesota P, 1986.

Young, Michael F.D. 'An Approach to the Study of Curricula as Socially Organized Knowledge.' *Knowledge and Control: New Directions for the Sociology of Knowledge*. Ed. Michael F.D. Young. London: Collier-Macmillan, 1971. 19–46.

8

Reading Readers

The foundational question of literary studies – underlying all critical speculation whether or not it is expressly 'theoretical' – may well be that of the relationship between 'literature' and 'life.' This is now commonly cast as a question of the relationship between 'reading' and 'resistance': that is, what is the consonance or causality between our most basic disciplinary practice and political life? It is a query that structures both feminist and Marxist literary scholarship, and has spilled into recent reader-response work.

In part because of the range of their use, however, these terms do not occur with consistency. The first item seems less problematic, but this stability is false since 'reading' may denote either the passage from one end of a book to the other or a rigorously rhetorical examination. The definition of 'resistance' will vary widely from context to context. Subjective and psychoanalytically based theories refer to a resistance to self-knowledge. Political projects such as feminism often postulate a 'resisting reader,' in Judith Fetterley's term; while social reproduction analysts like Henry Giroux attempt to discern how teacher and student resistance may be possible and effective. All forms of inquiry have recourse to a de Manian notion of resistance; that is, a resistance to rhetorical reading, to reading the text's resistances. Thus, while there is a considerable terminological overlap, the embedding of these terms in a variety of fields causes divergences as well. From a psychoanalytic perspective, resistance (while necessary) is to be overcome or worked through; for political theorists, it is to be strengthened and maintained; on a de Manian definition, resistance is an inevitability, inscribed into the project as such.

Current work 'between' the disciplines intends to bridge some of these differences. For example, a Lacanian theory would appear to span the psychoanalytic and feminist definitions of 'resistance' by configuring resistance as a transference to the supposed knowledge of the analyst (a knowledge which is, in the end, the analysand's self-knowledge); by extension, teacher or text occupy a usefully illusory position of stable authority. This 'occupation,' however, remains problematic from a feminist point of view, since the positions of analysand/analyst or student/teacher are currently gender-determined; thus the question of resistance recurs. In another interdisciplinary bridging, titled 'Deconstruction, Feminism, and Pedagogy,' Barbara Johnson shows how the 'impersonal' and rhetorical pedagogic program of Paul de Man's 'Resistance to Theory' and the 'personal' feminist pedagogy of the multi-authored volume *Gendered Subjects* stand in relations of interactive complementarity and sharp critique, and asks 'whether each is not in reality haunted by the ghost of the other' (44).

It would appear that such questions are most productively asked and answered across heuristic and disciplinary boundaries – and certainly the potential of inter- or even non-disciplinary inquiry drives both women's studies and new literary-theoretical work. But is interdisciplinarity always enriching, cumulative, synergistic? Or is it possible for something to be replaced or displaced in the transaction, a loss with consequences for women? It is this problem of transference, in its several senses, that emerges in an interesting interdisciplinary case.

In late 1987, the journal *College English* devoted two special issues to 'psychoanalysis and pedagogy' in literature and composition study (a boundary-breaking topic *par excellence*). Of the seven essays and two editorial prefaces, two of the nine pieces are by women; numbers alone suggest that it is primarily men who hold the role of analysts of 'psychoanalysis and pedagogy.' Thus in this instance of cross-disciplinarity, the representation of women seems to reflect, not the literary disciplines, in which women are numerous, but the psychoanalytic establishment, where women are common as analysands and rare as analysts. (Since so much new psychoanalytic examination has occurred under the banner of 'psychoanalysis and feminism,' this under-representation is doubly striking.) Other aspects of the editorial organization of the volumes may be relevant as well. Of the two women-authored pieces, both are co-authored; further, the two woman-authored pieces are placed in the first and second position in the first issue, after the editor's preface.

Is there, one asks, any connection between the editorial placement of the pieces and their topics or approaches? The woman-authored essays diverge from the other seven pieces in two distinct ways. Each deals with the specifics of teaching *a* text, and each therefore takes 'psycho-analysis and pedagogy' to mean psychoanalytic text-reading practices. Barbara Johnson and Marjorie Garber provide an essay on ways of reading *The Secret Sharer*, while Patricia Donahue and Ellen Quandahl discuss the teaching of psychoanalytic literature, focusing on the use of 'Dora' in an academic upgrading classroom. The choice of a textually mediated 'impersonalism' by the feminist authors, and the status of co-author for all the women, suggest that this 'de-authorization' may be a conscious strategy of these contributors, in pieces that are both experiential and impersonal, pedagogic and theoretical.

The other papers in the volume – and the ones to which I will now refer – are all single-authored by men, and all assume by 'psychoanalysis and pedagogy' that the classroom situation is, or should be, or cannot help but be, like analysis and the analytic setting. From this, it follows that the teacher does, or should, or inevitably must, occupy the position of the analyst. Most cite de Man to locate this 'personal' teaching in an impersonal or rhetorical study. All papers are to a degree Lacanian in orientation, if only through their system of citation, and hinge their arguments on the Lacanian configuration of 'resistance' as 'resistance to knowledge.' Thus 'transference' and 'resistance' are seen to be inextricably related since the student's transference to the teacher, or more precisely to the teacher's assumed knowledge, is viewed as the form that resistance to knowledge takes. A psychoanalytic pedagogy, as envisaged here, would foreground or ironize or dismantle the position of the teacher as a *'sujet supposé savoir,'* although the articles differ in their programs for this.

While an overview of the pieces risks blurring the considerable distinctions between them, three significant similarities may be noted of these five male-authored articles and the two prefaces. First, while the concept of the transference is central to these examinations, the idea of counter-transference is almost entirely absent. Second, there is little or no analysis of the material conditions and determinants of literary study, despite the fact that consideration of the analytic situation is central to clinical literature, which considers actions and reactions as framed by, and referrable to, this setting. Third, 'resistance' on its political definition is occluded by the psychoanalytic, or is seen as following from it, configured as the end result of working through (and envisaged as the attainment of an individual critical awareness of the ideological, rather than the development of a self in solidarity). The specific pedagogic consequences of these lacunae are illustrated in two passages, which are themselves established as pedagogically illustrative in the context of their respective articles.

The first is from Patrick McGee's 'Truth and Resistance: Teaching as a Form of Analysis,' in which a young woman asks the question 'Why is English so important?':

She was honest enough to admit that she had never cared for reading and found writing to be irrelevant to her life and interests. When I pointed out that English was her language and the medium of communication at her university, she quickly responded that she found it difficult to relate her everyday use of language, even at school, to what happens in an English course. She had no difficulty communicating directly through speech with her instructors and friends; but whenever she had to write or pay attention to how texts are written, she felt paralyzed. Writing on topics I had given, which involved thinking about rhetorical strategies and an audience, irritated her enormously ... She thought it should be enough to agree or disagree with, to like or dislike, an essay.

McGee goes on to comment: 'My student's attitude is not unrepresentative, and the least one can say is that her remarks illustrate the view that language-teaching involves not only eradicating ignorance but overcoming resistance' (672).

The second excerpt is from Gregory Jay's 'The Subject of Pedagogy':

One student recently expressed her frustration (a common one) with Joyce's *Dubliners*, saying that she got nothing from it, that it didn't mean anything to her. This led quite nicely into a discussion of how literary meaning doesn't exist like a scoop of ice-cream to be spooned and swallowed. It has to be produced actively by the reader, and so the class began a discussion of how we go about making meaning happen while we read. Is there a reason, historical or ideological or personal, why we can't at first 'see' something which the later adoption of a critical perspective suddenly brings into focus? How much about the positions of religion, class and gender in Joyce's Ireland do we need to know for *Dubliners* to mean something for us? In a given situation (a play, a football game, a bar-room seduction, a presidential news conference), what are the materials out of which meaning is being made, and by what common rules? (794)

These passages substantiate their respective authors' contentions that both pedagogy and psychoanalysis are questions of interpretive strategy – although they are perhaps illustrating this in ways the authors do not intend. The terms of the argument are thematized here, but also put into question, as they are quite literally questioned by the student interlocutors.

The lesson of the two stories is similar: meaning is not 'there' in the text but (in Jay's words) is 'produced actively by the reader,' and we 'mak[e] meaning happen while we read' (794). This is a lesson with which most teachers would surely agree, citing either textual complication or the liberatory potential of a 'writerly' perspective. The engenderment of the stories, however, alerts us to the fact that identification solely with the male narrative and not its (transcribed) female speech may be misleading.

In each case, the student is attempting to postulate her 'life' in some way as an epistemological base (an assumption, it should be noted, that the writers share, since they also assume that this is how literary study takes its bearings). Additionally, in each instance the student is expressing some dissatisfaction with classroom orientation and teaching materials (as, presumably, would the authors of the articles in 'Psychoanalysis and Pedagogy,' else there would be no need for the topic). How are these readers read, and what is the response to them? In the first instance – which sounds like an excerpt from 'Dora' – an 'irritated' and 'paralyzed' student who is perceived to be 'in difficulty' resists the instructor's 'pointings out' and his demands to 'think.' In the second case, the student's frustration (in fact, 'common' frustration) with Joyce is read as a symptom of the malaise of consumer culture – texts are not to be consumed and neither, we assume, should students expect to be spoon-fed.

While neither author would use these terms explicitly, the first student has been described as mildly hysteric, while the second seems to be suffering a petty neurosis. Mary Jacobus, in her response to Stanley Fish's 'Is There a Text in This Class?' notes the position of the woman student as anti-muse, the misapprehending 'fall doll who sets ... theoretical discourse in motion' (117). (This is an issue that will be dealt with in more detail in chapter 10.) The quoted excerpts from McGee and Jay set up gendered binaries of experience/analysis, opinion/thought, speech/writing, spontaneity/attention, unintentional communication / rhetorical strategy, blindness/insight, illness/health, with the woman student occupying the first position in each instance and the male professor the second. McGee puts it bluntly when he sees in the student's utterance an 'ignorance' which must be 'eradicated.' ('On De-Programming Freshman Platonists' is the subtitle of Gregory Ulmer's contribution to the issue.) But how does this lexis of 'eradication,' 'ignorance,' 'overcoming,' and 'de-programming' fit with the notion propounded by these authors that the instructor should give up the position of 'mastery'? It would seem that the teacher can occupy the position of analysand (who speaks more than he or she knows) only if the students' statements are stripped of referential value (say less than they think they say).

At this point, it would appear that the 'psychoanalytic' classroom is, in fact, traditionally literary, and in three ways. It maintains a post-Leavisite consonance between 'literature' and 'life,' while inverting a similar assertion made by the student questioners: for while they assume that 'life,' or their lives, are the base for their literary studies, the instructors assume that self-knowledge will be the end process of their endeavours. The premise that students do not have self-knowledge in the beginning but may develop it forms the second connection of the 'psychoanalytic' to the traditional classroom, in the maintenance of a set of therapeutic disciplinary rationales, elaborated most specifically in I.A. Richards's psychiatrizing of students but held by many professors through a general sense of student inadequacy. Third, the classroom scene presented here is also traditionally literary in the most literal sense: that is, the student-teacher relationship replicates that between the poetic object and (male) poet, and between the poem and critic. The way in which this educative and critical situation is grounded in, enacts a repetition of, a common literary structuration may be illustrated by one of the most poignant and economical sketches of this engenderment of interpretation.:

She dwelt among the untrodden ways
    Beside the springs of Dove
A Maid whom there were none to praise
    And very few to love;

A violet by a mossy stone
    Half-hidden from the eye!
– Fair as a star, when only one
    Is shining in the sky.

She lived unknown, and few could know
    When Lucy ceased to be;
But she is in her grave, and, oh,
    The difference to me!

Do structures which exclude women have their origins in the texts and text-reading practices by which women are valued and devalued? Can we attribute to literary forms and structures what Barbara Johnson has implied of rhetorical figures, when she writes:

... are the politics of violence already encoded in rhetorical figures as such? In other words, can the very essence of a political issue ... hinge on the structure of a figure? Is there any *inherent* connection between figurative language and questions of life and death, of who will wield and who will receive violence in a given human society? (184)

Wordsworth's 'She dwelt among the untrodden ways' is fully located in this rhetorical, logical, and political complex. It is a poem of praise and remembrance, in which the absent figure is figurally elevated over the poet while being, quite literally (in the poem's 'real'), beneath his feet. This starry elevation to the position of the Muse, and the fact that the unnamed woman is the subject of the poem, means she is doubly the generator of the discourse while remaining herself silent; dead before discourse begins. Thus, although it is the narrator who displays an expressive difficulty, it is 'she' who is wordless while the poet gets his words' worth.

One of the most striking and readily apparent features of 'She dwelt among the untrodden ways' is that such a simple poem, a poem which is about simplicity itself, should have so many aspects which are hard to understand. To catalogue a few: What are untrodden ways? This seems doubly oxymoronic, since ways are meant to be trodden (in fact, are trodden by definition) and if they are unused they become overgrown and are no longer identifiable as ways. How can one dwell 'among' ways? This defies spatial sense. 'None to praise' fits awkwardly in what is identifiably an encomium; we ask why those who loved her did not praise her; and we wonder about this mysterious 'few' and the narrator's past and present relation to them, and status as a lover or praiser. Our drive to narrativize this vanished past and the narrator-'Lucy' relationship puts us in an analogous relationship to the poet, whose own project, it would appear, is to read a hidden, unrecorded, or – perhaps most tragically – unheard text, which must first be reconstructed from a web of relational and associational adjacencies.

Thus the complex and often contradictory rhetorical structure of 'She dwelt among the untrodden ways,' with its stanzaic montage linking a series of images and metaphors which (in part because of that very seriality) appear attemptive. The 'violet by a mossy stone' stands, verb-less and visualizable, in an imagist perfection; but it is then completed by another couplet which stands grammatically in a relationship of apposition. The two images are in one respect compatible – the light point on a dark surround in each – but otherwise at odds, for what is buried and half-hidden in the first couplet is shining in solitary splen-dour in the second. Further, even those readers familiar with poetic con-vention start slightly at the seemingly backhanded praise of 'Fair as a star, when only one / Is shining in the sky.' This rather convoluted con-ceit seems not in the spirit of a poem which praises simplicity, and has done so to this point in a relatively straightforward way. The dash, which typographically signals, variously, continuity and sharp division, creates and emblematizes the oblique relationship of these two couplets, as does the slant rhyme of 'stone' and 'one.'

The third stanza confronts us with the impacted redundancy of 'unknown' and 'known' (made even more repetitive by the lilt of the line), as well as the euphemism of 'ceased to be.' The first lines are enjambed; and this running-on, like the dash, posits a series of concep-tual connections which, by this time, the reader may have some diffi-culty making, except on the level of affect. Further, the closing couplet could be read either as a torn-out cry of pain, moving in its grief-stricken diminishment of diction; or as an emotionally and ideationally impover-ished ending with a forced rhyme of 'know' and 'oh.' And finally it must be asked: what is the purpose of 'but' in the closing couplet? To what do these lines possibly stand in contradiction?

Some of these splits may be healed through a reference to generic and poetic convention, but others may not, and one effort to restore a tempo-rary consonance to the poem would go as follows. By dwelling 'among' the untrodden ways, 'Lucy' is thoroughly embedded in the natural (as in lines 5–6), and in a culture, or what there is of it ('few,' 'untrodden ways'), which is also naturalized. This notion of natural love takes away the sting of praiseless love; it is wordless, more or less immediate, and stands in distinct contrast to the poet's mediate and always deferred understanding, which the reader tracks in the rereading and rethinking of lines 3 and 4. Here, the inevitability of *post-facto* understanding takes on the terrible belatedness of the words said too late. This play between the none and the few, praise and love, is carried into the notion of the seen-yet-unseen or partially seen of lines 5 and 6; and to the distinction in lines 7 and 8, in all her singularity, of a love object who had been half-hidden – not by any neglect of the narrator's, but by her almost perfect blend with the nature-of-things. This selection of one from the sur-round, which then is best appreciated in this solitary display, is the motion of both praise and love, the choosing of one from among others. We are recalled, again, to the belatedness of this movement by the tran-sition from the present to the past tense, from the fullness of present – hence imaginative – vision to the actuality of the 'unknown,' from stanza two to stanza three, whose opening line forces the difference between the being known (of fame) and of being loved for one's true self. (The 'few' reminds us of that sort of love, by repeating the word from line 4.) This loving is reconfigured in the terrible ambiguity of 'ceased to be,' which links love to knowledge to grieving, but carries with it both the distantiation of the euphemism and the horrible imme-diacy of ascertaining an exact moment of death.

The shading of 'Lucy' from life to death is in keeping with the slow comings to light, the gradual advents and descents of the evening star poem which works counter to the Horatian ode and its epiphanic expec-tations. 'She dwelt' is in many senses a family member of the genre, dis-playing the identificatory ambiguities common to these verses of double identity (for the evening and morning star are the same). But this evening star poem also runs counter to the conventions while carrying them along, for the vocative 'o' which traditionally initiates address is reworked as a cry at the conclusion; and where it normally begins a movement to gradual union, here the sound signals the (doubly) irrevo-cable split of 'she' from 'me,' as does the entire poem, for these are its first and last words. The structure of this couplet, and of the entire poem, is that of an unrequited half of the cross of chiasmus. The star symbol folds into the symbol of the grave, which gives off no light, which totally absorbs *lucia*; this collapsing black hole is the 'oh' of grief, and it is the tightening circle of hermeneutic collapse, as the poem ends in the moment of crisis with which the ode traditionally begins. The hor-rible irony is that 'the difference' is that there *is* no difference. This is a world in which there is only 'me.'

The above treatment of the poem draws upon and disperses a number of critical approaches that could be, and have been, taken in deciphering this poem about decipherment. An interpretation that views the poem as primarily about 'nature,' about Lucy's prior and post-naturalization, sees the contradictions and illogicalities as a proof of natural plenitude, or of nature's dissolution of logical contradiction. From another per-spective, the poem is primarily concerned with loss and loneliness, a critical approach which might be considered faithfully thematic; the poem enacts the contextualizations and recontextualizations of mourning, and the diminishment of diction is a marker of grief. From a slightly different angle, the poem is about intepretational difficulty, stylistically signalled by the repetitions and contradictions noted above. These views have several points of interconnection, and all partake of what one might loosely term a 'New Critical' perspective, in assuming a consonance of form and ostensible content, a readerly re-enactment or working through of the verse, and an identification with the narrator, both affectively and in the attempt to restore the absent narrative line.

But reading and loss are here linked in another way, and this question may be plainly put: what is the relationship between (male) interpretation and (female) inaudibility? To answer this takes us more closely to the gender structures of literary texts and their study, and opens a reading in which form and content have less consonance (especially when 'she' brings the content and 'he' brings the form), in which it may be desirable to preserve readerly distance or resistance, and in which the 'she' in the poem must be kept in view as much as the narratorial 'me.' From such a perspective, 'woman' may be viewed, not as the text to be read – in this sense, the often drawn equation betwen body and text needs to be inflected – but as the absence of a text whose recreation, in the guise of creation, then becomes the poet's duty and desire. And this absent text is not a given, but the product of a prior act of 'unreading': is Lucy dead of 'natural' causes, or cannibalistically incorporated? are women silent, or are their words ingested?

At this point, it may appear that such an approach partakes too closely of the poem's fiction: 'Lucy,' after all, is a fictional creation and cannot speak and never did. The stakes may appear more clearly if the poem is given its alternate generic placement as an epitaph. Coleridge surmised that 'A slumber did my spirit seal' was an imaginary epitaph for the (still living) Dorothy Wordsworth; whether or not the actual subject of 'She dwelt' is the poet's sister, the alignment between love poetry and the advance epitaph appears. Such acts of prior 'unreading' underpin both literary and popular cultural production; and the muse, once a creature of no or few words (able, at least, to tell the poet to look to his own heart), is now most frequently figured as the dead female cipher – body – from Poe's Eleonora to *Twin Peaks*'s Laura Palmer – from which male action is born. In other words, 'She dwelt among the untrodden ways' may simply be a limit case of the love poem's ventriloquency, as put with eerie candour in another twilight verse, Wallace Stevens's 'Two Figures in Dense Violet Night':

Speak, even, as if I did not hear you speaking,
But spoke for you perfectly in my thoughts,
Conceiving words ...

In this economy, interpretation-as-substitution is the structure both of
the relationship of poet to poetic object and critic to poem, in a clearing
away of the text already in place. There is, therefore, a discomfitingly
close link between a post-mortem restitution and the cause of death (as
Hartman has noted for the 'Lucy' poems), between critical helpfulness
and aggression, between the disposal of the body and rhetorical disposition. And no one is in a better position to know this than the critical
'object' herself.

These students, or any students, are of course asking real questions and
making real statements. In the first case, the query being posed is: what
is the status in academic discourse of 'opinion' and one's own thoughts,
which probably have been developed in a different context? In the second case: are there really 'common' rules and meanings, especially if
this is the code of football games, presidential speeches, barroom seduc-
tions, and male authors? If students are raising the central questions of
literary study and literary theory – of interpretation and system and
power – why is the response to their questions informed by a 'reading'
that takes their statements purely as a symptom? Or, to be more specific,
why is the text of the student supplanted or supplied by the instructor
in day-to-day classroom life?
    It is important not to overlook the obvious reason – the sexual politics
of the teaching situation. At work, too, may be an unacknowledged
counter-transference, where the student is expected to become the 'analyst,' a silent, featureless, listener. I have noted above the recurrent slip-
page in literary studies from a text-reading to a therapeutic practice,
which rank-shifts students from the position of potential knowers to the
already-known. The lack of satisfactory elaboration of a concept of political 'resistance' – or a conflation of 'political' and 'psychoanalytic' resistances – leads to a dismissal of daily acts of classroom questioning or
dissatisfaction as the 'wrong' sort of resistance, even by instructors who
would align themselves with the goals of student empowerment.
    Thought on these questions could and does go in several directions.
One might develop a contrast between a 'bad' or masculinist personal
teaching and a 'good' or feminist personal teaching. The first term of an
engendered binary – voice, speech, for example – could be retrieved or

reasserted. Or the combination of seemingly opposite elements – experience, rhetoric – could be seen as itself the project for a feminist literary studies pedagogy. (It is at this point that the compatibility of feminist ideas of 'resistance' and de Manian 'resistance' becomes apparent.) One could assert the necessary imposition of an information-based teaching as a corrective for an endemic inclination to transference; even re-examine more distanced pedagogic forms such as the lecture. Or one could note the *a priori* impossibility of a truly 'psychoanalytic' pedagogy given the structural dissimilarity between the analytic and classroom situations and the fact that the teacher – always hiding a visible demand – can never be a mirror as the analyst can (Penley 133). The 'demand' may be personal; it is always institutional; and to ignore the demand is to ignore the conditions of teaching, in which the instructor is by definition both interactive and authoritative, both adjudicator and assessor. This consideration could lead to a questioning of the ethics of a de-authorized teaching if its existence is conditional on the misrecognition of academic power relations. Here 'bad' and 'good' personal teachings might be closer together than one would wish (a fact perhaps signalled by the rhetorical and topical manoeuvres of the women-authored *College English* pieces).

We could also ask whether it is possible for feminism to be anything other than the lost first term in interdisciplinary blendings and battles. It would at first seem so, at least from the instances given above, if one assumes that the case of *College English*, combining literature and theory, psychoanalysis and pedagogy, is the *exemplum* of interdisciplinariness. However, as I have argued, what has been displayed is for the most part a recasting in new guise of the traditional terms of English study, in slippages from 'text' to 'self' and the concurrent conflations of knowledge and style; in a teaching against mass culture; in a proposed learning for moral development. In the above passages, as I have tried to suggest, it is the absence of attention to the specific, gendered, scene of instruction and its institutional siting that has caused the omissions and regressions of the *College English* essays on the psychoanalytic classroom; and has allowed them to be read as instances of a purely 'personal' teaching against the essays' own descriptions of an impersonal, impossible, and discursive pedagogic style. This would suggest for feminist pedagogy – and other political or theorized pedagogy – a new sort of 'impersonal' analysis and teaching, which locates our 'personal' positions as teachers and students as 'impersonal,' socially constructed positions as well. To paraphrase Gregory Jay: how much about race, class, and gender in the classroom do we need to know before these interventions and interlocutions will mean something to us? Are the reasons historical, ideological, personal? And can this be the critical perspective which will bring into focus something which, to this point, we just can't see?

Works Cited

Culley, Margo, and Catherine Portuges. *Gendered Subjects: The Dynamics of Feminist Teaching.* Boston: Routledge and Kegan Paul, 1982.

de Man, Paul. 'The Resistance to Theory.' *Yale French Studies* 63 (1982): 3–20.

Fetterley, Judith. *The Resisting Reader: A Feminist Approach to American Fiction.* Bloomington, Ind.: Indiana UP, 1978.

Fish, Stanley. 'Is There a Text in This Class?' *Is There a Text in This Class? The Authority of Interpretive Communities.* Cambridge, Mass.: Harvard UP, 1980. 303–21.

Freud, Sigmund. 'Fragment of an Analysis of a Case of Hysteria.' *The Standard Edition of the Complete Psychological Works of Sigmund Freud.* Vol. 7. London: Hogarth P, 1974. 71–122.

Giroux, Henry. *Theory and Resistance in Education: A Pedagogy for the Opposition.* South Hadley, Mass.: Begin and Harvey, 1983.

Hartman, Geoffrey. 'The Interpreter's Freud.' *Raritan* (Fall 1984): 12–28.

Jacobus, Mary. 'Is There a Woman in This Text?' *New Literary History* 14, 2 (Winter 1983): 117–41.

Jay, Gregory S. 'The Subject of Pedagogy: Lessons in Psychoanalysis and Politics.' *College English* 49, 7 (Nov. 1987): 785–800.

Johnson, Barbara. 'Apostrophe, Animation, and Abortion.' *A World of Difference.* Baltimore and London: Johns Hopkins UP, 1987. 184–99.

– 'Deconstruction, Feminism, and Pedagogy.' *A World of Difference.* Op. cit. 42–6.

McGee, Patrick. 'Truth and Resistance: Teaching as a Form of Analysis.' *College English* 49, 6 (Oct. 1987): 667–78.

Penley, Constance. 'Teaching in Your Sleep: Feminism and Psychoanalysis.' *Theory in the Classroom.* Ed. Cary Nelson. Urbana and Chicago: U Illinois P, 1986. 129–48.

Stevens, Wallace. 'Two Figures in Dense Violet Night.' *The Collected Poems of Wallace Stevens.* New York: Knopf, 1967. 85–6.

Ulmer, Gregory L. 'Textshop for Psychoanalysis: On De-Programming Freshmen Platonists.' *College English* 49, 7 (Nov. 1987): 756–69.

Wordsworth, William. 'She dwelt among the untrodden ways.' *Poetical Works.* Ed. Thomas Hutchinson. London: Oxford UP, 1969. 86.

9

Charisma and Authority in Literary Study and Theory Study

The diacritical slashes of 'theory/pedagogy/politics,'[1] obliquely connecting and separating, postulate a series of permutations and combinations of the parts, of relations of adjacency, alternacy, and addition. As a provisional (perhaps utopian) liaison, retaining the marker of choice and division, 'theory/pedagogy/politics' models the problematic of theory study in the first decade of its current institutionalization.

But the institutionalization of theory has led, against the hopes and labours of many, to a teaching of theory rather than a theorized teaching. This has raised doubts of the actual or potential utility of theory to political action. 'Theory,' as it is now constituted in the academy, is the complex knowledge of a specialized few. That it is not everywhere accepted or integrated has only increased its moral claims, by permitting 'theory' to be aligned (much more readily than it is, perhaps, in fact) with marginalized cultural constituencies, and by facilitating a view of theory study as inherently counter-discursive or institutionally uncontaminated. This hypostatization of theory and the placement of theory practitioners have at times strengthened rather than challenged an entrenched disciplinary distribution of knowledge and power and especially have reinforced the appeal to charismatic authority by which this distribution is traditionally justified. To show in more detail how this situation has occurred, and its consequences, is my purpose here. I will argue that an endemic resistance to pedagogy, and a resultant lack of discipline-specific analysis of academic authority and practice, have allowed this state of affairs. But I will also suggest that increased attention to pedagogy and other activities of both teachers and students will help us to locate areas where resistance is possible and where there are increased opportunities for non-recuperable change. As S.P. Mohanty writes: 'The pedagogical context is ... the instance of the everyday and the contingent, but it is also the challenge of the need to *think* the institutional limits of the discursive. As such, it allows us to de-etherialize the claims of theory while offering the possibility of situating it in a network of determined relations' (Mohanty 151). Here, then, I use 'pedagogy' not in the sense of teaching techniques but as the most basic alignment of power and knowledge, effected in discipline-specific ways; and by 'politics' I confine myself here to the analysis of such authority and the question of doing effective cultural work in the academy.

That 'theory' already has, and always has had, both a pedagogy and a politics is made apparent by its etymology, by current use of the term, and by the traces of its dropped definitions. (We rarely refer, although we well might, to the 'theory' that was a body sent by the state to perform religious rites and sacrifices.) Derrida has taken direction from Heidegger's observations on the consequences of translation from Greek *theoria* to Latin *contemplatio* and thus into German. Similarly, in English we find 'theory' shifting from the thing observed to the act of seeing to the end product of that observation, until a theory is a proposition to be proven by argument rather than by verification. This transition is tracked in the *OED* citations, through negative definition (theory, as opposed to practice) and unfavourable definition (theoretical, not substantiated). Theory itself, without the article, is described as being 'in the abstract.' Faintly readable are the earlier and obsolete definitions of theory as a sight in both senses, the observed thing or spectacle (thus, of the Passion, 'there is no part but is a Theory of itselfe') as well as the act of viewing. There seems a lost epistemology here, replaced by a split between knower and known and a further hierarchization of knowledge, accomplished first through a privileging of vision (Derrida, 'White Mythology') and then through a metaphorized division of processes of knowing into direct and mirrored sightings. This transition (whether actual or mythic) is consequential, pedagogically, in a teleology of academic knowledge; politically, in structures of academic authority. (At the same time, however, acknowledgment both of the intrinsic metaphoricity of the theoretical and the etymological and historical production of 'theory' as a category undermines the terms on which a 'return' to a prelapsarian or pre-Cartesian epistemological unification could appear a potential solution to this.) The 'theory' which we practise and critique is always and intrinsically a 'meta-' theory – a theory described as either 'beautiful' (Bruss) or 'grand' (Skinner), and whose 'sudden' appearance (Bruss) or 'return' (Skinner) has made theory itself the object of much recent study.

The terminological conflict over the advent of theory – renaissance or epistemic break? – comes in part from the mixed timetables of the many disciplines which contribute to current theoretical study. But it also seems indicative of the state of the centre – literary studies – a discipline with a notoriously weak command both of its own history and of its status as a systematic field (Sosnoski). Richard Rorty has suggested that criticism moved in to fill the vacuum left by the 'professionalization' and asociality of philosophy (quoted in Mohanty 149). A space was also left through philosophy's abandonment of speech-act and natural-language analysis; and the recognition of contingent and mediate meaning and its linguistic and cultural construction has meant a turn to literary studies as the closest ally. To this, comparative studies, with its European orientation, and English studies, with its elastic departmental boundaries, were accommodating, leaving literary studies as the host of a body seen sometimes as guest, sometimes as parasite. This is more than a matter for ironic appreciation, for it is to be expected that the contours of literary study, and most especially of English study (which *is* literary study in the Anglo-American and, often, postcolonial academy), will form theoretical study as well. As Paul de Man has noted: 'Literary theory may now well have become a legitimate concern of philosophy, but it cannot be assimilated to it, either factually or theoretically. It contains a necessarily pragmatic moment that certainly adds a subversive element of unpredictability and makes it something of a wild card in the serious game of the theoretical disciplines' (de Man 8). Literary theory often seems both diffuse and unprincipled to philosophers; it may perhaps best be described (to use Whitehead's famous definition of electricity) not as a thing like St Paul's Cathedral, but as a way that things behave – once that behaviour is described, that's all there is to say about it. This is, as de Man points out, a systemic weakness, but it may also be a recovery of some of the sense of engaged observation embedded in the original concept of *theoria*.

Part of de Man's 'pragmatic' moment, then, is the vexed relationship between 'English' and 'theory,' in an anti-theoretical disciplinary bias. Chris Baldick has located that bias in the foundational work of Matthew Arnold, whose

radical curtailment of theoretical argument or explanation protects the urgency of empirical demonstration ('there') from closer scrutiny, while the evacuated realm of theory becomes vulnerable to invasion by cruder substitutes: first a certain vitalism, evident in Arnold's constant appeals to the authority of 'life' or to the 'instinct of self-preservation in humanity' and its various culturally-deter-mined manifestations; second, a quantitative calculus, which can be found at work in his assertion that morality is 'three-fourths of human life,' and in the curious argument that larger nations were more likely to be 'saved' than smaller ones because their enlightened minorities would be larger in absolute numbers. (Baldick 41–2)

Anti-intellectualism, then, stands in for theory rather than competing with it (Baldick 42). We can see this combination of 'vitalism' and 'quan-titative calculus' at work in a persistent yoking of moral purpose and vanguardism to be found from Leavis to heralds of the literacy 'crisis,' from New to newest critics.

In a manner which Baldick describes as 'homeopathic,' 'criticism' has always protected itself against 'science' by making its own claims to social utility and – especially in the United States in the 1950s – to sus-tained and systematic inquiry. 'Theory,' then, is the repressed of criti-cism. It is always uncannily returning, for so systematic has this anti-theoretical formulation been that there is at times little to distinguish it from 'theory' as we commonly define it. This paradox de Man unpacks in his accounting for contemporary resistance to theory, which he does by distinguishing between a criticism based on 'cultural' and 'ideologi-cal' normative principles and an 'impersonal' and consistent rhetorical study (de Man 6). De Man goes on to argue that contemporary theory, allied to grammar and logic rather than to reading and rhetoric, is thus equally anti-theoretical; and that resistance to theory comes not from 'outside' theory but constitutes its discourse. 'The Resistance to Theory,' however, presents more than a case for rethinking the current theoreti-cal project: it also makes claims for its political utility and pedagogic possibilities. Against accusations that literary theory is a reality-denying 'verbalism,' de Man painstakingly points out that 'literariness' and a-referentiality are not the same. Rather, 'what is in question is [lan-guage's] authority as a model for natur: 1 or phenomenal cognition'(11). De Man moves *en passant*, postulating b\. ι not picturing the political and ethical ends of literary study.

While the political issues occasion a certain rhetorical indirection, the pedagogic question precipitates a textual break. The piece first appeared in the issue of *Yale French Studies* examining 'Pedagogy as a Literary Genre' and is situated within recent debate over the relationship of scholarship, theory, and teaching. It asserts their 'complete' compatabil-ity, given theory as 'a controlled reflection on the formation of method'

(4). The elaborated introduction, the sketching of an 'impersonal' or rhe- torical pedagogy, and the equation throughout of rhetorical and reading study lead the reader to expect a finish to the frame. However, while de Man concludes with a critique of speech-act work, both reader-response and *Rezeptionaesthetik*, for its grammatical and psychological orientation, the issues which initiated these reflections are never taken up again, and the article ends suddenly. Thus while it opens up the possibility that the turn from notions of linguistic determinacy may permit the examination of linguistic determination, and while it most usefully cautions against a loosely psychologized teaching, 'The Resistance to Theory' does not itself effect the move from a rhetorical to a political project, and it dis- plays the endemic resistance to a pedagogy whose possibility it was designed to demonstrate.

Since language and literature form the largest area of study in all phases of teaching and scholarship (Bleich 4), with English by far pre- dominant, and since 'English' itself has been shaped at pivotal points by projects and directives that are essentially pedagogic, it may seem odd to speak of a persistent disciplinary resistance to pedagogy. By this, however, I mean a lack of sustained or self-reflexive attention to the scene of teaching and daily practices; a resistance intrinsic to the enter- prise, like the resistance to theory as de Man describes it. For if the resis- tance to theory may be conceived, if only provisionally, as 'a resistance to the use of language about language' (de Man 12), the resistance to pedagogy may equally be viewed as a resistance to talking about, or teaching about, teaching.

This becomes apparent whenever practitioners are faced with the exercise of examining (or even discussing) given structures, seen in the difficulty of initiating debate and the paucity of the arguments offered. There is for the most part no ongoing discourse on these topics. And while there has been much useful institutional analysis and disciplinary critique in recent years, it is primarily confined to 'higher' levels ('pro- fessionalization,' for example). Therefore, while theorists can often offer reasons for change, the legacy of this resistance to pedagogy leaves us without a good case for the 'teachability' of theory, and without a com- municable vision of what a theorized literary study might do or what useful work it might perform. By default, and under pressure, we often fall back on traditional defences of humanistic study. Too, we are often ill-equipped, albeit willing, to critique our own practices, to locate areas for reform and resistance, and to form liaisons within and without the academy. In order to analyse more fully the operations of knowledge and power within English studies, it would therefore be necessary to undertake a sustained and discipline-specific analysis of the mutually reinforcing interplay of pedagogic action and pedagogic authority (to use the terms of Bourdieu and Passeron), in a reading of our daily practices and their construction, relying on the sort of text analysis that is already our primary skill.

The seminar group – to outline the procedures for one such reading – is a basic instructional, social, and administrative unit at some institutions; and it probably represents for most instructors and many students the ideal situation of university study. It is, therefore, the real or imaginary 'scene' of English studies – almost intrinsic to English, given the adoption or adaptation of the German-model seminar by Canadian, British, and U.S. universities in the late 1800s (the founding years of 'English') and the development of its dynamics in the work of I.A. Richards (the moment of systematization of study). The seminar seemingly is a 'phalansteric circulatory space,' as described by Roland Barthes (*Roland Barthes* 171) in a reference to the socialist living community envisaged by Fourier, both withdrawn and active. (In this respect, Barthes's remarks are applicable to the undergraduate and Anglo-American seminar, although formulated for the seminar as an advanced study group.) The seminar, in short, seems designed for free expression of opinion, cooperative and cumulative exchange, and attention to the alterity of the other.

It stands, in these ways, in distinct contrast to the lecture. In comparing the European and U.S. pedagogic situations, de Man found the latter more satisfactory 'precisely because of the *contract* one has with the people one teaches. In Europe there is a bizarre separation on two completely different levels. It's concretely visible in the fact that you stand up there, on that chair [*sic*], with an abyss between you and the students, while here you sit at a table. I found bad faith involved in that ideological situation in Europe, worse than here' (quoted in Rosso 789). But this 'concrete visibility' has permitted a range of critiques, from GREPH's formulation of the conjunction of philosophy and the state to Barthes's dream of the seminar as free space, from Bourdieu to May '68. The seminar – in good faith, less 'ideological,' with everything on the table – seems designed to develop a 'misrecognition' (Bourdieu and Passeron) of the relations and determinants at work. How, then, might we develop an analysis of the tangled web of the social and heuristic function of the seminar group in its Anglo-American construction? Because of its 'fit' to literary study, and its detectable but deniable relations of authority, the seminar merits examination.

Like 'theory,' the 'seminar' has an English history and etymology in addition to its route through German lexis and practice. The *OED* gives a first citation in 1889, with the establishment of university-level seminars on the German model. The term also comes to signify any study group, although the connotations of advanced study persist. What is dropped is the equation of the word with 'seminary,' the religious inflexion of the term, and their mutual root in the Latin *seminarium* or 'seed-bed.' (Definitionally noted, but lost to use, is the early nineteenth-century employment of the term 'seminary' for a girls' school.) The dictionary points to the muted masculinization of the *seme*-seminar conjunction as Derrida has traced it in *Glas*, and to the double 'culture' of Western education, nurturing the individual and bending the twig to and through authority. Through botanical metaphors, the 'dissemination' model of knowledge erases the woman as transmitter or generator, allowing a direct male line of production and growth, and easing the anxiety about origin and originality.

This 'anxiety about the relations of authors to their words, anxiety about the relation of flesh-and-blood reality to conventional signs' (Hertz 70), produces the 'extravagance' of the seminar group as Neil Hertz has described it. What seems to be a circulation or exchange (Derrida, *Ear*), a 'closed-circuit of ideal communication,' is in fact 'a controlled linearity, a graded series':

... at the head of the line is 'the mind that composed *The Rape of the Lock*,' a mind whose learning is not something acquired but rather something 'deeply engrained' or ... 'deeply embedded.' Next in line, in a middleman's position, is the teacher, whose knowledge *is* acquired. Finally there are the students, presumably there to acquire the erudition their teacher already possesses in part. This is a familiar enough account of academic lineage, and it might be that at moments literary education comes to feel like that. But more often what happens is that – by a trick of the mind, call it a deeply embedded inclination to convert series into binary oppositions – the teacher's position is experienced (by the teacher, as well as by his class) not as a middle ground somewhere between his author and his students, but as a dramatic occupation, more or less earned, of the position of authority itself. (Hertz 66–7)

The interplay of anxiety, originality, and authority, of bodies and signs, creates the complex and unequal relations of the seminar group, in alignments which are difficult to negotiate and to critique. From the above, however, several features may be distinguished. The envisaging of the seminar group as a seemingly self-contained and self-regulating entity (much like a poem under New Critical criteria) works to counter recognition of its internal authority and institutional placement. The subject/object shifting noted by Hertz suits it to an Arnoldian contagion model of education (minds like minds) and a Richardsonian mimeticism (those minds like poems). The seminar is especially suited to professional and social formation on an Hegelian model precisely because it is so 'humanizing' and individual in orientation. This alerts us to the dangers of a supposedly non-directive (or, to use Bourdieu's term, an 'affectionate') teaching. At the same time, there are few who would not defend the seminar against 'budgetary' pressures for larger class sizes. And insofar as the seminar functions as a particularly usable model of the production of academic discourse, it has potential to be the site of self-reflexive learning. A working through of the resistance to pedagogy (which is, like the resistance to theory, at base a suspicion of self-reflexive inquiry) may help to turn 'rhetorical' study to political ends.

Literary criticism, despite whatever claims to disinterestedness, is always at base 'political,' postulating a certain relationship of 'individual' to 'society' and a mediating role for literature and literary study in this. Recent work on the establishment of English studies (Baldick) and its institutionalization in England and the United States (Bové, Cain, Doyle, Fekete, McCallum) has exposed the political contours of this academic neutrality and has assessed the aims and achievements of the more expressly engaged projects. Again, however, it has proven easier to examine scholarly than pedagogic work, no matter how inextricably intertwined we know them to be. This says much about the intense privatization and isolation of the classroom, and about the lack of written records of its practices. Yet pedagogy is as 'political' as scholarship, despite a persistent ivory-towerism that sees literary studies as a haven in a heartless university. As universities are further 'rationalized' – a term which points nicely to both empiricist fetishism and financial cutbacks – this illusion becomes easier to maintain. But as power is increasingly a matter of information control and symbolic manipulation, it is imperative to understand how education in language, literature, and 'literacy' is central to, rather than peripheral to, this process, and is more than a 'humanizing' face for technology and technological study. As the place where people do – and do not – become expert in symbolic skills, literary study merits examination at all levels.

In his sections of *Reproduction in Education, Society and Culture,* Pierre Bourdieu outlines the mutual dependence of pedagogy, pedagogic authority, and state authority in a series of formulations as tight and intricate as the situations they describe. He reminds us that there can be no place outside of power, and that 'pedagogic action' exercised without 'pedagogic authority' is 'a logical contradiction and a sociological impossibility' (12). Pedagogy, then, is not really a matter of the transmission of information – Jean-Claude Passeron, in a later section, amusingly demonstrates how little information is ever in circulation in a lecture – and neither does the authority of the instructor derive from the quantity of information or its truth value, although both these factors are ostensibly the case. There is, instead, a surplus to content: both teacher and teaching are already 'receivable' by the students precisely because of the legitimation 'already conferred on every pedagogic transmitter by the traditionally and institutionally guaranteed position he occupies in a relation of pedagogic communication' (21). This is independent of the 'degree of technical or charismatic authority of the transmitter' (21); however, it is through claims to such qualifications that the exercise of pedagogic authority is in turn justified, although these lines of power are occluded or made to seem the natural order of things. Thus the pedagogic situation is constructed to allow the misrecognition of that construction.

While Bourdieu has been critiqued (by Henry Giroux, for example) for the automatism and dystopianism of the reproduction model – points which he has attempted to accommodate in later work – the formulation sketched above gives some useful points of departure for the analysis of literary studies pedagogy. The notion of pedagogic content being in a surplus relation to information is useful for examining cases in which 'the relation of pedagogic communication can be maintained even when the information transmitted tends toward zero, as in ... some literary education' (21). Although pedagogic authority is institutionally conferred, it is justified by two traditional claims, either to the 'intrinsic strength of the true idea' or to special personal qualities or sensitivies; and these claims are discipline-specific. As seen in Hertz's description of pedagogic conflation, with the teacher's mind in a synecdochic relation to literature as a whole, in literary studies the two claims can amount to one and the same. This closeness of mind to material suggests that Max Weber's formulation of 'charisma' can be usefully redeployed on the small group level – a possibility for which Weber's theory of charismatic authority already allows. Particularly applicable would be Weber's notion of 'institutional authority,' as Bourdieu's work suggests. In applying the notion of charisma more generally, Bourdieu allows for a charisma which does not have its genesis in the personal qualities of an exceptional individual; while Weber's schema usefully supplements Bourdieu by introducing the 'problematic of the psychological genesis of representations of legitimacy' (Bourdieu 13). Both Weber's psychologism and Bourdieu's suggestion of receivability through authority point to the transferential elements of the pedagogic situation, and to the masking of instructor transference and counter-transference by professorial disinterestedness. The contributions made to this inquiry by psychoanalytic and feminist study indicate that 'charismatic' and 'patriarchal' authority may thus be closely allied, and in a way that Weber had not acknowledged.

'The space of the seminar is phalansteric,' writes Roland Barthes, 'i.e. in a sense fictive, novelistic. It is only the space of the circulation of subtle desires, mobile desires; it is, within the artifice of a sociality whose constituency is miraculously extenuated, according to a phrase of Nietzsche's: "the tangle of amorous relations"' (*Roland Barthes* 171). Barthes speaks for the hopes and wishes of many instructors when he envisages the seminar space as a utopia, within and withdrawn, personal yet political (Barthes, 'Writers'; Ungar). But there is much to be examined in Barthes avant-gardist dream of the seminar space as somehow miraculous, exempt, related to the body politic through its work of atonement, amendment, love. For it is in precisely this way that the social and socializing project of literary study has always been justified. Minds are formed through 'soft' disciplines and 'subtle' pedagogies; in the absence of a readily testable subject matter, these 'minds' and their achievements are frequently assessed on formal or even impressionistic grounds. Thus the popularity of the close reading assignment at the university level and its function as a 'touchstone' for assessing students; and thus the fact that male students in English are often seen as superior even when women have the higher grades (Weedon). What is inculcated and valued is a sensitivity or a style – and this style is, of course, gender-, race-, and class-specific. For women students, to take only one example, to be in the free, circulatory space of the seminar is often to be reduced to silence or to having one's remarks seen as perpetually adjacent (Krupnick, Elliott), despite the fact that the seminar is the place where a questioning, so-called feminine academic discourse should be most welcome. The English studies seminar, with its traditional mix of women students and male instructor, functions as the broad base of what is perhaps the steepest gender pyramid of all the disciplines (as noted in chapter 5), with a predominance of women in the early years and few at the 'top' of the profession. The current understanding of sexual harassment in the academy and its construal within existent power relations suggests that the erotic or 'amorous' classroom is a matter for careful critique, rather than unconditional celebration. While the seminar may well provide the best opportunity for teaching and learning, it cannot do this unless we pay attention to its particular construction, conditions, and institutional placement, and take this as a point of pedagogic orientation.

Much work has been devoted to the politics of theory study, most particularly, and pointedly, by Edward Said ('Reflections'; World). But even given the narrower definition I am using here, of 'politics' as effective cultural work in the academy, there is much to be done before theory, pedagogy, and politics may have a more than provisional alliance. A number of recent books and articles have been devoted to the question of theory teaching – and, in fewer cases, to theorized teaching. Most ask, or beg, the question of its 'teachability,' or solve the issue by confining examinations to what are generally considered the more learnable or applicable methods, such as structuralism. Many develop a strong rationale for theory teaching without an equally articulated plan of action; and without an underpinning institutional analysis, several promising lines of inquiry inevitably repeat that which they would or should critique.

'Subjective' criticisms, for example, given the innate psychologism of literary study and their own attention to readers and responses, have had the most to say about literary studies pedagogy, from Richards to Rosenblatt to reception theory. As 'subjective' teaching segues into a 'psychoanalytic' pedagogy, however, it demands close examination (which was attempted in the eighth chapter of this volume). (A so-called 'psychoanalytic' classroom, without the demands for a counter-transferential analysis, without the safeguards of psychoanalysis proper, and with all the existent pedagogic power relations firmly in place, is a dangerous place for students to be.) More restricted 'subjective' criticisms, and some very useful reader-oriented pedagogies, may still disempower students insofar as they are difficult to criticize and negotiate (McCormick); they may still tend to a 'therapeutic' (Elshtain) or 'personal' (de Man) pedagogy, under which the teacher not only knows, but knows the students, and knows best what is good for them. Such supposed attentiveness to students actually silences them by an a priori assumption about them, and revives the traditional role of the teacher as social worker or cultural missionary. To take a second and more specific case, the work of Gregory Ulmer – which provides a thoughtful and extended current examination of theory and pedagogy – repeats in practice much of what it disentangles in 'theory.' The establishment of the teacher-as-producer (of video or 'post(e)'-lecture) reasserts the one-way 'transmission' model of pedagogic communication that Ulmer has been at pains to unpack; while the teacher-as-performer (of 'scene' or discourse) re-embodies the style and charisma of the traditional literary studies pedagogue and 'his' fully achieved reading. And yet, as de Man's 'Resistance to Theory' would suggest, an 'impersonal' pedagogy achieved at the expense of considerations of the intersubjective, or the social, is neither a fully rhetorical nor a fully political teaching in its denial of the politics of rhetoric.

Rabbit-out-of-hat readings and monologic conference papers whose performances belie their contents are the too visible symptoms of a much more general predicament of theory studies today. Even critical practitioners find our efforts easily recuperated and our effectivity in doubt. If theory is seen as self-evidently useful and moral, then student questioning will be taken as a 'resistance' to be ignored or overcome, rather than as resistance upon which pedagogy may be constructed (Freire; Giroux). When theory is seen as difficult or specialized, something the instructor must demonstrate or epitomize, and when that difficulty or demonstration remains uncritiqued, then traditional pedagogic power is reinforced rather than challenged. When theory is construed as the counter-culture of literary study (while providing qualitative and quantitative assessments of students and their work), then students are asked to cooperate in an all-round misrecognition of the operations of institutional and pedagogic power. A 'conditional' analysis – conditional in both senses, as self-reflexive and cognizant of determinants, and as provisional – undertaken by both teachers and students, using the classroom, its situation, and its work as one example of the production of literary discourse, is, I suggest, a first step in teaching and learning theory theoretically. Which is to say, to teach and learn politically.

Note

1 This chapter was first prepared for the volume *Theory/Pedagogy/Politics: Texts for Change*, ed. Donald Morton and Mas'ud Zavarsadeh (U Illinois P, 1991).

Works Cited

Baldick, Chris. *The Social Mission of English Criticism, 1848–1942*. Oxford: Clarendon P, 1983.

Barthes, Roland. *Roland Barthes by Roland Barthes*. Trans. Richard Howard. New
York: Hill and Wang, 1977.

– 'Writers, Intellectuals, Teachers.' *Image/Music/Text*. Selected and trans.
Stephen Heath. Glasgow: Fontana, 1977. 190–215.

Bleich, David. *Subjective Criticism*. Baltimore: Johns Hopkins UP, 1978.

Bourdieu, Pierre, and Jean-Claude Passeron. *Reproduction in Education, Society
and Culture*. Trans. Richard Nice. London: Sage, 1977.

Bové, Paul. *Intellectuals in Power: A Genealogy of Critical Humanism*. New York:
Columbia UP, 1986.

Bruss, Elizabeth. *Beautiful Theories: The Spectacle of Discourse in Contemporary Criticism*. Baltimore: Johns Hopkins UP, 1982.

Cain, William. *The Crisis in Criticism: Theory, Literature, and Reform in English
Studies*. Baltimore: Johns Hopkins UP, 1984.

de Man, Paul. 'The Resistance to Theory.' *The Resistance to Theory*. Minneapolis:
U Minnesota P, 1986. 2–20.

Derrida, Jacques. *Glas*. Paris: Galilée, 1974.

– 'Otobiographies.' *The Ear of the Other: Otobiography, Transference, Translation*.
Ed. Christie V. McDonald. New York: Schocken, 1985. 1–38.

– 'White Mythology: Metaphor in the Text of Philosophy.' Trans. F.C.T. Moore.
New Literary History 6 (1974): 5–74.

Doyle, Brian. *English and Englishness*. London: Routledge, 1989.

Elliott, Patricia. 'The Silent Paradox: The Politics of Speaking in the University.'
Border/lines (Winter 1985–6): 21–3.

Elshtain, Jean Bethke. 'The Social Relations of the Classroom: A Moral and Political Perspective.' *Telos* 27 (1976): 97–110.

Fekete, John. *The Critical Twilight: Explorations in the Ideology of Anglo-American
Literary Theory from Eliot to McLuhan*. London: Routledge and Kegan Paul,
1977.

Freire, Paulo. *Pedagogy of the Oppressed*. Trans. Myra Bergman Ramos. New
York: Continuum, 1985.

Giroux, Henry. *Theory and Resistance in Education: A Pedagogy for the Opposition*.
South Hadley, Mass.: Bergin and Garvey, 1983.

Hertz, Neil. 'Two Extravagant Teachings.' *Yale French Studies* 63 (1982): 59–71.

Krupnick, Catherine G. 'Women and Men in the Classroom: Inequality and Its
Remedies.' *On Teaching and Learning: The Journal of the Harvard Danforth Center*
(May 1985): 18–25.

McCallum, Pamela. *Literature and Method: Towards a Critique of I.A. Richards, T.S. Eliot and F.R. Leavis.* Dublin: Gill and Macmillan, 1983.

McCormick, Kathleen. 'The New Paradigm in Literary Studies.' 'Literature in the High School' conference [GRIP project]. Carnegie-Mellon University, April 1987.

Mohanty, S.P. 'Radical Teaching, Radical Theory: The Ambiguous Politics of Meaning.' *Theory in the Classroom.* Ed. Cary Nelson. Urbana, Ill.: U Illinois P, 1986. 149–76.

Rosso, Stephano. 'An Interview with Paul de Man.' *Critical Inquiry* 12 (1986): 788–95.

Said, Edward. 'Reflections on Recent American "Left" Criticism.' *Boundary 2* 8, 1 (1979): 11–30.

– *The World, the Text, and the Critic.* Cambridge, Mass.: Harvard UP, 1983.

Skinner, Quentin. *The Return of Grand Theory in the Human Sciences.* Cambridge: Cambridge UP, 1985.

Sosnoski, James. 'Literary Studies as a Field for Inquiry.' *Boundary 2* 13, 2/3 (1985): 91–104.

Ulmer, Gregory. *Applied Grammatology: Post(e)-Pedagogy from Jacques Derrida to Joseph Beuys.* Baltimore: Johns Hopkins UP, 1985.

Ungar, Stephen. 'The Professor of Desire.' *Yale French Studies* 63 (1982): 80–97.

Weber, Max. *On Charisma and Institution Building.* Ed. and introd. S.N. Eisenstadt. Chicago: U Chicago P, 1968.

Weedon, Chris. 'Engendering Stereotypes.' *Literature/Teaching/Politics* 1 (1982): 37–49.

10

Does Controversy Have a Rhetoric?

... I will venture to say that this session had its origin in the dialogue between Wayne Booth and myself which centered on the rationale of the historical procedures in my book, *Natural Supernaturalism*. Hillis Miller, had, in all innocence, written a review of that book; he was cited and answered by Booth, then recited and re-answered by me, and so was sucked into the vortex of our exchange to make it now a dialogue of three. And given the demonstrated skill of our chairman in fomenting debates, who can predict how many others will be drawn into the vortex before it comes to an end? (Abrams 425)

The question raised by this chapter may at first seem contradictory or contra-logical, since the case could be made that controversies are by definition rhetorical; that is, a controversy is a form of linguistic exchange and as such is *a priori* rhetorical in some fashion or another. But what I hope to suggest is that controversies are generally perceived to be a-rhetorical or to have rhetorical features which are indecipherable or unreadable. The ensuing suspicion of controversy (that is, not of any controversy *per se* but of what one might call the structure, or non-structure, of controversy itself) results in a drive to organize academic dispute in the form of two-person debate and dialogue.

I would contend that the rhetoric of controversy (including its perceived lack of 'rhetoric') accounts in no small measure for much of what happens, not only in theoretical and critical discourse, but in day-to-day life in the academy. In particular, this distrust of controversy results in repeated, ongoing, and deeply institutionalized attempts to restore rhetorical order and proportion and direction where these are seen to be lacking. Whereas in controversy people and positions are perceived to be unstable, in the debate a structure of address and attribution is restored, as well as a certain expressive propriety. (We have, after all, centuries of treatises on the conduct of the debate, but none that I can find on the conduct of controversy.) I begin by examining the difference between controversy and debate, and give some examples from critical literature and daily life to show the tendency to resolve the first through establishment of the second. I then move on to a passage from Stanley Fish's 'Is There a Text in This Class?' – a text which is about the possibilities of debate, but which resolves this question less through the points it makes than through a rearrangement of rhetorical positions. Here, I will concentrate on the question of address, rather than style, because that seems to me to be the pressing theoretical/political question today.

While the *OED* finds little original distinction between a controversy and a debate, in practice we generally do. A debate is dialogic or dialectical, involving two sides or parties; it is staged or contained or managed in some form or another. A controversy, by contrast, is seen to be more wide-ranging, amorphous, multivocal. In particular, a controversy is thought to have, simultaneously, both too little and too much 'rhetoric,' to use the term loosely for a moment. Controversy is seen to have 'too little' rhetoric in the sense that it is perceived to lack a discernible structure of address that would be apparent in another sort of discursive format such as a debate. On the other hand, controversy is seen to have 'too much' rhetoric, since such features as figures and tone appear to be in a disproportionate and excessive ratio to the literal. The 'too little' rhetoric of an unclear structure of rhetorical address, with the 'too much' rhetoric of rhetorical features, results in an extreme instability both of attribution and of content. The question of who is speaking what and when becomes difficult to answer.

The above language situation may sound familiar, and it can be compared to others which are related. For the question of controversy currently overlaps with problems of gossip, rhetoric, and deconstruction.

First, controversy is seen to resemble gossip in its ungovernability, its lack of attribution, and its multiplicity. As Patricia Meyer Spacks writes of gossip in her book by that name, 'Gossip diverges ... from all other forms of art in lacking a conceivable audience (as well as a consciously structured form), and in spilling over, sometimes dangerously, into the real world. No spectator watches, no reader pursues a printed or written text, no auditor listens' (3). Gossip would appear to lie on the negative side of the oral/written, private/public, thus female/male, binaries. And yet, as Spacks notes, gossip threatens even the stability of this system. 'Gossip,' she writes, 'belongs to the realm of private, "natural" discourse, it often violates "the claims of civility," but it incorporates the possibility that people utterly lacking in public power may affect the views of figures who make things happen in the public sphere' (6–7). It is interesting to note recent attempts to both publish and structure gossip itself within the context of academic journals (the Gilbert and Gubar / Lentricchia exchange in *Critical Inquiry*, and the journal *Lingua Franca*, being two well-known examples). Jerome Christensen's 'From Rhetoric to Corporate Populism: A Romantic Critique of the Academy in an Age of High Gossip' notes the tendency of the press to cover the controversies of academic life – 'western civ.,' for example – by creating both verbally and visually a two-theorist standoff.

The suspicion of controversy and its peculiar 'rhetoric' often resembles the distrust of rhetoric itself; and the history of anti-rhetorical thinking helps to explain how something can be perceived as both deficient and excessive in rhetorical features. As Stanley Fish points out, the anti-rhetorical stance 'posits an *in*coherence at the heart (literally) of the self that is both rhetoric's victim and its source.' Since the 'self is always presented as divided, as the site of contesting forces' ('Rhetoric' 476), the status of both speaker and auditor is in question. Further, not only may the participants be themselves unstable or divided; they may be speaking with other voices or hearing with other ears. The structure of address is in crisis at this point, deficient precisely because too many are involved. The question of 'too much' rhetoric – that is, an excess of trope, figure, tone, and emotive force – is intrinsically related to this addressive instability. It is a commonplace of rhetorical treatises that an excess of rhetoric to content is a sign of insincerity; thus the problem for Longinus is the problem of the management of excess. Style in disproportion to the speaker's relationship or role is also disapproved; thus Horace cautions with the example of the inconsolable grief of paid mourners. The 'too little' rhetoric of a discernible structure of address (where speakers and their roles are in question) and the 'too much' rhetoric of features and figures are considered interdependent.

(Regional variations in the assessment of rhetoric should, however, be noted. While English Canada shares with the United States a suspicion of rhetorical imbalance – former Prime Minister Mulroney was distrusted as much for his *sententia* as his policies – certain sectors of the academy are less anti-rhetorical than their U.S. counterparts. While there is a continuing concern in the U.S. academy that rhetorical analysis is inadequate to the 'real' of urgent political conditions – racism, the

AIDS crisis, for example – in both English Canada and Quebec, discourse analysis is often considered the form of new work with the greatest political utility.)

Just as 'rhetoric' is now closely linked to deconstruction, so too has deconstruction seemed in recent years to be synonymous with controversy, with 'deconstruction' standing, however inaccurately, as a synecdoche for 'theory.' These points may be made from either a 'right' or a 'left' perspective (as Barbara Johnson has noted). The charges made against deconstructionism and its perceived rhetoric will be familiar to most and may be briefly sketched. Deconstructionism is suspect in large measure for its style and is viewed as obfuscating, slippery, or mandarin. In fact, deconstructionism is sometimes seen to be all style and no content; or, alternatively, to have a content which is disavowed but which the canny reader gleefully detects. The structures of address of deconstruction are viewed as unstable, although the observations on this are often contradictory, since deconstructionism is seen as simultaneously too diverse and too greatly centred on key figures. These figures are characterized as disingenuous or schizophrenic, living double lives in which one self disavows referentiality and the other scribbles grocery lists. All this is encapsulated in a later line from 'The Deconstructive Angel,' where Abrams writes:

For Derrida's chamber of texts is a sealed echo-chamber in which meanings are reduced to a ceaseless echolalia, a vertical and lateral reverberation from sign to sign of ghostly nonpresences emanating from no voice, intended by no one, referring to nothing, bombinating in a void. (431)

Here is the familiar relationship of unstable address ('no voice,' 'no one') to a disproportion of style and substance ('bombinating,' 'referring to nothing'). And yet the 'meaning' of Abrams's passage begins to reverberate in a disquieting way in the echo chamber of this text. The deconstructive situation is both attributable ('Derrida's chamber') and diffuse ('no voice,' 'no one'). Whose 'echolalia' is this? How are we to decide the grammatical undecidability of the 'ghostly nonpresences' themselves? (A 'reverberation ... of ghostly nonpresences'? A 'sign of ghostly nonpresences'?) While it may appear that, for Abrams, meaning and meaninglessness are most at issue, it seems to be the question of address and accountability that sets off echoes here.

When the topic is the rhetoric of rhetoric, debates take on a curiously abyssal quality, into which the anti-deconstructionist is as apt to tumble

as anyone else – a situation of which Abrams is fully conscious and
deploys to some advantage. He begins by quoting the famous lines from
'Prometheus Unbound' – '[I]f the Abysm / Could vomit forth its secrets:
but a voice / Is wanting ...' – and thus humorously places himself
'within' the project of deconstructionism by citing what might be
termed the emblematic deconstructionist text. Too, he is in a 'vortex'
(the term is used twice) of citations and responses. Abrams establishes
an interpretive and situational indecidability precisely to show that
undecidability is not really as undecidable as J. Hillis Miller might think,
since it is possible to have this exchange in the first place, and with a
minimum of misunderstanding. Is this, then, the secret of the abyss? It
would appear that the abyss of undecidability has some surprises still in
store; for it is exactly Abrams's answer – that there is a community of
shared interests – which will be turned against him in the next swirl of
the critical vortex, in the response to his response.

It is perhaps because of its intersections with all of gossip, rhetoric,
and deconstruction, that the controversy over the wartime writing of
Paul de Man was able to take on such enormous consequence in the
United States. While it is not possible to begin to trace here the rhetorical
and addressive complexities of the controversy, stretching over years
and across many constituencies and media, a few features may be
noted. 'Style' and tone very quickly became the subject to be analysed.
And the debate was notable for extraordinary rearrangements in structures of address – caused, in large part, by the actual and irrevocable
absence of their logical addressee. (The real question of the *Responses*
volume is responses to *whom*?) Attempts to place Derrida in a substitu-
tive relationship, to funnel controversy into debate, became notoriously
re-complicated in the process. The crisis of address caused not only the
sorts of prosopopoeic summonings, which one would expect, but also
remarkable switches, shuntings, reversals, and impersonations on the
part of the addressors. The anti-deconstructionists, curiously, were the
most ready to speak *for* deconstructionism; that is, to make the truth
come out from Paul de Man, to speak for him. One prominent theorist
accused others of irresponsibility for not acting on information which
they did not have but he did; he may be seen to be caught between the
incompatible demands of gossip (I already knew) and dissociation (I
never knew), both closely associated with controversy. The debate was
characterized, in my opinion, by the careful discrimination of points and
people on the part of deconstructionists purportedly wholly lacking in
judgment; and mass treatment of speakers and concepts by those who

labelled themselves independents. The questions at stake – of the ability to sustain intellectual uncertainty, of the willingness to take responsibility – were played out in the toleration, or lack of toleration, of controversy itself.

The structuring of criticism as debate is so endemic to the discipline that it can easily pass notice; in fact, the history of criticism can at times appear to be nothing but a series of great exchanges. For example, Con Davis and Schleifer's *Contemporary Literary Criticism*, a widely used undergraduate anthology, is organized to a large extent around critical debates (over 'The Purloined Letter,' speech acts, and so on), and even where essays are unrelated they are placed in a dialogic relationship to one another in the introductory sections. Part of the recent editorial alteration of journals in the United States – *Critical Inquiry*, most notably – is to encourage responses to articles, and to foreground the debate as a feature. (In some cases – to cite again the infamous Lentricchia / Gilbert and Gubar interchange, for example – the content of the pieces is more or less irrelevant, and the debate becomes an event, significant for having happened.) The debate is even a fledgling feature of the English-Canadian academic scene, initiated by the pairing of Linda Hutcheon and Len Findlay on the topic of 'postmodernism' in *English Studies in Canada*, for example; although the decorum, even impersonality, of the exchange would indicate some differences in the national scholarly culture.

Day-to-day academic life also offers examples of the controversy-to-debate movement. To women's eyes, the gender inequalities of the academy are often most glaringly displayed in the spectacle of competetive academic debate; debate which is either resolutely man-to-man or embarrassingly Oedipal or a combination. The 'star system' in the United States is often seen as a way of sanctioning and regulating discourse, although it might be more profitably viewed, symptomatically, as an effect rather than as a cause of certain forms of academic structuration. Many of us have encountered the discomfiting experience of giving an invited lecture or job talk at another university, and then facing responses which range from the obliquely unintelligible to the overtly hostile. Here, the unfortunate speaker functions as a relay for controversies in place long before she or he arrived on the scene, but which seem to find public expression only when a suitably dialogic structure is available. Conference arrangements and rearrangements offer a particularly common, sometimes comic, example of the debate formula and resistances to it. Taking chairs off the stage to sit at the level of the audience, or refusing to use a podium or microphone, are often the opening gestures of feminist panels, for example. What was distinctive about the 'Theory Group' of ACCUTE for many years was not so much the material discussed – since the group continued even when the main sessions became 'theorized' – but the mode by which the discussion was handled, with no papers or moderators. These examples show the prevalence of the debate format, if only through the perceived need for conscious efforts against it. The increasing popularity of the debate-as-structure may well be directly related to anxieties about conflict in the academy, or the sense that there are now too many voices.

While recent theoretical work has increasingly turned to the analysis of the institution and determinants of literary study, little attention has been given to the debate as a structure of academic life. There are, however, some exceptions. Father Walter Ong's 'Agonistic Structures in Academia' gives a history of the deep intrication of male aggresivity and academic disputation. For Ong, ceremonial academic combat is doubly 'rhetorical' – it is rooted in oral culture, which is for Ong more agonistic than the literate, and it has historically been, and continues to be, developed in the study and inculcation of rhetoric and oratory. The oral and thus agonistic has persisted in a residual and uneven way well into the twentieth century. For Ong, coeducation is responsible for the demise of combative structures, and his feelings on this topic are mixed, since the waning of institutionalized combat has allowed the 'more dangerous' confrontations of student protest. (Here, interestingly, women are seen as representing, not the 'oral,' but the incursion of the 'written' into the academy.) The structure of feeling of many academics – the pulls of democracy and elitism, controversy and debate – have rarely been more clearly displayed than in Ong's piece. In her two responses to Ong's work, Diana Hume George draws out the gender implications of Ong's rhetorical/political theory and presents a utopian vision, conceived in Miltonic terms, of a post-feminist (or prelapsarian) academic sexual harmony, to counter the nostalgia for agonistic debate.

For Gerald Graff in *Professing Literature*, however, academic conflict is both historical fact and structural necessity. He suggests that it is inaccurate to contrast a disputatious and contentious present to an imagined consensual disciplinary past; rather, conflict is endemic to, almost definitive of, the discipline, occasioned by multiple social demands, battling disciplinary paradigms, and the development of 'English' itself through series of disciplinary exclusions and inclusions. Graff's book is also a good example of the way in which controversy is structured, since he frames his history as a series of debates in which some points of view emerge as victors and others persist in a subtextual form, if at all. However, a history of successive debates, structured as disciplinary dialectic, cannot take account of the 'voices off,' the people and points of view not included in these already dominant, if contending, positions. The question of who and what is represented in the first place remains to be answered.

To examine this question, I will now turn to a text which is exemplary in a number of ways. It is, first of all, about the very subject under discussion here; that is, it is about the possibilities of academic debate, the very question of being on different 'sides.' It is not a new text, but for that reason is useful, since it is located at a particularly crucial and contentious time in the entry of 'theory' into the academy, and begins with a response to the Abrams response examined above. And it shows in a particularly interesting way how theoretical combat is, as much as anything else, an arrangement and rearrangement of rhetorical positions. Last, Fish's 'Is There a Text in This Class?' has itself been a prime generator of debate.

Mary Jacobus, in *her* response to Fish – entitled 'Is There a Woman in This Text?' – has noted the sexual politics of certain stagings of theoretical and critical discourse, in which a textual triangulation 'characteristically invokes its third (female) term only in the interests of the original rivalry and works to get rid of the woman, leaving theorist and theorist face to face' (119). However, while Jacobus looks at the politics of gender – who is speaking and who is not – I wish to focus more closely on how certain sorts of rhetorical rearrangement are accomplished in the first place.

The opening passage of 'Is There a Text in This Class?' has achieved a certain notoreity:

On the first day of the new semester a colleague at Johns Hopkins University was approached by a student who, as it turned out, had just taken a course from me. She put to him what I think you would agree is a perfectly straightforward question: 'Is there a text in this class?' Responding with a confidence so perfect that he was unaware of it (although in telling the story, he refers to this moment as 'walking into the trap'), my colleague said, 'Yes; it's the *Norton Anthology of Literature*,' whereupon the trap (set not by the student but by the infinite capacity of language for being appropriated) was sprung: 'No, no,' she said. 'I mean in this class do we believe in poems and things, or is it just us?' Now it is possible (and for many tempting) to read this anecdote as an illustration of the dangers that follow upon listening to people like me who preach the instability of the text and the unavailability of determinate meanings; but in what follows I will try to read it as an illustration of how baseless the fear of these dangers really is. ('Text' 305)

This anecdote accommodates us, as jokes do, and discomfits us, as do jokes at the expense of others. It is a story in which the knowledge of a teacher and of a student are compared and found different, as one would expect *a priori*. The joke here is 'on' the professor since – and this comes from a distinction Fish will later develop – the student has a more sophisticated knowledge of the meaning of 'text' than the person who teaches the meaning of texts. The disorder created by plot is simultaneously settled by style, for the vagueness, repetition, and ungrammaticality of the student's utterance – the absences of precise pronoun referent and parallel construction – show her not to be fully in control of her own knowledge; just as her use of the verb 'believe' suggests that she cannot recognize knowledge for what it is. The joke, then, is really 'on' the student. We may call this text 1, purportedly a reporting of what happened and what was said. (Without questioning the account's accuracy, it may be noted that secondary revision allows the professor a semicolon after his interjection, an unusual marker in the transcription of speech, which gives a sense of gravity to his reply. It has also been pointed out to me that there is no such work as the *Norton Anthology of Literature*.)

If this is text 1, we also have fragments of an overarching and implied text 2. Here the colleague tells the story to the narrator with added commentary ('walking into the trap'), as he presumably has told it on other occasions ('... in telling the story, he refers ...'), probably for other reasons than the examination of situate meaning. Here we are meant to see the incident not as a joke 'on' the student or 'on' the professor, but as a joke the professor tells 'on' himself. The point is that the professor *can* tell a joke on himself, can now see the joke in a way that the student could not at the time and presumably never will, even if she reads Fish's book. (And perhaps not even then, since she didn't get it the first time although she had prior instruction as 'one of Fish's victims' – a term by which the colleague later describes her.) Although the student has a double command of the word 'text,' the professor displays the higher ordering skills of an ironizing self-reflexivity: the stability of professorial knowledge is maintained.

It is with this particular professorial knowledge that the narrator's discourse merges and diverges, in the text we could call text 3. The references to 'a colleague' and 'my colleague' suggest an alliance – note the pronominal tree of 'my colleague' and 'his' student, and the change of possession of 'one of Fish's victims' in the exchange ritual known as 'the first day of the new semester' – an alliance formed in the overlap of texts 2 and 3 in the ambiguity of 'responding with a confidence so perfect that he was unaware of it.' Whether this is a recognition of the narrator's, or a later realization of the colleague's, a part of the 'as it turned out,' is unclear. But while the colleague knows that he has walked into a trap, he does not understand how it is sprung. Text 3, the narrator's, serves as a lucid explanation and a living example of its mechanisms.

Text 3 is a trap, and we are its victims. (Jokes, as Freud reminds us, are always both seductive and aggressive.) This is the narrator's text with its slightly elaborated introduction which both invites us (with a 'once upon a time' preamble) and interpellates us (by direct address). It allows an open-door admission policy of readers and listeners, by the geniality and generality of the first lines and the equally broad reach of 'I'm sure you will agree' – an assumption safely made, even at this early stage, since the statement allows for those who think it is straightforward; those who know that some might think so; and those who understand the whys and why nots of all of this. Because this elaborated introduction leads us to expect something from 'Fish' at the end, a finish to the frame, the actual conclusion seems inadequate, especially when it is followed by a negative moral, a summation of what the story *doesn't* mean. What we do get is a punch-line – rather weak, but still enough to knock the student right out of this debate on linguistic determinacy – and while this satisfies the plot demands of text 1 and the structure of jokes, it does not provide an equal finish to text 2 (the discourse of the now wiser professor), nor does it suitably frame text 3, for reasons noted.

However, the conclusions to these stories have already been given to us, but earlier on, and are available anaphorically. Just as the ending to the professor's story was given in the first set of parentheses (the rueful recognition that he had been trapped), so the conclusion to text 3 has already been made in the second set (with the explanation of how that trap works). The narrative is aranged to serve first and foremost the requirements of the joke – this rhetorically assists the entire piece, for these are the opening lines of a talk. But just as the first parenthetical statement served both to ally and distinguish the positions of narrator and professor (for the narrator understands something the professor only knows about), so the second ties our divergent notions to the narrator's (for he will tell us about something we presumably know but not in the way that he does). That the mainspring mechanism is 'the infinite capacity of language ...' is an aside made at the next-to-last moment of this other first-day ritual, the overt or covert placement test. Prompted, we have the right answer just in time and can be 'in' on the joke.

The opening lines of 'Is There a Text in This Class?' compel and impel assent in a way that Fish has noted of Freud's 'From the History of an Infantile Neurosis.' Freud accuses his detractors and sceptics of clinging to the old and comfortable and turning their backs on the new. Since this is the very predicament of the infantile neurotic then, Fish notes,

the conditions of being an infantile neurotic and of being an opponent of Freud turn out to be one and the same. It is a master-stroke which accomplishes several things at once: whatever Freud's opponents might say about his handling of the present case is discredited in advance, because they are too much like its subject; and more importantly, Freud's reader is simultaneously introduced to the opinions of those opponents and inoculated against their effect ... ('Withholding' 532)

Here, we lend assent to the theory of situate meaning not only because we are seeing examples of of it – a misunderstanding, and a joke – but because it is the only position available to us if we do not wish to be classed with the unknowing or the credulous.

This has been accomplished through a swift sleight-of-hand arrangement of positions; for while it may appear that the student has in fact disappeared, her place is available to be filled, although we would prefer it not be filled by us. There is, however, a candidate of whose presence the reader has been warned in the appended preface: 'These essays have a double origin, in the incident that gave them their title, and in Meyer Abrams's recently published paper "How To Do Things with Texts," a forthright attack on the work of Jacques Derrida, Harold Bloom, and me' ('Text' 303). Here Fish summarizes arguments later made in greater detail. He attends to Abrams's accusation that Fish and other 'New Readers' deny their own theory of linguistic and cognitive determinacy by writing meaningful and communicative papers. To this Fish responds that Abrams can understand him not because meaning is determinate but because they speak from within the same set of interests. The sceptics, then, 'do not realize' (304) that communication occurs only within such a system; 'nor do they realize' (304) that such an understanding is enough. While ostensibly this is a rebuttal, it is also implicitly a charge, that Abrams does not know what he knows because he does not understand the mechanism of his own discourse.

What has developed by this point is an homology between the textual structure I have described above and the communication situation of 'Is There a Text in This Class?' itself. Abrams is placed both as the 'colleague' – the man who does not know what and how he knows – and as the 'student,' whose words 'or is it just us?' parody Abrams's charge of new readerly relativism. What seems a joke 'on' Fish – he sets himself up as perennially misunderstood and misinterpreted – is actually a joke 'on' Abrams. Abrams has been rank-shifted from a generator of one discourse to the character in another, and no points made against Abrams's ideas in the pages to follow are as effective as this rhetorical and narrative restructuration.

The examples given above are not, perhaps, unique to theoretical discourse. The concerns and issues of intellectual debate, the questions of responsibility and propriety, have always been present. What is interpretation, after all, than the act of speaking *for* another? What is citation, except the act of speaking *as* another? Or debate, except the act of speaking *instead* of another? But I would suggest that the current intensification of the 'debate' formula is in a direct relation to concerns about controversy, and if it is not immediately consequential, it still has a signifying power as an index to contemporary life in the academy. And it is of more than 'academic' significance. In Canada today, for example, perhaps no question is of greater cultural urgency than the controversy over the appropriation of the myths and symbolics of Native people. This controversy is currently staged in both the newspapers and the alternative press as a 'debate' between European-descent writers, in a mimetic rehearsal of the original problem. Both the issue and its selective staging raise the question of speaking on, for, and through, and its rhetorical and ethical repercussions.

Slavoj Žižek begins *The Sublime Object of Ideology* by asking why certain theoretical debates achieve prominence and become the grid by which discussions are structured. Žižek notes that the Habermas-Foucault interchange has taken priority over, replaced 'in a kind of metaphorical substitution' (1–2), the Lacan-Althusser debate which Žižek finds more far-reaching. As Žižek writes, 'there is something enigmatic in the sudden eclipse of the Althusserian school: it cannot be explained away in terms of a theoretical defeat.' The 'traumatic kernel' of Althusser's theory, as he sees it, is uncertainty; this is what must be repressed through such acts of 'theoretical amnesia'(1). Žižek attempts to retrieve the theoretical uncanny and proposes a new form of both a philosophical and political dialectics, in which the impossibility of absolute knowledge, the necessity of suspension, are inscribed into the project as such. I hope I have suggested that this would be a matter not only of ideational, but of rhetorical and positional, rearrangements.

Works Cited

Abrams, M.H. 'The Deconstructive Angel.' *Critical Inquiry* 3, 3 (Spring 1977): 425–38.

Christensen, Jerome. 'From Rhetoric to Corporate Populism: A Romantic Critique of the Academy in an Age of High Gossip.' *Critical Inquiry* 16 (Winter 1990): 438–65.

Davis, Robert Con, and Ronald Schleifer, eds. *Contemporary Literary Criticism: Literary and Cultural Studies.* 2d ed. New York: Longman, 1989.

Findlay, Len. 'Otherwise Engaged: Postmodernism and the Resistance to History.' *English Studies in Canada* 14, 4 (Dec. 1988): 383–99.

Fish, Stanley. 'Is There a Text in This Class?' *'Is There a Text in This Class?' The Authority of Interpretive Communities.* Cambridge, Mass.: Harvard UP, 1980. 303–21.

– 'Rhetoric.' *Doing What Comes Naturally: Change, Rhetoric, and the Practice of Theory in Literary and Legal Studies.* Durham, N.C.: Duke UP, 1989. 471–502.

– 'Withholding the Missing Portion: Psychoanalysis and Rhetoric.' *Doing What Comes Naturally.* Op. cit. 525–54.

George, Diana Hume. 'The Miltonic Ideal: A Paradigm for the Structure of Relations between Men and Women in Academia.' *College English* 40, 8 (April 1979): 864–70.

– 'Stumbling on Melons: Sexual Dialectics and Discrimination in English Departments.' *English Literature: Opening Up the Canon; Selected Papers from the English Institute 1979.* Ed. Leslie A. Fielder and Houston A. Baker, Jr. New Series 4. Baltimore: Johns Hopkins UP, 1981. 107–36.

Gilbert, Sandra M., and Susan Gubar. 'The Man on the Dump versus the United Dames of America; or, What Does Frank Lentricchia Want?' *Critical Inquiry* 14, 2 (Winter 1988): 386–406.

Graff, Gerald. *Professing Literature: An Institutional History.* Chicago: U Chicago P, 1987.

Hamacher, Werner, Neil Hertz, and Thomas Keenan, eds. *Responses: On Paul de Man's Wartime Journalism.* Lincoln, Neb.: U Nebraska P, 1989.

Hutcheon, Linda. 'The Postmodern Problematizing of History.' *English Studies in Canada* 14, 4 (Dec. 1988): 365–82.

Jacobus, Mary. 'Is There a Woman in This Text?' *New Literary History* 14, 2 (Winter 1983): 117–41.

Johnson, Barbara. 'Is Writerliness Conservative?' *A World of Difference.* Baltimore: Johns Hopkins UP, 1987. 25–31.

Ong, Walter J. 'Agonistic Structures in Academia: Past to Present.' *Daedalus* 103 (1974): 229–38.

– 'Agonistic Structures in Academia: Past to Present.' [Expanded version.] *Interchange* [Ontario Institute for Studies in Education] 5, 4 (1974) 1–12.

– 'Comment.' *College English* 40, 8 (April 1979): 871–73.

Spacks, Patricia Meyer. *Gossip.* New York: Knopf, 1985.

Žižek, Slavoj. *The Sublime Object of Ideology.* London: Verso, 1989.

PART III: RESOURCES

11

English Studies in Canada to 1945: A Bibliographic Essay

Some of the more interesting theoretical work of recent years has focused on the institutions of criticism and of the teaching and learning of literature. This work best operates from a strong sense of the local and historical. It has been difficult to undertake such examination for English Canada, however, as the materials have not appeared to be readily available. The following should be read simply as a guide to such resources, but even a preliminary overview suggests that the situation of English studies in Canada is unique: in the length of its history; in its intrication with public and political life; in its uses and generation of critical material; in its goals and communities.

Thinking about the institutionalization of literary study in the nineteenth century requires a historically specific definition of those two terms. Early in the century, educators speak of 'literary' education (as opposed to the teaching of divinity); thus, for example, Queen's is envisaged by its founders as a 'Literary and Theological Seminary.' While Victoria College in the early 1840s includes practical and scientific treatises in its literature courses, somewhat later the term specifies any non-scientific writing. Throughout the century, 'literary' education can also refer to education in the vernacular, and the term characteristically refers to a wide variety of poetry and prose, including historical accounts, essays, and biography.

'Institutionalization' also needs definition, for institutionalization in higher education is only one way by which literary study becomes established in a colonial culture. Mechanics' institutes, literary and historical societies, newspapers, reading groups, and public lecture series are all important; and the study of literature throughout the nineteenth century is intricated with public and political life, and often its progressive aspects. For example, the reformer Joseph Howe wrote on both 'Eloquence' and 'Shakspeare' [sic]; the revolutionary William Lyon Mackenzie was a bookseller, and founder of a lending library; and the Toronto Women's Literary Club, after working for coeducation at the University of Toronto, reconstituted itself as the Canadian Woman's Suffrage Association.

At the moment, there are few extended studies pertaining to English studies in Canada, but they deserve special mention. Robin Harris's *English Studies at Toronto: A History* is the only full departmental history; and it provides, as well, useful contextual material about developments in the rest of the country. (This departmental history, along with his *History of Higher Education in Canada* and the higher education bibliographies by Harris, and Harris and Tremblay, provided the starting place for this research.) Margery Fee's 'English-Canadian Literary Criticism, 1890–1950: Defining and Establishing a National Literature' contextualizes national (and nationalist) criticism, both popular and academic, and studies key figures; her analysis of Romantic-nationalist criticism is abbreviated in the *Canadian Encyclopedia* entry on 'Criticism.' Henry Hubert traces 'The Development of English Studies in Nineteenth-Century Anglo-Canadian Colleges,' examining the eventual development away from rhetorical study to an idealist literary work. Robert Morgan's 'English Studies as Cultural Production in Ontario 1860–1920' is concerned with English studies at the primary and secondary levels, but provides a thorough analysis of educational debates of the day, examining the relationship of English studies to nation building.

Thanks to the work of Nan Johnson and Henry Hubert, the early years of rhetoric and literature teaching are the most thoroughly researched of all periods. Johnson surveys 'The Study of English Composition in Canadian Schools: 1800–1900' and then extends this examination to higher education in 'English Composition, Rhetoric, and English Studies at Nineteenth-Century Canadian Colleges and Universities.' In her ground-breaking 'Rhetoric and Belles-Lettres in the Canadian Academy,' Johnson details the persistence and consequences of the British model of education for 'Taste,' and surveys curricula and common texts. Her book detailing the philosophical and theoretical bases of *Nineteenth-Century Rhetoric in North America* is not concerned specifically with Canada, but does draw comparisons between the United States and Canada (especially regarding the withering of oratorical instruction here). In a shorter study, 'The Vernacular in Nineteenth-Century Anglophone Colleges,' Henry Hubert examines the battling attitudes to vernacular education of Scottish and anglophone traditions. Anne Tayler's 'McCulloch to deMille [sic]: Scottish Influences on the Teaching of Composition and Rhetoric in Nineteenth-Century Canada' surveys teaching in the mid years of the last century and provides a useful overview of the texts used; while Alistair Tilson's 'Who Now Reads *Spalding*?' examines the deployment of this particularly popular text. The first chapter of Harris's history (1988) gives a synopsis of the development of English studies in Canada during 1842–89; the years to 1950 are surveyed in the *Encyclopedia Canadiana* entry on 'English Study in the English-Language Universities,' co-authored by A.S.P. Woodhouse and Harris.

Two works by Charles Phillips provide useful background on rhetorical education at the lower levels. Phillips's textbook *The Development of Education in Canada* contains a succinct overview of reading and grammar instruction in the nineteenth century (470–82), while 'The Teaching of English in Ontario, 1800–1900' covers contemporary debates on this topic. W.P. Seary describes the literature studied in primary and secondary schools in the late years of the nineteenth century in 'Nova Scotian Culture Fifty Years Ago'; while Laurence Walker demonstrates, in 'Grammar Teaching in Alberta, 1905–1985,' the persistence of nineteenth-century theories of grammar teaching. The relationship of literacy and literacy teaching to citizenship formation is analysed in two important articles by Bruce Curtis – 'The Speller Expelled: Disciplining the Common Reader in Canada West,' and '"Littery Merrit," "Useful Knowledge," and the Organization of Township Libraries in Canada West, 1840–60.' Robert Morgan also considers the relationship of 'English' to state formation in Ontario in 'The "Englishness" of English Teaching.' Harvey Graff's *The Literacy Myth: Literacy and Social Structure in the Nineteenth-Century City*, a frequently cited work, provides historical documentation of reading levels in mid-nineteenth-century Upper Canada and shows how 'literacy' and 'illiteracy' become modes of social categorization. As a primary source, the *Canada Educational Monthly* (under its various titles) offers many articles on the teaching of English at all levels (especially in the issues of the late 1880s) and regular publication of matriculation examinations.

Programs for public education plead the value of literary instruction, as early as Stephen Dickson's 1799 *Considerations on the Establishment of a College in Quebec for the Instruction of Youth in Literature and Philosophy*. Such instruction is featured by 1818 in the Pictou Academy founded by Thomas McCulloch. (McCulloch defends arts instruction in *The Nature and Uses of a Liberal Education*; and his educational philosophy is examined by Anne Tayler, and by D.C. Harvey in 'Dr. Thomas McCulloch and Liberal Education.') But it is Egerton Ryerson who most firmly establishes literary education in this country. The 1842 prospectus of Victoria College shows English as mandatory at both the academy and college levels, with English language and literature studied by the first division, and rhetoric and belles-lettres by the second. Ryerson defended this innovation in his famous *Inaugural Address*:

The admission of an ENGLISH DEPARTMENT of *Language, Science,* and *Literature,* into a Collegiate Institution, may, I am aware, be regarded by some as a novelty, or innovation; but, as it appears to me, it is such a novelty as were, at one time, the Telescope, the Microscope, the Compass, the Inductive System of Philosophy, and, even, English Periodical Literature itself. After much reflection on the subject, it is my strong conviction that the absence of an English Department in our Collegiate Institutes of Learning in this Province, would be a defect of an injurious character. Why should there be provision for the teaching of dead and foreign languages, and none for the teaching of our own vernacular tongue, is a phenomenon for which I can assign no reason but custom and prejudice ... It is our native language – the language of our firesides, our commerce, our laws, our literature. The study of it should, therefore, occupy a leading, as well as a primary place, in the education of our youth. (10–11)

The first chapter of A.B. McKillop's *A Disciplined Intelligence* examines Ryerson's influential address as an attempt to relate academic inquiry to moral concern. While there are many general works on Ryerson, Morgan devotes specific attention to the role of Ryerson (and the school inspector and professor of moral philosophy George Paxton Young) in the development of English studies.

It would appear that other colleges were soon to follow Victoria's lead. The *Canadian Educational Directory* for 1857–8, for example, shows English literature taught throughout the undergraduate program at University College, with rhetoric added in the junior year (Hodgins 49); while at McGill literature is taught in the first year and rhetoric in the fourth (70); and at Bishop's the curriculum offers, more generally, 'English Literature and Composition' (88). Literature study is sufficiently well established by this time that 1858 marks the founding of the Molson Chair at McGill.

The Maritime provinces provide two interesting early figures. Baron d'Avray – doctor, diplomat, political satirist, and the eventual model for

'Dr. Martell' in Joseph Conrad's *Suspense* (Hamilton 318) – was professor of modern languages at the University of New Brunswick. W.B. Hamilton examines 'Marshall d'Avray: Precursor of Modern Education'; while in 'Creative Moments in the Culture of the Maritime Provinces,' A.G. Bailey sees in d'Avray the beginnings of the rich Fredericton intellectual tradition which would culminate with the Confederation poets. An 1871 *Oration* praises classical learning as the highest form but defends vernacular literature and local history as indispensable to a well-rounded education.

The eccentric polymath James De Mille, professor of history and rhetoric at Dalhousie College, Halifax, was being considered for the chair of rhetoric at Harvard at the time of his early death. His respected *The Elements of Rhetoric* (1878) recommends the study of rhetoric as even more essential for readers than for writers (iv) and proposes the addition of rhetorical analysis to the more usual philological and historical examinations. Contemporaries of De Mille's bemoaned the fact that his book was pre-empted by another appearing the same year (Patterson 140); presumably this was Adams Sherman Hill's *The Principles of Rhetoric*.

Archibald MacMechan has left a delightful portrait of 'De Mille, the Man and the Writer,' while Allan Bevan details the material that Mac-Mechan collected when working on an uncompleted biography. Carole Gerson (1983) gives a useful overview of De Mille's literary career; and G.G. Patterson sketches this very popular teacher. A spirited defence of liberal education informs De Mille's inaugural speech at Acadia and his two Dalhousie addresses. The extraordinary *A Strange Manuscript Found in a Copper Cylinder*, written at the same time as the *Elements*, is a 'theoretical,' if parodic, reflection on problems of criticism and interpretation.

Janet Scarfe's 'Letters and Affection: The Recruitment and Responsibilities of Academics in English-Speaking Universities in British North America in the Mid-Nineteenth Century' provides both useful background and glimpses into the classrooms of some early professors, including De Mille. Regional differences abound. At the University of New Brunswick in 1880, for example, Thomas Harrison – teacher of Bliss Carman and Charles G.D. Roberts – emphasized poetry and criticism, and taught Addison, Macaulay, and Johnson's *Lives of the Poets*, along with standard rhetoric texts; while at Queen's the philosophically inclined George Ferguson took a historical and philological approach, and assigned Max Müller's *Science of Language* (360–1).

Daniel (later Sir Daniel) Wilson was appointed to the chair of history and English literature at University College, Toronto, in 1853, and occupied that post for much of the rest of the century. This distinguished ethnographer and prehistorian was less qualified as a literary scholar, although he produced reviews and sonnets and a biographical study of Chatterton. (He also wrote some of the earliest reviews of Canadian poetry throughout the 1850s, and under his editorship the *Canadian Journal*, a primarily scientific magazine of the Canadian Institute, began to include literary criticism.) But, as A.B. McKillop notes in the section of *A Disciplined Intelligence* devoted to Wilson, the 'aesthetic bent of Wilson's mind' formed both his literary and scientific work (105). In another study, 'Evolution, Ethnology, and Poetic Fancy,' McKillop shows the overlap of Wilson's interests in his *Caliban: The Missing Link*, which combines Shakespeare study and Darwinian-informed ethnohistory. H.H. Langton's *Sir Daniel Wilson: A Memoir*, based on Wilson's journal entries and letters, is a thorough overview of his career, although it concentrates on his university presidency. For Wilson, language study was the base for literary work, and thus (as he dauntingly intoned) '... we must aim at a system of study which in its honor work shall embrace the Moeso-Gothic of Uphilas, the Icelandic, the Anglo-Saxon of Alfred and the Saxon Chronicle, and the Middle English of writers from the Ormulum and Layamon's "Brut" to Langland and Gower; as well as the influence of the Scandinavian and the Romance languages on the English grammar and vocabulary' (*Address ... 1888* 8). He appeared, however, to have seen this study as anything but dry, and felt that 'English at Junior Matriculation,' with its emphasis on obscure grammar, ill prepared students for university study. Wilson's views on vernacular education were aired in an important debate with Ryerson, as analysed by Hubert (1991); Harris details the development of the curriculum under Wilson and describes the texts he used (1988: 11–26).

The 1889 appointment of a first professor of English at the University of Toronto was to be the subject of an extraordinary public controversy, involving debate about both the hiring of Canadian nationals and the goals of literary study. Throughout this period, the press was alert to literary matters. (See, for example, the coverage of the Modern Language Association of Ontario: 'Annual Meeting of the Modern Language Association,' 'Discussing the Modern Tongues,' and various items in the *Toronto Daily Mail*.) The eventual choice, W.J. Alexander, was the first professor of English in Canada to be expressly trained in the discipline, for he matriculated in 1873 into the 'department of English, French and History' at Toronto and did advanced work in English at London (*Testimonials in Favour of William John Alexander*).

In *The Study of Literature*, his 1884 inaugural address as the Munro Professor at Dalhousie, Alexander had defended vernacular literary study as an accessible source of 'aesthetic culture' (19). Alexander's 1889 Toronto address, similarly titled, adds a more fully developed program for English studies. Here he reverses Wilson's priorities by seeing the study of literature as paramount; further, he assigns such study a central importance since 'in all departments of study, written authorities must be submitted to the crucible of higher criticism' (9). He advocates a 'natural method' (25) in which the study of works is followed by the study of literary history and intellectual context, and only then can the student make 'profitable use' of the critics (26). His 'aim of forming a complete image of the thought of an age' (30) has been shared by many other scholars at Toronto over the years; and Alexander's 'natural method' underpins many curricula even today. Another, similarly titled piece some ten years later is more practical than programmatic. He describes English as a distinct discipline, differing from history by its concern with language and feeling, and sees criticism as an inversion of the creative process, with the student's task to 'attain to the state of mind which the writer intended to embody' (vii). Alexander remained interested in English education at all levels. His piece on 'Literature' in the *Methods in Teaching* volume, intended for teachers-in-training, suggests that children can best be taught when literature is related to concrete experiences; while an address made to classics graduates, entitled 'Graduates' Reading – Literature,' advises the busy teacher on selections for evening reading.

Alexander's popular lectures had to be scheduled in the largest hall on campus. M.W. Wallace's 'Memoir' surveys Alexander's career and describes him as a teacher; while in 'Critic and Teacher,' A.S.P. Woodhouse lists his work and assesses him as a post-Romantic. In 'Staff, 1890–1953,' Woodhouse credits Alexander with building the University College department, describing curricular innovations and the new faculty he hired. Harris devotes some pages to the curriculum and examinations under Alexander (1988: 29–48). The numerous collections and composition texts he organized and edited are further evidence of his practical criticism; and his article 'The Purpose of *Shorter Poems* and Its Use in the Class,' as well as the various introductions to the many editions of *Select Poems*, demonstrate in detail his intent for such volumes. (These texts are fully listed in the Woodhouse bibliography.)

Archibald MacMechan, educated at Toronto and Johns Hopkins, replaced Alexander at Dalhousie in 1889 and remained there until his retirement. (MacMechan's background and educational philosophy are described in his *Testimonials*, and Carl Klinck also provides a biography in 'Professor MacMechan, Native of Western Ontario.') His inaugural address *Concerning the Oldest English Literature* is a case for treating Anglo-Saxon poetry in a literary rather than philological manner, for 'there is food there for the lover of pure poetry' (22). MacMechan's essay 'Child of the Ballads' charmingly recounts his awkward undergraduate encounter with 'the Harvard great,' and other tales of his student years. C.L. Bennet has written three tributes to MacMechan, listing the accomplishments of this versatile scholar. Both Wilhelmina Gordon and G.G. Sedgewick remember their teacher; Sedgewick's is an amusing description of MacMechan's pedagogic style, recreating a class on Kipling in the fall of '98. S.E.D. Shortt's detailed 'Archibald MacMechan: Romantic Idealist' takes MacMechan as a representative intellectual figure of the transition years.

Charles G.D. Roberts's career as a junior professor of English and other subjects at King's College in Windsor, Nova Scotia, provides another typical career, and both he and his cousin Bliss Carman were attuned to disciplinary developments at Harvard and Johns Hopkins. (See the letters edited by Boone and by Gundy. The biographies of Roberts by Adams and Pomeroy both devote a section to Roberts's academic career.) Roberts's 1888 essay 'The Teaching of English,' published in the *Christian Union*, envisages a vital, literary study instead of mere labour in the 'Valley of Dry Bones' of syntax and analysis. This call for 'culture, intellectual and moral' (488), appeared in the same issue as the editorial announcement of the death of Matthew Arnold; and Roberts's own program is in large measure Arnoldian.

'Fidelis' (the writer Agnes Maule Machar) concurs with 'The True Principles of Teaching English' laid down in Roberts's piece; and Archibald Lampman also appears to share the views of his fellow poet, to judge from his account in the 'Mermaid Inn' column of the martyrdom of *Paradise Lost*:

They read it; they declaim it rhetorically; they get it by heart; they analyze it sentence by sentence; they parse it word for word; they study its language syllable by syllable, following each word to its remotest kindred in Latin, Greek, Saxon, old high German, Lithuanian, or Sanscrit [*sic*]; they turn it into prose and back again into verse; they hunt up all the allusions; they make themselves acquainted with parallel passages; they discuss it historically, geographically, critically; they tear and worry and torture the lines of the great poem till they are littered out as dry and innutritive as a worm-eaten codfish. When all this has been done the student's mind is perhaps the acuter for the mental training, but he wishes never to hear the name of *Paradise Lost* again. (5 Nov. 1892; Davies 186–7).

His not disinterested solution to the 'problem of pedantry' – which Lampman considered especially pronounced in Canada – was the recommendation of a 'lecturing guild' of writers to talk at the universities (18 March 1893; Davies 275–6).

Scholars, too, were convinced of the need for new methods for these new subjects. A.H. Reynar, professor of English literature and modern languages at Victoria College (then in Cobourg), notes in 1889 that 'grammar, rhetoric, philology, history, mythology, etc. etc.' are useful in their own way and 'moreover, these things can be put down in black and white to appease the examination demon who is going up and down the land seeking whom he may devour, and they may be put into annotations, and expanded into books'; but 'culture is a law written in the heart and in the mind' (129). He makes practical suggestions, including the encouragement of fiction reading for pleasure. Another program is provided by a contemporary, the energetic William Morley Tweedie of Mount Allison, who taught at that institution for fifty years. The principles of his inaugural address are implemented in the 1888 honours program, with its backbone of Old and Middle English, and its thoroughly historical, chronological, and contextual study of the Renaissance, the eighteenth century, and the Romantics. University historian John Reid relates Tweedie's critical work to textual and higher criticism (1:222).

James Cappon, Scottish born and educated, held the chair of English at Queen's for thirty-one years and was a staunch defender of the humanities. The unanimous selection of Cappon was praised by the editors of the *Week*, who (bearing in mind the Toronto controversy) saw his inauguration as a wise solution in times when, 'if the advocates of the old order were bigoted and prejudiced against all innovations, it can hardly be denied that many of the modern school are self-satisfied and conceited ...' ('The Study of English Literature' 741). Cappon's educational philosophy is expressed in several polemical pieces, apart from his inaugural, which was published in full by the *Kingston British Whig*. 'Is Ontario to Abandon Classical Education?' he demands, defending Latin as a compulsory component of English teacher education. 'Literature for the Young: Notes on the High School Reader' criticizes a widely used textbook; here Cappon favours interest and reading-level over the principles of comprehensive coverage. An address to the Modern Language Association in Toronto, published in 1890 as 'Subjects and Methods in the Teaching of English,' examines a school edition of 'Lay of the Last Minstrel' and the draft curricula for the junior matriculation and Toronto honours programs. (Replies by J.E. Wetherell and William Houston continue the debates on whether reading of criticism impedes student self-reliance, and whether the 'canon' should be expanded to include *Lorna Doone*.) A later piece, entitled 'Edward Caird: A Reminiscence,' is as much a statement of Cappon's own creed as it is a memory of the Scottish moral philosopher; but his 1917 address to the University of Toronto's English Association on the Celtic renaissance shows a willingness to keep up-to-date, although the symbolists among the students debated his contention that the poet should have a 'rationalised concept' (see Cooper).

W.E. McNeill provides his memories of Cappon, who 'came out of a Scotland that still talked proudly of Thomas Carlyle, just seven years dead' (74). In 'James Cappon: The Ideal in Culture,' S.E.D. Shortt shows that Cappon saw literature study as the study of life, and he gives a portrait of Cappon as a Canadian Arnoldian and lists his writings.

The career of the Reverend Professor William Clark of Trinity College provides an interesting example of the overlap of higher and public education of that day. Initially a professor of mental and moral philosophy, but then to be the college's first professor of English, Clark was a popular public speaker on literary matters who treated his material personally and, often, elegiacally. ('He's dead now, poor fellow,' often commenced his lectures on authors [Reed 94].) A useful example of popular literary education is provided by the 1892 publication of a series of lectures on Tennyson (complete with suggestions for primary and secondary reading); another lecture on 'Books and Reading' encourages reading as an enrichment for day-to-day life. This well-developed connection between literary and popular education allows English to be seen as integral to the schooling of women. In 1869, when Hitchin College for women was opened at Queen's, a special class on English was offered by John Clark Murray. In the next year, rhetoric and logic, English, and natural history were the three courses approved by the senate for women (Neatby 133). John William Dawson, president of McGill and a dedicated proponent of women's rights, felt that the classical training men received was both too diffuse and 'one-sided.' Literary education for women might more profitably combine rhetoric, composition, and philological study in 'Saxon and Celtic sources'; in addition, the learner should acquire 'some other cultivated tongue, either ancient or modern,' and through this, understanding of the 'laws of language' (*Educated Women* 8). Dawson pronounced women capable of undertaking study of Hebrew or Chinese, Assyrian or Chaldean.

At Toronto, the entry of women into University College centred around the modern languages, precipitated by the awarding of the modern language entrance scholarship to Alice Cummings in 1879, before women were admitted to lectures (see Squair; and Ford). The influx of women into the modern languages was to continue for some decades. A 1928 overview, *Modern Language Instruction in Canada*, devoted a separate section to 'Women Students in Modern Languages' and noted that as early as 1889 half the Toronto honours English students were women. At the same time, however, popular women's fiction of the transition years often details not only the literary aspirations of women, but their failure. Part of the particular poignancy of L.M. Montgomery's *Anne of Green Gables*, for example, is that family duties prevent Anne from taking up the Avery Fellowship in English Language and Literature, which she struggled to earn; while L.V. MacKinnon's *Miriam of Queen's* concludes with the protagonist's career as a 'professor' of English and history at the Halifax Ladies College giving way to love interests.

While literature was at times seen as especially suited to women's talents, literary matters were frequently in the public eye. Matthew Arnold's ten-day speaking tour in 1884, to Toronto, Ottawa, Quebec City, and Montreal, occasioned keen interest and detailed press coverage; these are the subject of Barbara Opala's 'Matthew Arnold in Canada' and Clifford Holland's 'Canada Greets the Apostle of Culture.' While Arnold's ideas were sympathetically received and influential, the reception was not uncritical. Arnold's equation of 'race' and 'nation' and – most scandalously – his anti-Catholic remarks occasioned outrage in Quebec and spirited retaliation by Louis Fréchette (Opala 91–112). 'Science and Literature' sparked discussion about literary education in a new land, while the concept of the critical 'remnant' in 'Numbers' was considered by some undemocratic (Opala 38–47). The house poet of the *Toronto Evening News* greeted Arnold humorously but conditionally:

Dear friend, if thou would'st so be called
Talk on the topics of the place

Tell us what votes, and how, were polled
In that corrupt Algoma case.

Alas! not sweetness and not light,
Can ever in our ears supplant
Your views upon the boundary fight,
Or that Pacific railway grant.
('To M. Arnold ... Greetings!'; quoted in Opala 33)

As Pat Jasen has demonstrated in 'Arnoldian Humanism, English Studies, and the Canadian University,' English was able to move into the
centre of university studies in Canada precisely because of its Arnoldian
mission; she sees Alexander as a primary proponent of these views and
traces a continuing influence. A succinct contemporary statement is provided by University College lecturer D.R. Keys, assessing in 1896 'Our
Debt as Teachers to Matthew Arnold.'

The impact of Oscar Wilde on literary study here is less easy to discern, since many of his engagements took place after universities had let
out for the summer. But 'Ruskin' versus 'Wilde' was a familiar structure
of aesthetic debate especially among undergraduates, and Wilde established some continuing connections with writers during his 1882 speaking engagements here, as detailed by Kevin O'Brien in 'Oscar Wilde and
Canadian Artists.' (O'Brien's *Oscar Wilde in Canada: An Apostle for the
Arts* is a more extended study.) It may also be that Wilde's influence is
less documented since at many of his engagements the audience was
primarily women. One hundred and forty students of the Wesleyan
Ladies College in Hamilton and their principal and literature professor,
Dr Alexander Burns, braved church elders to attend Wilde's Hamilton
talk; and Wilde addressed the students the next day on 'The Relation of
Art to Other Studies' (O'Brien, *Apostle* 114–16).

The nineteenth century provides a miscellany of thoughts and polem-
ics on the teaching of English. One work of especial interest is Rev. H.
Esson's 1852 *Strictures on the Present Method of Teaching the English Language*. A professor of mental and moral philosophy at Knox College,
Esson develops a theory of the sign in which linguistic order is reflective
of natural order, and bases a program for language instruction upon
this. In 1886 John Watson of Queen's presents a commonsensical case
for the improving powers of 'The Study of Literature.' Theodore Arnold
Haultain's 'Can English Literature Be Taught?' (1887) remarks that
English literature, 'whether, how, and why it ought to be taught, is at

present a sort of *campus philosophorum'* (19) but notes that 'aesthetic and philosophical criticism have by us been by no means relegated to the insignificant places which ... have been their fate in the British Isles' (20). Haultain supports his argument with examples of junior matriculation and teacher certification examination questions. These issues were soon to trickle down to the secondary level, and 'Baie Chaleur' in 1888 advocates redesign of the 'Study of English Literature' at the secondary level with new developments in the discipline in mind. A student's-eye view of the discipline is provided by commonly used study guides, such as the *Synoptical View of the Literature for University and Teachers' Examinations ...*, a 'masterplots' guide to 'Warren Hastings' and various Coleridge poems, with practice questions added. Copp publishers issued many examination guides; see, for example, *English Literature for 1890, for University and Departmental Examinations*.

A number of overviews of the intellectual condition of Canada provide valuable background. George Renny Young's 1842 *On Colonial Literature, Science and Education* is an unjustly neglected (albeit idiosyncratic) series of lectures to the Halifax Institute, presenting a comprehensive program for government-sponsored colonial education, which concludes with a discussion of the relationship of oratory and rhetoric to public life. Three years later, William Scott Burn ingeniously makes *The Connection between Literature and Commerce*, providing a sweeping overview of all world history to prove that commerce is the 'grand moving power' (15) of literature. James Douglas in 1875 writes of 'The Intellectual Progress of Canada during the Last Fifty Years, and the Present State of Its Literature,' and is very critical of colonial culture. He gives statistics on book-buying and university graduations to show that literary culture was lagging far behind the scientific. John George Bourinot paints a more positive picture in 'The Intellectual Development of the Canadian People: An Historical Review,' which appeared in four instalments in 1880 and 1881, surveying the 'Effect of Social and Political Changes on Mental Development,' 'Education,' 'Journalism,' and 'Native Literature.' George Stewart's section on 'Literature in Canada,' part of an overview of Canadian culture prepared in 1887 for the Canadian Club of New York, uses the term 'literature' to signify intellectual achievement more generally, and describes the evolution of the intellectual infrastructure of literary and historical societies, archives, and publishing houses. John Dent's 1881 survey of 'Literature and Journalism' also defines 'literature' generally as intellectual work, and lists the varieties produced. Most famously, Bourinot's 1893 *Our Intellectual*

Strength and Weakness, first an address to the recently formed Royal Society, surveys institutions of national literatures and letters, and intellectual and political achievement; it is a generous, imperialist, biculturalist, and sometimes explicitly Arnoldian program for cultural development. His *Bibliography of the Members of the Royal Society of Canada*, produced in the next year, is a most valuable record of scholarly production at the end of the century, although most of the works listed are historical or scientific.

Later scholars also provide analyses of the intellectual culture and literary taste of the day. Reginald Watters examines 'The Study of Canadian Literature since 1840,' surveying reviews and the rise of scholarship; while C.T. Bissell analyses 'Literary Taste in Central Canada during the Late Nineteenth Century' as demonstrated in the *Week*, and discerns a distaste for experimentation and the overtly intellectual among the author-critics of the day. In 'Opinion,' Bissell concentrates on student literary taste in the Toronto *Varsity* of the '80s and '90s. Carole Gerson's *A Purer Taste: The Writing and Reading of Fiction in English in Nineteenth-Century Canada* is the most sustained examination of this topic, with extensive reference to reviews of the day. George Parker's *The Beginnings of the Book Trade in Canada* documents the publishing industry here, with useful sections on colonial education, libraries, and mechanics' institutes.

William Morton Payne's important 1894 survey of *English in American Universities*, a collection of pieces originally published in the *Dial*, provides a point of comparison between Canadian and U.S. departments at the close of the century, and a strong sense of the sort of training (at Johns Hopkins and Harvard, for example) which formed many Canadian scholars. It is interesting to note that the book is presented as a rebuttal to the influential Canadian Goldwin Smith, for 'even so sound a thinker as Goldwin Smith has recently doubted the success of the new Oxford school of English literature, on the ground that the subject does not easily lend itself to the traditional sort of examination' (18).

By the 1900s, then, while the Oxbridge study of English was in its infancy (although studies at London and the Scottish universities had been in place much earlier), and while cases for vernacular study were still being mustered in the U.S. academy, the study of literature *as* literature – a so-called 'rhetorical' or even 'aesthetic' criticism – was as much as sixty years old in English Canada.

The twentieth century first brought advances in individual critical work, and then the development of a stronger scholarly infrastructure;

and many of these developments can be traced in the career of just one man. The indefatigable Watson Kirkconnell is the subject of a biographical sketch by J.R.C. Perkin, but the fullest account is provided by Kirkconnell himself in his memoirs, *A Slice of Canada*, which include a chapter on his teaching career. Of particular interest are his memories of an early association of English professors, and it is worth quoting this passage at length:

In the 1920s, some Prairie scholars in English, having felt keenly their isolation from one another, decided to do something about it. Hence arose an annual 'English Conference' held at Saskatoon for two days in 1926 and at Edmonton for two days in 1927. At Saskatoon, our hosts were R.A. Wilson, head of the English department, who, as an old disciple of John Watson, had just completed an erudite volume on the metaphysical implications of language, and J.M. Lothian, a Glasgow M.A. who had taught in Italy and had studied the relations of the Italian and the English Renaissance drama. At Edmonton, Edmund Kemper Broadus, an irascible and aristocratic Virginian, whose specialties were Southern slang and the English laureateship, made us at home, but warned us not to speak to him each morning until three cups of coffee had restored his faith in the world. The conferences were a great success. As teachers, we discussed such professional matters as remedial English (referred to us by the National Conference of Canadian Universities for study), high school curricula, the proper character of examination papers, and modern philosophies of education. Equally important were scholarly papers in which individuals put some of their special research wares on the table and received the criticism and encouragement of men in their own field.

In May 1928, the delegates moved east by invitation to an 'English Conference' at University College, Toronto. Our host was Malcolm Wallace, a specialist in Milton's prose and the life of Sir Philip Sidney, but the centre of the stage was taken by explosively irrepressible Garnet Sedgewick from the University of British Columbia and the punctilious but mellow scholar, Archibald MacMechan, from Dalhousie. 'Archie' spoke on Matthew Arnold's *Merope*, and it was my task to supplement his paper with one on French and Italian dramas on the same theme by Voltaire, Alfieri, and Maffei (all borrowed a month earlier from the University of Toronto Library). This 1928 meeting, with representatives present from Vancouver and Halifax, marked the widest geographical extension of the 'English Conferences.' It was also the last of them. The financial crash of 1929 dragged universities down along with the rest of the community, and harassed university presidents, who had largely financed our meetings, were forced to withhold supply. The three golden interludes had revealed, however, that notable encouragement can come from a foregathering of kindred spirits and that a surprising amount of first-class material was in the making or vainly awaiting publication. (234)

Sedgewick's 'The Unity of the Humanities' is described in its published form as a talk to 'the first conference of Professors of English in Canada.' Pondering the relationship of English to classics and history, Sedgewick asserts that it is, happily, 'just in those extraneous fields that safety for English studies lies' (358), envisaging a wide-ranging and revitalized interdisciplinarity. This piece also details the establishment of honours essays and independent study projects in the UBC honours program; while his later 'Of Disillusionment in Freshmen' recounts experiences teaching some of the bleaker modern poets to young undergraduates. The colourful Sedgewick – Kittredge student and founding chair of the UBC department – is remembered by G.P.V. Akrigg in *Sedgewick: The Man and His Achievement*, and he features prominently in *The Way We Were*, a collection of reminiscences by UBC alumnae/i (a collection which also provides a vignette of Ira Dilworth by Sam Roddin). Earle Birney's autobiographical *Spreading Time* provides a full account of undergraduate life in the UBC program. Again, Sedgewick is a major figure; and he also appears in Birney's *Down the Long Table*, the *roman à clef* adventures of a graduate student in mediaeval literature who flirts with communism and the League for Social Reconstruction in the '30s.

Other men mentioned by Kirkconnell have left memoirs or are remembered by others. E.K. Broadus, Virginia-born and Harvard-educated, chaired the Alberta department for many years, and much of Lovat Dickson's *The Ante-Room* is devoted to memories of Broadus and his teaching. (Dickson also details his own early career as a teacher.) Broadus is at the centre of R.D. McMaster's article on 'The Department of English, 1908–1982,' along with his successor R.K. Gordon. And other figures from the years between the wars have left their marks. Orlando John Stevenson of the Ontario Agricultural College (later Guelph), and its chair from 1916, wrote a regular column called 'The English Department' in the *Ontario Agricultural College Review* from 1928 to 1939. Some of these anecdotes and meditations are collected as *Through the Years*, while Stevenson's *Reminiscences* mention his education at Toronto, a lecture by Alexander on Browning, and a talk by Carman at OAC. Pelham Edgar, whose career spanned some forty years at Victoria College and twenty-five as its chair, unfortunately completed only three sections of his autobiography, whose fragments have been collected by Northrop Frye as *Across My Path*. (His 'A Confession of Faith and a Protest' is an interestingly Arnoldian attack on Canadian philistinism.) Edgar is, however, remembered by others: see Northrop Frye's introduction to the collection and his tribute to this 'Dean of Critics,' as well as Wilfrid Eggleston's reminiscences in *Literary Friends* (111–24). Fee's extended study of Edgar's critical career provides much biographical information (1981: 237–69); an overview is also provided by Sandra Campbell in 'The Canadian Literary Career of Professor Pelham Edgar.' As editor of both the *Canadian Forum* and the *University of Toronto Quarterly*, E.K. Brown was a formidable and formative intellectual presence in Canada, teaching at University College and then Manitoba, and remaining involved in Canadian cultural issues after his move to Chicago. Fee provides a study of his critical career (1981: 326–58); the later correspondence between Brown and Duncan Campbell Scott, edited by R.L. McDougall, also provides useful information, as do Leon Edel (1953) and David Staines (1977; 1979). Staines's account of Brown's life and writings is supplemented by Fee (1980). John Ferns's survey of A.J.M. Smith's work devotes a few pages to his academic career. Notable women scholars of the period have lives which are less documented. A brief profile of Wilhelmina Gordon of Queen's is provided by John Dewar; and Mossie May Kirkwood is remembered in her roles as scholar and dean in *Sanctam Hildam Canimus* (ed. B. Sutton). Alison Prentice sees Kirkwood as exemplary of the 'Scholarly Passion' of women in the early years of this century, and relates Kirkwood's achievements to her life and times.

Undergraduate memoirs also exist. Claude Bissell's *Halfway Up Parnassus* fondly reflects on the '30s at University College, with particular memories of A.S.P. Woodhouse and Herbert Davis; Northrop Frye remembers his own undergraduate years in the 'Foreword' to the Harris history, and these are detailed as well in the John Ayre biography of Frye. An intimate account of undergraduate literary life is given by Leon Edel in his *Memories of the Montreal Group* at McGill; while Philip Marchand's *Marshall McLuhan: The Medium and the Messenger* devotes a chapter to McLuhan's undergraduate years in the Manitoba program. The unpublished diaries of UNB and Toronto undergraduate Alfred G. Bailey appear in the article by J. Paul Grayson and L.M. Grayson, 'Canadian Literary and Other Elites: The Historical and Institutional Bases of Shared Realities,' which examines social formation through undergraduate education.

These important early years of the discipline provide some famous scholarly upheavals. J.D. Logan's broadside *Dalhousie University and Canadian Literature* attacked both MacMechan and Dalhousie for ignoring the Canadian literature of which Logan was so strong, and so early, a proponent. For Logan, the teaching of Canadian literature is not only a national but a spiritual necessity, for 'a written literature and the written appreciations of that literature are a spiritual history of a people' (2). The battle raged through pamphlet, letters, and the columns of the Halifax *Morning Chronicle*. Toby Foshay's *J.D. Logan, Canadian Man of Letters* gives a biographical and bibliographic study of this tenacious man.

A sheaf of talks in Logan's archives is proudly headed 'First Formal Lectures on Canadian Literature in Any Canadian University (Acadia).' According to Logan, Canadian literature was first taught at Acadia, then Wesleyan University in Winnipeg, then McGill, then Victoria College, Toronto, although Desmond Pacey suggests the first course was taught in 1906 by J.B. Reynolds at Macdonald Institute (Guelph) (McDougall 1988: 1226). In 'Teaching Canadian Literature in the Universities,' Logan gives a detailed description of the courses he and Vernon Rhodenizer taught at Acadia. Evidence of this new interest is given in Eggleston's narrative of 'Carman at Calgary and Queen's'; Fee gives an extended account of the development of Canadian literature courses in Canadian universities of the '20s (1981: 217–36); and a brief history of the incorporation of Canadian materials is presented by R.L. McDougall as 'Literature in English: Teaching.' (Rhodenizer's own career is examined in 'Dr. V.B. Rhodenizer,' by S.E. MacGregor; while he himself wrote a sketch of 'English at Acadia: 1918–52.') Later studies of Canadian literature 'canonization' in the period are provided by Carole Gerson's 'The Canon between the Wars' and Dermot McCarthy's 'Early Canadian Literary Histories and the Function of a Canon.'

A further controversy centred on the replacement of Cappon as departmental head at Queen's in 1919; the conflicts and controversies are worthy of C.P. Snow and are detailed in Gibson's history of Queen's (51–5). In all, 'an assorted procession of six heads and acting heads ... passed in and out of the English department in as many years' (Gibson 55), until the eventual selection of George Herbert Clarke, who was to hold the position for eighteen years. (Clarke is profiled in a sketch by David Dewar; as is, more briefly, his colleague James Roy.) The appointment of G.B. Harrison as his successor was equally baroque, involving first a rejected offer to A.S.P. Woodhouse and then a choice between Harrison (King's College, University of London) and the poet A.J.M. Smith (an expatriate at Michigan State), in which E.K. Brown,

Sedgewick, and Vincent Massey were called upon for advice (Gibson 235–7).

Some fictional or semi-fictional accounts give a glimpse of the state of English between the wars. Wyndham Lewis taught at Assumption College in Windsor (later part of the University of Windsor), lecturing on a variety of topics including philosophy of literature. *Self Condemned*, while the story of a teacher of history, presents one picture of the smaller colleges of the day; and J. Stanley Murphy, C.S.B., is later to reminisce about 'Wyndham Lewis at Windsor.' Assumption College compares well to the English departments at the University of Michigan and Michigan State, which Wyndham Lewis described in a letter to T.S. Eliot as 'a group of old hacks teaching English, though they have some difficulty in speaking it, supported by a deferential group of young hacks, [who] entertain one to liquorless and beerless six o'clock suppers ...' (13 March 1945; *Letters* 380). E.A. McCourt's *Music at the Close* presents, in part, a fictitious account of one year in the life of an English student in a Prairie university of the mid-1920s.

The first half of the century provides a series of statements and polemical revisionings of English studies. In 1903 English is seen as an important part of the solution to the question: '*How Can Canadian Universities Best Benefit the Profession of Journalism, as a Means of Moulding and Elevating Public Opinion?*' O.J. Stevenson's 1904 *The Study of Literature*, his published dissertation in pedagogy, gives practical and philosophical considerations on the use of English to train the child as 'a social agent'; while ignoring higher education, it develops a set of powerful rationales for English study. In the same year, J.F. MacDonald takes a more traditional direction and makes a case for reintroducing elocution as an element of the university English program. In 1908 Samuel Dawson makes *A Plea for Literature* in his presidential address to the Royal Society. Literature, he asserts, is the study of human life; but the Royal Society neglects this area in favour of the scientific. In 1930 R.S. Knox of University College praises 'The Educational Value of the Study of Literature' and finds himself in agreement with England's Newbolt report. English, however, should not just replace the classics by turning into a modern 'greats'; not only thought, but aesthetics, must be taught.

While there was a growing unanimity about the importance of English study, theories about how it should be taught differed widely throughout the first half of the century. A.F.B. Clark (a pivotal figure in the development of French studies, but then in the University College English group) had in 1913 created an uproar by advocating 'The Rehabilitation of Modern Languages' through abolition of philological requirements, while in 'Literary Scholarship in Canadian Universities' (1930) he extends his argument to include English studies. Since the disciplinary groundwork has now been laid, 'we must ally ourselves with other disciplines, psychology, economics, aesthetics; we must build up a philosophy of literature' (245). In response, H. Steinhauer deplores 'philological slavery' (323); later issues provide other comments, and E.K. Brown asking, 'Shall We Adopt the French Doctorate?' in lieu of the German-style Ph.D.

There are numerous analyses of the state of English throughout the first fifty years, and they sometimes give a glimpse of the workings of different departments. Reginald Bateman, first professor of English at Saskatchewan from 1909 until his untimely death in the First World War, gave two interesting lectures on 'The Teaching of English.' He suggests that sensitive assimilation precede analysis of 'form, structure, philology, and exact meaning' (49), and he recommends the development of 'vocal culture' as a teaching tool. A second lecture uses the example of Browning to show how works are profitably studied in their historical context. E.K. Broadus examines 'Weakness in English among Undergraduates and Graduates in Canadian Universities' in 1927 and finds Toronto's casual assignment of papers, and the 'grind of themes' (88) at the newer universities, equally unsatisfactory. He recommends the action taken at Harvard, where a committee representing all departments is responsible for testing and improving student writing; and the next year reports the implementation of this plan at Alberta as 'A Plan for Dealing with Weakness in English.' Rev. Father Francis Archambault describes 'The Teaching of English in the University of Montreal and Affiliated Colleges,' showing the place of English in the classical colleges. Grammar, translation, and recitation compose the curriculum, although some students go on Saturdays to a literature course at Université de Montréal. Eric Duthie's 1936 'English in Askelon' attributes the deplorable state of freshman writing to their love of films and trashy fiction; illiteracy, for him, is really a problem of lack of literary appreciation. In 'Humane Scholarship in the Humanities,' E.K. Brown gives his perspective on the curricular innovations at Iowa and Chicago and, while finding much to disagree with, concurs that specialization not only of subject matter but approach seems to be inevitable. G.B. Harrison's 1944 'Department of English' looks at the special burden placed on English departments by the rest of the university. ('So much is written in these days about the sad decay of the Humanities that a Professor of

English is from time to time overwhelmed almost by a sense of personal sin' [378].) He examines the fourfold function of composition, survey, honours, and graduate teaching, with sensible suggestions for improving and revitalizing each area. Although the semi-autobiographical *Profession of English* gives little attention to his years at Queen's, the shape of the Queen's program may be seen as a practical application of Harrison's principles (see Gibson 237–41). In 'Respectfully Submitted' in 1945, Sister Maura of Mount Saint Vincent makes reference to the rich literary heritage of the Maritime provinces and envisages a four-year program that will combine literary study with creative writing, to produce students who are both 'makers' and 'knowers' of literature. Another program for experimental literary education is examined in Heather Murray's history of the dramatic and rhetorical education provided by the Margaret Eaton School of Literature and Expression in the first quarter of this century.

There are numerous overviews of scholarship and criticism of the period. In his thorough survey of 'English-Canadian Literature,' written for the 1913 compendium history *Canada and Its Provinces,* Thomas Guthrie Marquis notes that criticism had been haphazard until very recent years, 'but there are now, mainly in universities, a number of men who are exerting a wide influence by giving sound critical standards and thus elevating literary taste in the Dominion' (529). While J.D. Logan considers Marquis a good example of new critical work, he is to disagree with Marquis's assessments of others. Logan's 1917 *Aesthetic Criticism in Canada: Its Aims, Methods and Status* begins by sorting critics of the time into the Traditional, the Academic, and the Pragmatic, to advocate a more constructive, contextualized, and pedagogic criticism. This work deserves serious retrospective attention as the first attempt to provide, in Logan's terms, a 'criticism of criticism' (8). In a 1939 article, Pelham Edgar surveys 'Literary Criticism in Canada' back to the mid-nineteenth century, and is disappointed by a general weakness; a brighter picture is painted in the later 'Creative Criticism in Canada,' where the work of Barker Fairley, Charles Cochrane, and Northrop Frye indicates new directions. Frye himself tracks the development of innovative critical work in 'Across the River and Out of the Trees' and in his famous 'Conclusion' to the *Literary History of Canada.*

More recently, Carl Klinck looks at 'Bookmen and Scholars' in the early years of the century and analyses how Canadian literary history was intricated with more general historical research. This may be another reason for the predominance of historical criticism here: and this historical trend is seen as definitive by Laura Groening in 'Modern-izing Academia,' her review of the Harris history. (Heather Murray's 'Resistance and Reception: Backgrounds to Theory in English-Canada,' reprinted in this volume, also examines the evolution of this historical criticism.) Millar MacLure's 'Literary Scholarship' is the most thorough documentation of scholarly work prior to 1960. MacLure traces the ini-tial intrication of scholarship with public education and catalogues the variety of work produced in the modern languages; while a more focused study, by Alvin Lee, looks at the development of teaching and scholarship at Victoria College.

University magazines of the time provide more evidence of this schol-arly and professional growth, and back issues of the *Rebel* (University College, Toronto), with their monthly descriptions of English Associa-tion addresses and debates, remain an important record of undergradu-ate literary culture in the 1910s. Robert McDougall defends 'The University Quarterlies' as valuable culturally and as an inevitable devel-opment of publishing specialization; George Woodcock's 'When the Past Becomes History' links the quarterlies to the growth of the essay in Canada. More specifically, Kenneth Hoeppner analyses 'The Image of the Reader in the Literary Essays Published in *Queen's Quarterly*, 1893–1929'; *UTQ* editor Roy Daniells has recorded 'A Quarter-Century of the Quarterly'; and W.J. Keith and B.-Z. Shek examine 'A Half-Century of *UTQ*,' concentrating on its role as a clearing-house for Canadian letters. More generally, Ann Cowan's study of the *Canadian Forum* demon-strates the intrication of academic and political concerns, the importance of English department personnel to this journal, and its important criti-cal function. Maria Tippett's *Making Culture* provides a thorough over-view of literary and cultural clubs and parallel institutes in the twentieth century, prior to the Massey Commission.

Despite the growth of scholarship in the pre–Second World War years, 1945 found humanities departments in a perilous position. Already endangered by the war effort (McGill and Queen's had both considered closing their English departments for the duration), human-ities departments seemed equally ill-suited to the postwar program of education for national prosperity. Thus the end of the war occasioned intense reassessment of the humanities and their role in the university and in the society at large. John Brebner's *Scholarship for Canada: The Function of Graduate Studies* is a cross-country tally of graduate training and funding; most thoroughly, the massive survey of *The Humanities in Canada*, begun by Watson Kirkconnell and A.S.P. Woodhouse in 1944, details everything from library resources to teaching hours. It is still useful for its history of humanities education, and for the survey in 'Appendix D' of publications and work-in-progress. Charles Glicksberg's 1943 study of 'Literary Criticism and Science' is emblematic of this time. Ostensibly a plea for an *entente cordiale* between the two cultures, it may also be read as an attempt to reposition humanities studies in the postwar world. As Patricia Jasen has suggested in her study of 'The English Canadian Liberal Arts Curriculum: An Intellectual History, 1800–1950,' both Arnoldianism and the new twentieth-century emphasis on the 'professionalism' of criticism had allowed English to assume, in the inter-war years, a central position in the humanities. Whether or not it would be able to retain that position is the story of the next fifty years.

Works Cited

This bibliography lists published material pertaining to the development of English studies in Canada in the formative years. It is not a history of literary criticism or scholarship in English Canada, nor of 'CanLit' studies and criticism, although it overlaps with these areas from time to time. Rather, I have tried to locate and describe material which would be useful in constructing a critical history of English studies and teaching at the university level. I have included some items relating to education at other levels to show the range of professorial activity and application of critical principles, and to provide relevant background. Material to be found in readily available reference sources – such as encyclopaedias or the *Dictionary of Canadian Biography* – is not for the most part listed here; nor is obituary material unless the items are substantial.

This bibliography is restricted to published material. But much more remains to be discovered in university and departmental archives, and in the oral histories of members of the profession. This bibliography has not systematically surveyed newspapers or periodicals, since most are not yet indexed; some items are given, however, and the deep intrication of 'literary' and 'popular' culture, especially in the nineteenth century, suggests that there are more to be found. Of particular interest will be literary magazines (including student and society publications) and those devoted to education (for the early journals treat all education levels).

When a work is very rare, a location or bibliographic reference is given. If the text has been put on fiche by the Canadian Institute for Historical Microreproductions, the citation is followed by the CIHM number.

Adams, John Coldwell. *Sir Charles God Damn: The Life of Sir Charles G.D. Roberts*. Toronto: U Toronto P, 1986.

Akrigg, G.P.V. *Sedgewick: The Man and His Achievement. Being the Eleventh Garnett Sedgewick Memorial Lecture*. [Vancouver]: Department of English, U British Columbia, 1980. Rpt. *The Way We Were: Anecdote ... Antic ... Absurdity at the University of British Columbia*. [Vancouver]: UBC Alumni Assoc., 1987. 2–10.

Alexander, W.J. 'Graduates' Reading – Literature.' *Proceedings of the Thirty-Eighth Annual Convention of the Ontario Educational Association*. Toronto: Rowsell and Hutchison, [1899]. 264–72.

– 'Introduction: The Study of Literature.' *Select Poems: Being the Literature Prescribed for the Junior Matriculation and Junior Leaving Examinations, 1898*. Toronto: Copp Clark, 1897. vii–xxii. [CIHM 57989]

– 'Literature.' *Methods in Teaching*. Ed. J.J. Tilley. Toronto: George N. Morang, 1899. 30–66. [CIHM 33968]

– 'The Purpose of *Shorter Poems* and Its Use in the Class.' *The School* 20, 8 (April 1932): 683–91.

– *The Study of Literature: Inaugural Address Delivered at the Convocation of Dalhousie University, Halifax, N.S., Oct. 28th, 1884*. Halifax: Office of the Nova Scotia Printing Co., 1884. [CIHM 08835]

– *The Study of Literature: Inaugural Lecture Delivered in the Convocation Hall, October 12th, 1889*. Toronto: Rowsell and Hutchison, 1889. Rpt. *Canada Educational Monthly and 'School Magazine'* 11 (1 Nov. 1889): 337–43. Rpt. *The Week* 6, 52 (29 Nov. 1889): 823–4; 7, 1 (6 Dec. 1889): 9–10. Rpt. as 'A Lecture on Literature.' *Select Poems 1908*. Toronto: Copp, 1907. vii–xxiv. [CIHM 01350]

'Annual Meeting of the Modern Language Association.' *Toronto World* (3 Jan. 1889): 1.

Archambault, Francis (Rev. Father). 'The Teaching of English in the University of Montreal and Affiliated Colleges.' *National Conference of Canadian Universities Proceedings* (1932): 50–4.

Ayre, John. *Northrop Frye: A Biography*. Toronto: Random House, 1989.

Bailey, A.G. 'Creative Moments in the Culture of the Maritime Provinces.' *Dalhousie Review* 29, 3 (Oct. 1949): 231–44.

Bateman, Reginald. 'The Teaching of English: Two Lectures Given to the Class in Education in the University.' *Reginald Bateman, Teacher and Soldier: A Memorial Volume of Selections from His Lectures and Other Writings*. London: H. Southeran, 1922. 36–62.

Bennet, C.L. 'Archibald MacMechan.' *Papers of the Bibliographical Society of Canada* 3 (1964): 17–26.

– 'Dr. Archibald MacMechan.' *The Alumni News, Dalhousie University* 19, 3 (Oct. 1962): 3–5, 16.

- 'A Scholar and a Gentleman.' [Re: MacMechan.] *Dalhousie Review* 13, 3 (Autumn 1933): 378–81.

Bevan, Allan R. 'James De Mille and Archibald MacMechan.' *Dalhousie Review* 35, 3 (Autumn 1955): 201–15.

Birney, Earle. *Down the Long Table*. Toronto: McClelland and Stewart, 1955.

- *Spreading Time: Remarks on Canadian Writing and Writers. Book I: 1904–1949*. Montreal: Vehicule P, 1980.

Bissell, Claude T. *Halfway Up Parnassus: A Personal Account of the University of Toronto 1932–1971*. Toronto: U Toronto P, 1974.

- 'Literary Taste in Central Canada during the Late Nineteenth Century.' *Canadian Historical Review* 31, 3 (Sept. 1950): 237–51. Rpt. *Canadian History since Confederation*. Ed. B. Hodgins and R. Page. Georgetown, Ont.: Irwin-Dorsey, 1972. 157–70.

- 'Opinion.' *University College: A Portrait 1853–1953*. Ed. C.T. Bissell. Toronto: U Toronto P, 1953. 84–111.

Boone, Laurel, ed. *The Collected Letters of Charles G.D. Roberts*. Fredericton, N.B.: Goose Lane Editions, 1989.

Bourinot, John George. *Bibliography of the Members of the Royal Society of Canada*. N.p.: By Order of the Society, 1894.

- 'The Intellectual Development of the Canadian People: An Historical Review.' *Rose-Belford's Canadian Monthly and National Review* 5 (Dec. 1880): 628–37; 6 (Jan. 1881): 3–14; 6 (Feb. 1881): 108–24; 6 (Mar. 1881): 219–34. Rpt. Toronto: Hunter, Rose, 1881.

- *Our Intellectual Strength and Weakness: A Short Historical and Critical Review of Literature, Art and Education in Canada*. [Royal Society of Canada Series.] Montreal: Foster Brown, 1893. Rpt. *Our Intellectual Strength and Weakness, 'English-Canadian Literature,' 'French-Canadian Literature.'* [By J.G. Bourinot, T.G. Guthrie, and C. Roy.] Toronto: U Toronto P, 1973. [CIHM 00205]

Brebner, John Bartlet. *Scholarship for Canada: The Function of Graduate Studies*. Ottawa: Canadian Social Science Research Council, 1945.

Broadus, E.K. 'A Plan for Dealing with Weakness in English.' *National Conference of Canadian Universities Proceedings* (1928): 95–9.

- 'Weakness in English among Undergraduates and Graduates in Canadian Universities.' *National Conference of Canadian Universities Proceedings* (1927): 79–97.

Brown, E.K. 'Humane Scholarship in the Humanities.' *University of Toronto Quarterly* 11, 2 (Jan. 1942): 217–25.

- 'Shall We Adopt the French Doctorate?' *Canadian Forum* 10, 118 (July 1930): 363–4.

Burn, W.S. *The Connection between Literature and Commerce. In Two Essays, Read before the Literary and Historical Society of Toronto.* Toronto: H & W Rowsell, 1845. [CIHM 67299]

Campbell, Sandra M. 'The Canadian Literary Career of Professor Pelham Edgar.' Diss. U of Ottawa 1983.

Cappon, James. 'Edward Caird: A Reminiscence.' *Queen's Quarterly* 16 (Jan. 1909): 266–82.

– 'Is Ontario to Abandon Classical Education?' *Queen's Quarterly* 12, 2 (Oct. 1904): 190–206.

– 'Literature for the Young: Notes on the High School Reader.' *Queen's Quarterly* 1 (July 1893): 27–39.

– 'Prof. Cappon's Address.' *Kingston British Whig* (17 Oct. 1889): 2. [Queen's]

– 'Subjects and Methods in the Teaching of English.' *Canada Educational Monthly and 'School Magazine'* 12, 1 (Jan. 1890): 8–14; 12, 2 (Feb. 1890): 45–9.

'Chaleur, Baie.' 'Study of English Literature.' *Canada Educational Monthly and 'School Magazine'* 10, 5 (May 1888): 168–72.

Clark, A.F.B. 'Literary Scholarship in Canadian Universities.' *Canadian Forum* 10, 115 (April 1930): 244–6; 248.

– 'The Rehabilitation of Modern Languages.' *University Monthly* [Toronto] 15, 1 (Nov. 1913): 20–33.

Clark, William (Rev.). 'Books and Reading.' *Canadian Educational Monthly and 'School Magazine'* 11, 3 (March 1889): 85–91; 11, 4 (April 1889) 121–5; 11, 5 (May 1889): 161–4.

– [Professor Clark's lectures on Tennyson:] 'I. Early Poems.' *The Week* 9, 47 (21 Oct. 1892): 741; 'II. The Princess.' *The Week* 9, 48 (28 Oct. 1892): 757–8; 'III. In Memoriam.' *The Week* 9, 49 (4 Nov. 1892): 773–4; 'IV. Maud.' *The Week* 9, 50 (11 Nov. 1892): 789–90; 'V. Idylls of the King.' *The Week* 9, 51 (18 Nov. 1892): 805–6; 'VI. The Drama.' *The Week* 9, 52 (25 Nov. 1892): 821–2; 'VII. Later Poems.' *The Week* 10, 1 (2 Dec. 1892): 5–7.

Cooper, Christina C. 'Professor Cappon at the English Association.' *The Rebel* 2, 3 (Dec. 1917): 103–4. [U Toronto Archives]

Cowan, Ann Stephenson. 'The Canadian Forum 1920–1950: An Historical Study in Canadian Literary Theory and Practice.' Thesis, Carleton U, 1974.

Curtis, Bruce. '"Littery Merrit," "Useful Knowledge," and the Organization of Township Libraries in Canada West, 1840–60.' *Ontario History* 78, 4 (Dec. 1986): 285–311.

– 'The Speller Expelled: Disciplining the Common Reader in Canada West.' *Canadian Review of Sociology and Anthropology* 22, 3 (1985): 346–68.

Daniells, Roy. 'A Quarter-Century of the Quarterly.' *University of Toronto Quarterly* 25, 1 (Oct. 1955): 3–9.

Davies, Barrie, ed. *At the Mermaid Inn: Wilfred Campbell, Archibald Lampman, Duncan Campbell Scott in 'The Globe' 1887–93.* Toronto: U Toronto P, 1979.

d'Avray, Joseph Marshall De Brett Marechal [Baron]. *Oration by Professor D'Avray [sic], at the Encenia of the University of New Brunswick, June 1871.* Fredericton, N.B.: n.p., [1871?]. [CIHM 05739]

Dawson, John William. *Educated Women: An Address Delivered before the Delta Sigma Society of McGill University, December 1889.* Montreal [?]: private circulation, 1889. [CIHM 03665]

Dawson, Samuel Edward. 'President's Address: A Plea for Literature.' *Proceedings and Transactions of the Royal Society of Canada.* 3d ser., 2 (1908): 51–68. Rpt. *A Plea for Literature: Presidential Address before the Royal Society on May 26, 1908.* Montreal: Renouf, 1908.

De Mille, James. *The Elements of Rhetoric.* New York: Harper and Brothers, 1878. [CIHM 06019]

– 'Inaugural Address' [at Acadia College]. *Christian Watchman* [Saint John, N.B.] 1, 24 (12 June 1861): [1–2]. [National Library]

– 'Professor DeMill's [sic] Address.' *Dalhousie Gazette* 4 [old series 11], 1 [whole no. 107] (23 Nov. 1878): 1–7; 4 [old series 11] 2 [whole no. 108] (7 Dec. 1878): 13–17.

– 'Professor D'Mill's [sic] Inaugural Address.' *Dalhousie Gazette* 6, 1 (15 Nov. 1873): 1–6.

– *A Strange Manuscript Found in a Copper Cylinder.* London: Chatto and Windus, 1888.

Dent, John Charles. 'Literature and Journalism.' *The Last Forty Years: Canada since the Union of 1841.* 2 vols. Toronto: George Virtue, 1881. 555–93.

Dewar, David G. 'George Herbert Clarke.' *Queen's Profiles.* Kingston, Ont.: Office of Endowment and Public Relations of Queen's University, 1951. 47–54.

– 'James Alexander Roy.' *Queen's Profiles.* Op. cit. 117–24.

– 'Wilhelmina Gordon.' *Queen's Profiles.* Op. cit. 85–8.

Dickson, Lovat. *The Ante-Room.* Toronto: Macmillan, 1959.

Dickson, Stephen. *Considerations on the Establishment of a College in Quebec for the Instruction of Youth in Literature and Philosophy.* Quebec: New Printing Office, 1799. [Tremaine] [Public Records Office, London]

'Discussing the Modern Tongues.' *Toronto World* (4 Jan. 1889): 1.

Douglas, James. 'The Intellectual Progress of Canada during the Last Fifty Years, and the Present State of Its Literature.' *Canadian Monthly and National Review* 7, 6 (June 1875): 465–76.

Duthie, Eric. 'English in Askelon.' [Part II of 'Canada: An Illiterate Nation?'] *Queen's Quarterly* 43 (Spring 1936): 43–50.

Edel, Leon. 'Editor's Foreword.' *Willa Cather: A Critical Biography.* By E.K. Brown; completed by Leon Edel. New York: Knopf, 1953. xvii–xxiv.

– *Memories of the Montreal Group: The Pratt Lecture.* St John's, Nfld: Dept. of English, Memorial University of Newfoundland, 1986.

Edgar, Pelham. *Across My Path.* Ed. H.N. Frye. Toronto: Ryerson, 1952.

- 'A Confession of Faith and a Protest.' *University Magazine* [McGill] 8 (April 1909): 305–15.
- 'Creative Criticism in Canada.' *Across My Path.* Op. cit. 77–89.
- 'Literary Criticism in Canada.' *University of Toronto Quarterly* 8, 4 (July 1939): 420–30. Rpt. *Across My Path.* Op. cit. 118–28.

Eggleston, Wilfrid. 'Carman at Calgary and Queen's.' *Literary Friends.* Ottawa: Borealis, 1980. 8–16.
- *Literary Friends.* Ottawa: Borealis, 1980.

English Literature for 1890, for University and Departmental Examinations. Toronto: Copp, 1890.

Esson, Henry (Rev.) *Strictures on the Present Method of Teaching the English Language and Suggestions for Its Improvement.* Toronto: J. Cleland, 1852. [Dalhousie] [CIHM 56038]

Fee, Margery. 'Criticism,' in 'Literature in English: Theory and Criticism.' *The Canadian Encyclopedia.* 2d ed. 4 vols. Edmonton: Hurtig, 1988. 2:1228.
- 'English-Canadian Literary Criticism, 1890–1950: Defining and Establishing a National Literature.' Diss. U of Toronto 1981.
- 'On E.K. Brown.' *Canadian Literature* 86 (Autumn 1980): 142–3.

Ferns, John. *A.J.M. Smith.* Boston: Twayne, 1979.

'Fidelis' [Agnes Maule Machar]. 'The True Principles of Teaching English.' *Canada Educational Monthly and 'School Magazine'* 11, 2 (Feb. 1889): 46–8.

Ford, Anne Rochon. *A Path Not Strewn with Roses: One Hundred Years of Women at the University of Toronto 1884–1984.* Toronto: U Toronto P, 1985.

Foshay, Toby A. *J.D. Logan, Canadian Man of Letters: A Bio-critical and Bibliographical Study with a Checklist of the Logan Papers in the Acadia University Library.* Wolfville, N.S.: Lancelot Press [Acadia University Library], 1982.
- 'John Daniel Logan (1869–1929): Biography, Bibliography and Checklist of the Logan Papers in the Acadia University Library.' Thesis, Acadia U, 1981.

Frye, Northrop [H.N.]. 'Across the River and Out of the Trees.' *University of Toronto Quarterly* 50, 1 (Autumn 1980): 1–14. Rpt. *The Arts in Canada: The Last Fifty Years.* Ed. W.J. Keith and B.-Z. Shek. Toronto: U Toronto P, 1980. 1–14. Rpt. *Divisions on a Ground: Essays on Canadian Culture.* Ed. and introd. James Polk. Toronto: Anansi, 1982. 26–40.
- 'Conclusion.' *Literary History of Canada: Canadian Literature in English.* Ed. Carl F. Klinck. 2d ed. 3 vols. Toronto: U Toronto P, 1976. 2:333–61.
- 'Dean of Critics.' *Canadian Forum* 28, 334 (Nov. 1948): 169–70.
- 'Editor's Introduction.' *Across My Path.* By Pelham Edgar. Ed. H.N. Frye. Toronto: Ryerson, 1952. vii–xi.
- 'Foreword.' *English Studies at Toronto: A History.* By Robin S. Harris. Toronto: U Toronto P, 1988. ix–xii.

Gerson, Carole. 'The Canon between the Wars: Field-notes of a Feminist Literary Archaeologist.' *Canadian Canons: Essays in Literary Value*. Ed. Robert Lecker. Toronto: U Toronto P, 1991. 46–56.

– *A Purer Taste: The Writing and Reading of Fiction in English in Nineteenth-Century Canada*. Toronto: U Toronto P, 1989.

– *Three Writers of Victorian Canada and Their Works*. Downsview, Ont.: ECW Press, 1983.

Gibson, Frederick W. *Queen's University. Vol. II 1917–1961*. Kingston and Montreal: McGill-Queen's UP, 1983.

Glicksberg, Charles I. 'Literary Criticism and Science.' *University of Toronto Quarterly* 12, 4 (July 1943): 485–96.

Gordon, Wilhelmina. 'Archibald MacMechan.' *Queen's Quarterly* 40 (Nov. 1933): 635–40.

Graff, Harvey J. *The Literacy Myth: Literacy and Social Structure in the Nineteenth-Century City*. New York: Academic P, 1979.

Grayson, J. Paul, and L.M. Grayson. 'Canadian Literary and Other Elites: The Historical and Institutional Bases of Shared Realities.' *Canadian Review of Sociology and Anthropology* 17, 4 (1980): 338–56.

Groening, Laura. 'Modernizing Academia: An American and a Canadian Vision.' *Dalhousie Review* 67, 4 (Winter 1987–8): 511–22.

Gundy, H. Pearson, ed. *Letters of Bliss Carman*. Kingston and Montreal: McGill-Queen's UP, 1981.

Hamilton, W.B. 'Marshall d'Avray: Precursor of Modern Education.' *Profiles of Canadian Educators*. Ed. Robert S. Patterson et al. Toronto: D.C. Heath, 1974.

Harris, Robin S. *English Studies at Toronto: A History*. Toronto: U Toronto P, 1988.

– *A History of Higher Education in Canada, 1663–1960*. Toronto: U Toronto P, 1976.

– *Supplement 1965 to A Bibliography of Higher Education in Toronto*. Studies in Higher Education in Canada, No. 3. Toronto: U Toronto P, 1965.

– *Supplement 1971 to A Bibliography of Higher Education in Canada*. Studies in Higher Education in Canada, No. 5. Toronto: U Toronto P, 1971.

– and A. Tremblay. *A Bibliography of Higher Education in Canada*. Studies in Higher Education in Canada, No. 1. Toronto: U Toronto P, 1960.

Harrison, G.B. 'Department of English.' *Queen's Quarterly* 51, 4 (Winter 1944–5): 378–89.

– *Profession of English*. New York: Harcourt, Brace, and World, 1962.

Harvey, D.C. 'Dr. Thomas McCulloch and Liberal Education.' *Dalhousie Review* 23, 3 (Oct. 1943): 352–62.

Haultain, T. Arnold. 'Can English Literature Be Taught?' *The Week* 5, 2 (Dec. 8, 1887): 19–20.

Hill, Adams Sherman. *The Principles of Rhetoric and Their Application; With an Appendix Comprising General Rules for Punctuation.* New York: Harper, 1878.

Hodgins, Thomas, ed. *The Canadian Educational Directory and Calendar for 1857–58: Containing an Account of the Schools, Colleges, and Universities; the Professions; Scientific and Literary Institutions; Decisions of the Courts on School Questions, &c. &c.* Toronto: MacLear and Co., 1857. [CIHM 22636]

Hoeppner, Kenneth. 'The Image of the Reader in Literary Essays Published in *Queen's Quarterly,* 1893–1929.' *Prefaces and Literary Manifestoes / Préfaces et manifestes littéraires.* Ed. E.D. Blodgett and A.G. Purdy with S. Tötösy de Zepetnek. Edmonton: Research Institute for Comparative Literature, U Alberta, 1990. 171–80.

Holland, Clifford G. 'Canada Greets the Apostle of Culture.' *Dalhousie Review* 63, 2 (Summer 1983): 242–55.

Houston, William. 'The Proposed English Curriculum for Matriculation.' *Canada Educational Monthly and 'School Magazine'* 12 (March 1890): 90–2.

'How Can Canadian Universities Best Benefit the Profession of Journalism, as a Means of Moulding and Elevating Public Opinion?' [*Journalism and the University.*] Ed. editors of *Queen's Quarterly.* Toronto: Copp Clark, 1903.

Howe, Joseph. 'Eloquence.' *Poems and Essays.* Montreal: John Lovell, 1874. Rpt. Toronto: U Toronto P, 1973. 219–47.

– 'Shakspeare' [*sic*]. *Poems and Essays.* Op. cit. 190–218.

Hubert, Henry. 'The Development of English Studies in Nineteenth-Century Anglo-Canadian Colleges.' Diss. U of British Columbia 1989.

– 'The Vernacular in Nineteenth-Century Anglophone Colleges.' *Canadian Literature* 131 (Winter 1991): 131–42.

Jasen, Pat. 'Arnoldian Humanism, English Studies, and the Canadian University.' *Queen's Quarterly* 95, 3 (Autumn 1988): 550–66.

– 'The English Canadian Liberal Arts Curriculum: An Intellectual History, 1800–1950.' Diss. U of Manitoba 1987.

Johnson, Nan. 'English Composition, Rhetoric, and English Studies at Nineteenth-Century Canadian Colleges and Universities.' *English Quarterly* 20, 4 (Winter 1987): 296–304.

– *Nineteenth-Century Rhetoric in North America.* Carbondale, Ill.: Southern Illinois UP, 1991.

– 'Rhetoric and Belles Lettres in the Canadian Academy: An Historical Analysis.' *College English* 50, 8 (Dec. 1988): 861–73.

– 'The Study of English Composition in Canadian Schools: 1800–1900.' *English Quarterly* 20, 3 (Fall 1987): 205–17.

Keith, W.J., and B.-Z. Shek. 'A Half-Century of *UTQ*.' *University of Toronto*

Quarterly 50, 1 (Fall 1980): 146–54. Rpt. *The Arts in Canada: The Last Fifty Years.* Ed. W.J. Keith and B.-Z. Shek. Toronto: U Toronto P, 1980. 146–54.

Keys, D.R. 'Our Debt as Teachers to Matthew Arnold.' *Proceedings of the 35th Annual Convention of the Ontario Educational Association. Held in Toronto on the 7th, 8th and 9th of April 1896.* Toronto: C. Blackett Robinson, 1896. 126–36.

Kirkconnell, Watson. *A Slice of Canada: Memoirs.* Toronto: U Toronto P, 1967.

– and A.S.P. Woodhouse. *The Humanities in Canada.* Ottawa: Humanities Research Council of Canada, 1947.

Klinck, Carl F. 'Bookmen and Scholars.' *Aspects of Nineteenth-Century Ontario: Essays Presented to James J. Talman.* Ed. F.H. Armstrong et al. Toronto: U Toronto P, 1974. 327–33.

– 'Professor MacMechan, Native of Western Ontario.' *Waterloo Historical Society Annual Report* 40 (1952): 38–40.

Knox, R.S. 'The Educational Value of the Study of Literature.' *National Conference of Canadian Universities Proceedings* (1930): 56–64.

Langton, H.H. *Sir Daniel Wilson: A Memoir.* Toronto: Thomas Nelson, 1929.

Lee, Alvin A. 'Victoria's Contribution to Canadian Literary Culture.' *From Cobourg to Toronto: Victoria University in Retrospect: The Sesquicentennial Lectures.* Toronto: Board of Regents, Victoria University, 1989. 69–85.

Lewis, Wyndham. *The Letters of Wyndham Lewis.* Ed. W.K. Rose. London: Methuen, 1963.

– *Self Condemned.* London: Methuen, 1954. Rpt. New Canadian Library. Toronto: McClelland and Stewart, 1974. Rpt. Santa Barbara, Calif.: Black Sparrow P, 1983.

Logan, J.D. *Aesthetic Criticism in Canada: Its Aims, Methods and Status. Being a Short Propaedeutic to the Appreciation of the Fine Arts and the Writing of Criticism, on Literature, Painting and Dramatic and Musical Performances.* Toronto: McClelland, Goodchild and Stewart, 1917.

– *Dalhousie University and Canadian Literature. Being the History of an Attempt to Have Canadian Literature Included in the Curriculum of Dalhousie University. With a Criticism and Justification.* Halifax: the author, 1922.

– 'First Formal Lectures on Canadian Literature in Any Canadian University (Acadia).' Acadia University Archives, Logan collection, box 9, env. 83.

– 'Teaching Canadian Literature in the Universities.' *Canadian Bookman* 2, 4 (Dec. 1920): 61–2.

McCarthy, Dermot. 'Early Canadian Literary Histories and the Function of a Canon.' *Canadian Canons: Essays in Literary Value.* Ed. Robert Lecker. Toronto: U of Toronto P, 1991. 31–45.

McCourt, E.A. *Music at the Close.* Toronto: Ryerson, 1947. Rpt. New Canadian Library. Toronto: McClelland and Stewart, 1966.

McCulloch, Thomas (Rev.). *The Nature and Uses of a Liberal Education Illustrated: Being the Lecture Delivered at the Opening of the Building, Erected for the Accommodation of the Classes of the Pictou Academical Institution.* Halifax: A.H. Holland, Printer, 1819. [CIHM 63419]

MacDonald, J.F. 'Public Speaking as a College Subject.' *Queen's Quarterly* 16, 2 (Oct. 1908): 149–51.

McDougall, Robert L. 'Literature in English: Teaching.' *The Canadian Encyclopedia.* 2d ed. 4 vols. Edmonton: Hurtig, 1988. 2:1226–7.

– *The Poet and the Critic: A Literary Correspondence between D.C. Scott and E.K. Brown.* Ottawa: Carleton UP, 1983.

– 'The University Quarterlies.' *Canadian Forum* 38 (Feb. 1959): 253–5.

MacGregor, Stella Elaine Small. 'Dr. V.B. Rhodenizer: A Bibliographical and Critical Sketch.' Thesis, Acadia U, 1954.

McKillop, A.B. *A Disciplined Intelligence: Critical Inquiry and Canadian Thought in the Victorian Era.* Montreal: McGill-Queen's UP, 1979.

– 'Evolution, Ethnology, and Poetic Fancy: Sir Daniel Wilson and Mid-Victorian Science.' *Science, Pseudo-Science and Society.* Ed. Margaret J. Osler et al. Waterloo, Ont.: Wilfrid Laurier Press [Calgary Institute for the Humanities], 1980. 193–214. Rpt. as 'Evolution, Ethnology, and Poetic Fancy.' *Contours of Canadian Thought.* Toronto: U Toronto P, 1987. 43–58.

MacKinnon, Lilian Vaux. *Miriam of Queen's.* Toronto: McClelland and Stewart, 1921.

MacLure, Millar. 'Literary Scholarship.' *Literary History of Canada: Canadian Literature in English.* Ed. Carl F. Klinck. 2d ed. 3 vols. Toronto: U Toronto P, 1976. 2:53–74.

McMaster, Rowland D. 'The Department of English 1908–1932.' *Folio* [University of Alberta] 19, 14 (30 Sept. 1982): 5–12.

MacMechan, Archibald. 'Child of the Ballads.' *The Life of a Little College and Other Papers.* Boston: Houghton Mifflin, 1914. 165–77.

– *Concerning the Oldest English Literature: Inaugural Address Delivered at the Convocation of Dalhousie University, Halifax, N.S., Sept. 26th, 1889.* Halifax: James Bowes and Sons, 1889. [CIHM 27175]

– 'De Mille, the Man and the Writer.' *Canadian Magazine* 27, 5 (1906): 404–16.

McNeill, W.E. 'James Cappon.' *Some Great Men of Queen's.* Ed. R.C. Wallace. Toronto: Ryerson, 1941. 71–93.

Marchand, Philip. *Marshall McLuhan: The Medium and the Messenger.* Toronto: Random House, 1989.

Marquis, Thomas Guthrie. *English-Canadian Literature.* Toronto: Glasgow, Brooks, and Co., 1913. Rpt. 'English-Canadian Literature.' *Canada and Its Provinces: A History of the Canadian People and Their Institutions By One Hundred*

Associates. Ed. Adam Shortt and Arthur G. Doughty. 22 vols. Toronto: Glasgow, Brooks and Co., 1914. 12:493–589. Rpt. *Our Intellectual Strength and Weakness,* 'English-Canadian Literature,' 'French-Canadian Literature.' [By J.G. Bourinot, T.G. Marquis, and C. Roy.] Toronto: U Toronto P, 1973.

Maura, Sister. 'Respectfully Submitted.' *Dalhousie Review* 24, 4 (Jan. 1945): 438–42.

Montgomery, Lucy Maude. *Anne of Green Gables.* Boston: L.C. Page, 1908.

Morgan, Robert James. 'English Studies as Cultural Production in Ontario 1860–1920.' Diss. U of Toronto 1987.

– 'The "Englishness" of English Teaching.' *Bringing English to Order: The History and Politics of a School Subject.* Ed. Ivor Goodson and Peter Medway. London: Falmer P, 1990. 197–241.

Murphy, J. Stanley, C.S.B. 'Wyndham Lewis at Windsor.' *Canadian Literature* 35 (Winter 1968): 9–19. Rpt. *Wyndham Lewis in Canada.* Ed. George Woodcock. Vancouver: U British Columbia Publications Centre, 1971. 30–40.

Murray, Heather. 'Making the Modern: Twenty-Five Years of the Margaret Eaton School of Literature and Expression.' *Essays in Theatre / Etudes théâtrales* 10, 1 (Nov. 1991): 39–57.

– 'Resistance and Reception: Backgrounds to Theory in English-Canada.' *Signature* 4 (Winter 1990): 49–67.

Neatby, Hilda. *Queen's University. Vol. I 1841–1917.* Ed. Frederick W. Gibson and Roger Graham. Montreal: McGill-Queen's UP, 1978.

O'Brien, Kevin. 'Oscar Wilde and Canadian Artists.' *Antigonish Review* 1, 4 (Winter 1971): 11–28.

– *Oscar Wilde in Canada: An Apostle for the Arts.* Toronto: Personal Library, 1982.

Opala, Beatrice Barbara. 'Matthew Arnold in Canada.' Thesis, McGill U, 1968.

Parker, George L. *The Beginnings of the Book Trade in Canada.* Toronto: U Toronto P, 1985.

Patterson, George Geddie. 'Concerning James DeMille [sic], M.A.' *More Studies in Nova Scotia History.* By A.J. Crockett and George Geddie Patterson. Halifax: Imperial Publishing Co., 1941. 120–48.

Payne, William Morton, ed. *English in American Universities, by Professors in the English Departments of Twenty Representative Institutions.* Boston: D.C. Heath and Co., 1895.

Perkin, J.R.C. *Morning in His Heart: The Life and Writings of Watson Kirkconnell.* [With bibliography by James B. Snelson.] Wolfville, N.S.: Lancelot Press [Acadia University Library], 1986.

Phillips, Charles E. *The Development of Education in Canada.* Toronto: W.J. Gage, 1957.

– 'The Teaching of English in Ontario, 1800–1900.' Diss. D. Paed. U of Toronto 1935.

Pomeroy, Elsie. *Sir Charles G.D. Roberts: A Biography*. Toronto: Ryerson, 1943.

Prentice, Alison. 'Scholarly Passion: Two Persons Who Caught It.' *Historical Studies in Education / Revue d'histoire de l'éducation* 1, 1 (Spring/printemps 1989): 7–27.

Reed, T.A., ed. *A History of the University of Trinity College Toronto, 1852–1952*. Toronto: U Toronto P, 1952.

Reid, John G. *Mount Allison University: A History, to 1963*. 2 vols. Toronto: U Toronto P, 1984.

Reynar, A.H. 'Literature and Culture.' *Canada Educational Monthly and 'School Magazine'* 11, 4 (April 1889): 125–31.

Rhodenizer, V.B. 'English at Acadia: 1918–52.' *Acadia Bulletin* 38, 3 (May 1952): 2–6.

Roberts, Charles G.D. 'The Teaching of English.' *Christian Union* 37, 16 (19 April 1888): 488–9.

Roddin, Sam. 'An Encounter with Ira Dilworth.' *The Way We Were: Anecdote ... Antic ... Absurdity at the University of British Columbia*. [Vancouver]: UBC Alumni Assoc., 1987. 24–5.

Ryerson, Egerton (Rev.). *Inaugural Address on the Nature and Advantages of an English and Liberal Education*. Toronto: By Order of the Board of Trustees and Visitors, 1842. [CIHM 21866]

Scarfe, Janet C. 'Letters and Affection: The Recruitment and Responsibilities of Academics in English-Speaking Universities in British North America in the Mid-Nineteenth Century.' Diss. U of Toronto 1982.

Seary, V.P. 'Nova Scotian Culture Fifty Years Ago.' *Dalhousie Review* 15 (Oct. 1935): 276–84.

Sedgewick, G.G. 'A.M. [Archibald MacMechan].' *Dalhousie Review* 13 (1934): 451–8.

– 'Of Disillusionment in Freshmen.' *Queen's Quarterly* 39, 4 (Nov. 1932): 704–9.

– 'The Unity of the Humanities.' *Dalhousie Review* 8 (1928–9): 357–67.

Shortt, S.E.D. 'Archibald MacMechan: Romantic Idealist.' *The Search for an Ideal: Six Canadian Intellectuals and Their Convictions in an Age of Transition, 1890–1930*. Toronto: U Toronto P, 1976. 41–57.

– 'James Cappon: The Ideal in Culture.' *The Search for an Ideal*. Op. cit. 59–75.

Squair, John. *I. Admission of Women to the University of Toronto and University College. II. Rectification of a Passage in 'Alumni Associations in the University of Toronto' (1922)*. Toronto: U Toronto P, 1926. [Victoria College Canadiana]

Staines, David. 'E.K. Brown (1905–1951): The Critic and His Writings.' *Canadian Literature* 83 (Winter 1979): 176–89.

– 'Introduction.' *Responses and Evaluations: Essays on Canada*. By E.K. Brown. Ed.

David Staines. New Canadian Library. Toronto: McClelland and Stewart, 1977. vii–xvi.

Steinhauer, H. 'Why We Have No Great Canadian Scholars.' *Canadian Forum* 10, 117 (June 1930): 321–3.

Stevenson, O.J. *Reminiscences*. Guelph, Ont.: private circulation, 1951.

– *The Study of Literature*. Thesis, U of Toronto, 1904. Rpt. Toronto: Morang, 1904.

– *Through the Years*. Toronto: Ryerson, 1952.

Stewart, George. 'Literature in Canada.' *Canadian Leaves, History, Art, Science, Literature, Commerce: A Series of Papers Read before the Canadian Club of New York*. New York: Napoleon Thompson, 1887. 129–44.

'The Study of English Literature.' *The Week* 6, 47 (25 Oct. 1889): 741.

Sutton, Barbara, ed. *Sanctam Hildam Canimus: A Collection of Reminiscences*. Toronto: St Hilda's College [U Toronto P], 1988.

A Synoptical View of the Literature for University and Teachers' Examinations for 1886, with the Characteristics of Each Selection Illustrated by Numerous References, Also a Series of Examination Papers. A Valuable Aid to Candidates by an Experienced Teacher. Collingwood, Ont.: E.S. Brown, 1886. [CIHM 27781]

Tayler, Anne. 'McCulloch to deMille [*sic*]: Scottish Influences on the Teaching of Composition and Rhetoric in Nineteenth-Century Canada.' *Proceedings of the Canadian Society for the History of Rhetoric*. Ed. John Stephen Martin and Christine Mason Sutherland. Calgary: Canadian Society for the History of Rhetoric, 1986. 69–90.

Testimonials in Favour of William John Alexander, B.A. (Lond.), Ph.D. (J.H.U.), Munro Professor of English Language and Literature in Dalhousie College and University, Halifax, N.S., and Formerly Fellow of the Johns Hopkins University, Candidate for Professorship of English in the University of Toronto. Halifax: Nova Scotia Printing Co., 1888. [CIHM 24672]

Testimonials of Archibald MacMechan, B.A. (Toronto). Submitted With an Application for the Chair of English at Queen's College, Kingston. N.p.: privately pub., [1888]. [Dalhousie]

Tilson, Alistair. 'Who Now reads Spalding?' *English Studies in Canada* 17, 4 (Dec. 1991): 469–80.

Tippett, Maria. *Making Culture: English-Canadian Institutions and the Arts before the Massey Commission*. Toronto: U Toronto P, 1990.

Toronto Daily Mail [items on the meeting of the Modern Language Association of Ontario]: 'Learned Linguistics: Annual Meeting of the Modern Language Association' (3 Jan. 1889): 4; 'Learned Linguistics: Annual Meeting of the Modern Language Association of Ontario' (4 Jan. 1889): 2; 'Modern Languages' (8 Jan. 1889): 4.

Walker, Laurence. 'Grammar Teaching in Alberta, 1905–1985.' *English Quarterly* 18, 3 (Fall 1985): 24–34.

Wallace, M.W. 'Memoir [of W.J. Alexander].' *University of Toronto Quarterly* 14, 1 (Oct. 1944): 1–8.

Watson, John. 'The Study of Literature.' *Canada Educational Monthly and 'School Magazine'* 8, 2 (Feb. 1886): 48–53.

Watters, Reginald Eyre. 'The Study of Canadian Literature since 1840.' *Essays and Articles on Canadian and American Literature.* Ed. Thomas Vincent, George Parker, and Stephen Bonnycastle. Occasional Papers of the Dept. of English, R.M.C., no. 3. Kingston, Ont.: Royal Military College of Canada, 1980. 164–71.

The Way We Were. Anecdote ... Antic ... Absurdity at the University of British Columbia. [Vancouver]: UBC Alumni Assoc., 1987.

Wetherell, J.E. 'A Recent Criticism.' *Canada Educational Monthly and 'School Magazine'* 12, 2 (Feb. 1890): 59–64.

Wilson, Daniel (Sir). *Address at the Convocation of the University of Toronto and University College, October 19, 1888.* Toronto: Rowsell and Hutchison, 1888. [CIHM 25979]

– *Caliban: The Missing Link.* London: Macmillan, 1883.

– 'English at Junior Matriculation.' *Canada Educational Monthly and 'School Magazine'* 11, 3 (March 1889): 81–5.

'Women Students in Modern Languages.' *Modern Language Instruction in Canada.* 2 vols. [Publications of the American and Canadian Committees on Modern Languages, vol. 6.] Toronto: U Toronto P, 1928. 1:468–74.

Woodcock, George. 'When the Past Becomes History: The Half-Century in Non-Fiction Prose.' *University of Toronto Quarterly* 50 (Autumn 1980): 90–101. Rpt. *The Arts in Canada: The Last Fifty Years.* Ed. W.J. Keith and B.-Z. Shek. Toronto: U Toronto P, 1980. 90–101.

Woodhouse, A.S.P. 'Critic and Teacher [W.J. Alexander].' *University of Toronto Quarterly* 14, 1 (Oct. 1944): 8–33.

– 'Staff, 1890–1953.' *University College: A Portrait.* Ed. C.T. Bissell. Toronto: U Toronto P, 1953. 51–83.

– and R.S. Harris. 'English Study in the English-Language Universities.' *Encyclopedia Canadiana.* Toronto: Grolier, 1957. 4:12–16.

Young, George Renny. *On Colonial Literature, Science and Education. Written with a View of Improving the Literary, Educational, and Public Institutions of British North America. In Three Volumes: Vol. I.* Halifax: J.H. Crosskill and Co., 1842. [CIHM 42536]

12

English Studies in Canada, 1945–1991: A Handlist

The following is a handlist of works pertaining to English studies in Canada after 1945. Here, rather than the bibliographic essay of the preceding chapter, a handlist format has been chosen (with annotations offered when the title is especially cryptic) on the assumption that readers will have a stronger overview of the discipline's recent past and will be able to make sense of the entries. The two bibliographies are distinguished by the time period treated; for example, a recently published work dealing with the nineteenth century would appear in the preceding chapter. Here, the principle of organization is by date of publication.

The type of material included is similar for both chapters. All material is published, with the exception of one set of important oral history tapes. Reviews are not listed, but review essays are when they deal with institutional issues; while material from commonly available reference sources is for the most part omitted. The only newsletters listed are the early issues of the *Humanities Association Bulletin* (which provided space for early ACUTE news); the *ACUTE Theory Group Newsletter*; and more recent issues of the *ACUTE/ACCUTE Newsletter*, which contain brief articles on professional concerns. Both *Inkshed* and the *CACE Newsletter*, omitted here, are sources of further information; the annual 'Letters in Canada' issue of *University of Toronto Quarterly* is the most thorough survey of scholarship. Further biographical information is available from encyclopaedias and from the 'Biographical Sketches of Dead Fellows' which appear in the *Proceedings and Transactions of the Royal Society of Canada*.

'English Studies' is defined to mean the study and teaching of English language and literature in higher education with the exception of English as a second language. Items pertaining to elementary and secondary teaching are listed when they contribute in a general way to examination of the discipline or provide information about professorial activity. (While Northrop Frye's influence is especially extensive, I documented only his Canadian impact, relying on Robert Denham's bibliography to locate that material.)

1945–1949

Alexander, Henry. 'A Programme for English.' *Queen's Quarterly* 54, 1 (Spring 1947): 34–46.

Bentley, J.A. 'Undergraduate Disparagement of Milton.' *Dalhousie Review* 25, 4 (Jan. 1946): 421–32.

Brebner, John Bartlett. *Scholarship for Canada: The Function of Graduate Studies.* Ottawa: Canadian Social Science Research Council, 1945.

Diltz, Bert Case. *Pierian Spring: Reflections on Education and the Teaching of English.* Toronto: Clarke, Irwin, 1946. [on training for secondary teaching, by an influential professor of education]

– *Poetic Pilgrimage: An Essay in Education.* Toronto: Clarke, Irwin, 1942.

Frye, Northrop [H.N.]. 'The Function of Criticism at the Present Time.' *University of Toronto Quarterly* 19, 1 (Oct. 1949): 1–16.

Kirkconnell, Watson, and A.S.P. Woodhouse. *The Humanities in Canada.* Ottawa: Humanities Research Council of Canada, 1947. [On the writing of the report, see Kirkconnell 1967 and Lebel 1975; for updates of the report, see Priestley 1964 and Wiles 1966.]

Voaden, Herman. 'Dramatic Art in Canadian Higher Education.' *The Humanities in Canada.* By Watson Kirkconnell and A.S.P. Woodhouse. Op. cit. 228–36.

Woodhouse, A.S.P. 'Undergraduate and Graduate Studies.' *National Conference of Canadian Universities Proceedings* (1946): 81–2.

1950–1959

Association of Canadian Teachers of English. *Inaugural Report and Prospectus.* N.p.: The Association, 1957.

Bateson, F.W. 'Teaching of Literature: A Reply to Mr. (Thomas Stearns) Eliot.' *University of Toronto Quarterly* 25, 1 (Oct. 1955): 38–46.

Canada. Royal Commission on National Development in the Arts, Letters and Sciences. *Report of the Royal Commission on National Development in the Arts, Letters and Sciences.* Ottawa: King's Printer, 1951. Selections rpt. as *Royal Commission Studies: A Selection of Essays Prepared for the Royal Commission on National Development in the Arts, Letters and Sciences.* Ottawa: Edmond Cloutier (King's Printer), 1951. [Massey Commission; see Wallace 1951 and Shea 1952.]

Canadian Conference of University Teachers of English. *Report and Minutes of the Conference Held at Toronto, May 21–23, 1952.* Toronto: CCUTE, 1952.

Daniells, Roy. 'Proposal for a Canadian Association of University Teachers of English.' *Humanities Association Bulletin* 20 (Jan. 1957): 2.

– 'A Quarter-Century of the Quarterly.' *University of Toronto Quarterly* 25, 1 (Oct. 1955): 3–9. [its critical orientation]

Diltz, Bert Case. *The Sense of Wonder: Observations on Education and the Teaching of English.* Toronto: McClelland and Stewart, 1953.

Edgar, Pelham. 'Creative Criticism in Canada.' *Across My Path.* Ed. H.N. Frye. Toronto: Ryerson, 1952. 77–89.

Elder, A.T. 'The Teaching of English to Science Students at the University of Alberta.' *Canadian Conference of Pharmaceutical Faculties* 11, 5 (1958): 98–102.

Frye, Northrop [H.N.]. 'Humanities in a New World.' *Three Lectures: University of Toronto Installation Lectures, 1958.* Toronto: U Toronto P, 1958. 9–23. Rpt. *Four Essays.* Toronto: U Toronto P, 1960. 15–29. Rpt. *Form and Idea.* Ed. Morton Bloomfield and Edwin W. Robbins. 2d ed. New York: Macmillan, 1961. 162–81. Rpt. *Divisions on a Ground: Essays on Canadian Culture.* Ed. and introd. James Polk. Toronto: Anansi, 1982. 102–17.

– 'The Study of English in Canada.' *Dalhousie Review* 38, 1 (Spring 1958): 1–7. Rpt. *On Education.* Toronto: Fitzhenry and Whiteside, 1988. 22–8.

Harris, R.S. 'The Place of English Studies in a University Program of General Education: A Study Based on the Practices of English-Speaking Universities and Colleges of Canada in 1951–52.' Diss. U of Michigan 1953.

Kirkconnell, Watson. 'The Humanities.' *Canadian Education Today: A Symposium.* Ed. Joseph Katz. Toronto: McGraw-Hill, 1956. 200–10.

McDougall, Robert L. 'The University Quarterlies.' *Canadian Forum* 38 (Feb. 1959): 253–5.

MacKinnon, M.H.M. *Problems Past and Prospective of English Departments.* N.p.: Conference of University Teachers of English, 1957.

MacLure, Millar. 'Literary Scholarship.' *The Culture of Contemporary Canada.* Ed. Julian Park. Toronto: Ryerson, 1957; Ithaca, N.Y.: Cornell UP, 1957. 222–41. [includes selective bibliography of literary scholarship in Canada]

Neatby, Hilda. *So Little for the Mind.* Toronto: Clarke, Irwin, 1953. [influential indictment of education: 'What Goes On in the Schools I: The Art of Communication: English' 132–56]

Pacey, Desmond. 'Literary Criticism in Canada.' *University of Toronto Quarterly* 19, 2 (Jan. 1950): 113–19.

Peter, John. 'New Lamps for Old: Modern Critical Methods and the Teaching of English.' *Dalhousie Review* 32, 3 (Autumn 1952): 175–83.

Phelps, Arthur L. 'Literature and Society.' *Educational Record of the Province of Quebec* 66, 2 (April-June 1950): 97–9.

'The Poet and the University: A Symposium.' *Humanities Association Bulletin* 20 (Jan. 1957): 4–14. [Earle Birney, Louis Dudek, Eli Mandel, James Reaney, Frank Scott, Wilfred Watson, E.J. Pratt, Alfred Bailey]

Priestley, F.E.L. 'Creative Scholarship.' *The Arts in Canada: A Stock-Taking at Mid-Century.* Ed. Malcolm Ross. [Toronto]: Macmillan, 1958. 98–101.

Rhodenizer, V.B. 'Literature and Life.' *Canadian Author and Bookman* 35 (Spring 1959): 18–20.

Robbins, William. 'English as an Integrating Study.' *University of British Columbia Education Bulletin* [later *Journal of Education*] 1 (1957): 39–49.

Seary, E.R. 'The Place of Linguistics in English Studies.' *Canadian Journal of Linguistics* 1, 2 (Oct. 1955): 9–13.

Shea, Albert A., ed. *Culture in Canada: A Study of the Findings of the Royal Commission on National Development in the Arts, Letters and Sciences (1949–1951).* Toronto: CORE Pub., 1952. [See Canada. Royal Commission 1951.]

Stedmond, J.M. 'The Modern Critic: British, American and Canadian.' *College English* 17, 8 (May 1956): 427–33.

Wallace, Malcolm. 'The Humanities.' *Royal Commission Studies: A Selection of Essays Prepared for the Royal Commission on National Development in the Arts, Letters and Sciences.* Ottawa: Edmond Cloutier (King's Printer), 1951. 99–118. [See Canada. Royal Commission 1951.]

Whalley, George. 'Scholarship and Criticism.' *University of Toronto Quarterly* 29, 1 (Oct. 1959): 33–45. Rpt. *Academic Discourse.* Ed. John Enck. New York: Appleton-Century-Crofts, 1964. 150–62. Rpt. *The Practice of Modern Literary Scholarship.* Ed. S.P. Zitner. Glenview, Ill.: Scott, Foresman, 1966. 1–13.

Woodhouse, A.S.P. 'The Humanities.' ['Problems in Securing Staff.'] *Canada's Crisis in Higher Education: Proceedings of a Conference Held by the National Conference of Canadian Universities at Ottawa, November 12–14, 1956.* Ed. Claude T. Bissell. Toronto: U Toronto P, 1957. 127–47.

– 'The Nature and Function of the Humanities.' *Proceedings and Transactions of the Royal Society of Canada* 3d ser., 46 (1952) [section 2]: 1–17.

– 'The Place of Literature in the Humanities.' *Man and Learning in Modern Society: Papers and Addresses Delivered at the Inauguration of Charles E. Odegaard as President of the University of Washington, November 6 and 7, 1958.* Seattle: U Washington P, 1959. 111–25.

– 'The University Preparation of Teachers of English.' *English Studies at Toronto:*

A History. By Robin S. Harris. Toronto: U Toronto P, 1988. 292–6. [talk delivered in 1951]
- and R.S. Harris. 'English Study in the English-Language Universities.' *Encyclopedia Canadiana.* Toronto: Grolier, 1958. Rpt. 1975. 4: 12–16.

1960–1969

Association of Canadian University Teachers of English. *Ad Hoc Committee on Standards in English Composition for University Admission.* By Roy Wiles. N.p.: ACUTE, 1963. Rpt. *Association of Canadian University Teachers of English Report: Nineteen Hundred and Sixty Three.* N.p.: ACUTE, 1963. 8–10. [Wiles Report]
Bilsland, J.W. 'On the Teaching of the Drama.' *English Quarterly* 1, 1 (Summer 1968): 41–51.
Birney, Earle. 'The Writer and the Canadian University.' *Humanities Association Bulletin* 12, 3 (Spring 1962): 85–91.
Bush, Douglas. 'A.S.P. Woodhouse, Scholar, Critic, Humanist.' *Essays in English Literature from the Renaissance to the Victorian Age Presented to A.S.P. Woodhouse.* Ed. Millar MacLure and Frank Watt. Toronto: U Toronto P, 1964. 320–33. Rpt. *Engaged and Disengaged.* Cambridge, Mass.: Harvard UP, 1966. 79–96.
Campbell, M., et al. 'Report of the English Study Committee.' *Design for Learning.* Ed. H.N. Frye. Toronto: U Toronto P, 1962. 19–78. [See Ontario Institute for Studies in Education 1968.]
Daniells, Roy. 'Literary Studies in Canada.' *Scholarship in Canada, 1967: Achievement and Outlook. Symposium Presented to Section II of the Royal Society of Canada in 1967.* Ed. R.H. Hubbard. Introd. Watson Kirkconnell. Toronto: U Toronto P, 1968. 29–39.
- 'Ned Pratt: Two Recollections. II: The Special Quality.' *Canadian Literature* 21 (Summer 1964): 10–12.
deBruyn, Jan. 'Maintenance of Teaching Standards in Freshman English.' *Journal of Education* [U British Columbia] 8 (1963): 77–81.
Deverell, Frederick A. *Canadian Bibliography of Reading and Literature Instruction (English) 1760 to 1959.* Vancouver: Copp, Clark, 1963.
Diltz, Bert Case. *Stranger than Fiction.* Toronto: McClelland and Stewart, [1969]. [autobiography]
Dudek, Louis. 'Poetry as a Way of Life.' *English Quarterly* 1, 1 (Summer 1968): 7–17.
Frye, Northrop [H.N.]. 'The Critical Discipline.' *Canadian Universities of Today: Symposium Presented to the Royal Society of Canada in 1960 / Les Universités canadiennes aujourd'hui: Colloque presenté à la Société Royale du Canada en 1960.* Ed. George Stanley and Guy Sylvestre. Toronto: U Toronto P, 1961. 30–7. Rpt. *On Education.* Toronto: Fitzhenry and Whiteside, 1988. 29–37.

- 'The Developing Imagination.' *Learning in Language and Literature*. [By. H.N. Frye and A.R. MacKinnon.] Cambridge, Mass.: [Graduate School of Education of Harvard U] Harvard UP, 1963. 31–58.
- *The Educated Imagination*. The Massey Lectures, second series. Toronto: Canadian Broadcasting Corporation, 1963. [proposals for literature teaching]
- 'Elementary Teaching and Elemental Scholarship.' *PMLA* 79, 2 (May 1964): 11–18. Rpt. *The Stubborn Structure: Essays on Criticism and Society*. Ithaca, N.Y.: Cornell UP, 1970. 90–105.
- 'Introduction.' *Design for Learning: Reports Submitted to the Joint Committee of the Toronto Board of Education and the University of Toronto*. Ed. H.N. Frye. Toronto: U Toronto P, 1962. 3–17. Rpt. in part *The Making of Meaning*. Ed. Anne E. Bertoff. Montclair, N.J.: Boynton/Cook, 1981. 191–6. Rpt. *On Education*. Toronto: Fitzhenry and Whiteside, 1988. 46–61.
- 'Ned Pratt: Two Recollections. I: The Personal Legend.' *Canadian Literature* 21 (Summer 1964): 6–9.
- 'Northrop Frye Talks to Bruce Mickleburgh.' Part I 'The Only Genuine Revolution.' *Monday Morning* 3, 6 (Feb. 1969): 20–6. Part II. 'The Role of Literature.' ['Educating the Imagination.'] *Monday Morning* 3, 7 (Mar. 1969): 22–8.
- 'Research and Graduate Education in the Humanities.' *Journal of the Proceedings and Addresses of the Twentieth Annual Conference of the Association of Graduate Schools in the Association of Canadian Universities*. Ed. Gordon Whaley. Austin: U Texas P, 1968. 37–43.
- 'The Social Importance of Literature.' *Educational Courier* 39 (Nov.- Dec. 1968): 19–23. Rpt. *On Education*. Toronto: Fitzhenry and Whiteside, 1988. 74–82.
- Gajadharsingh, J. 'An Evaluation of the Pre-Service Education Programmes Provided by Western Canadian Universities for High School Teachers of English.' Thesis, U of Saskatchewan, 1966.
- Harlow, Robert. 'Bastard Bohemia: Creative Writing in the Universities.' *Canadian Literature* 27 (Winter 1966): 32–43.
- Hubbard, R.H., ed. *Scholarship in Canada, 1967: Achievement and Outlook: Symposium Presented to Section II of the Royal Society of Canada in 1967*. Introd. by Watson Kirkconnell. Toronto: U Toronto P, 1968.
- Kirkconnell, Watson. *A Slice of Canada: Memoirs*. Toronto: U Toronto P, 1967.
- Livesay, Dorothy. 'A Creative Climate for English Teaching.' *English Quarterly* 1, 1 (Summer 1968): 31–8.
- Lynch, M. 'A Canadian Record?' *Canadian Speech Journal* 2, 1 (1969): 13–17. [teaching of public speaking]
- McCourt, Edward. *Fasting Friar*. Toronto: McClelland and Stewart, 1963. [novel of departmental politics]

MacLennan, H. 'The Author as Teacher.' *McGill Journal of Education* 3, 1 (Spring 1968): 3–11.

McLuhan, Marshall. [Interview with Bruce Mickleburgh and Jack Wilson]. Part I. 'The Password.' ['The Password Is Involvement.'] *Monday Morning* 2, 1(Sept. 1967): 18–21. Part II. 'The Next 30 Years.' ['How Can We Equip Ourselves for the Next 30 Years?'] *Monday Morning* 2, 2 (Oct. 1967): 15–18.

McPherson, Hugo. 'Roy Daniells Humanist.' *British Columbia Library Quarterly* 24, 1 (July 1966): 29–35.

Mandel, E. 'Revolution and Reaction: Directions in English Studies.' *English Quarterly* 2, 1 (Jan. 1969): 7–15. [See Simpson 1969.]

Mardon, Ernest G. *Guide to English Studies*. Lethbridge, Alta.: [U of Lethbridge], 1968.

Martin, Walter R. '"Discovery" in the Teaching of Literature.' *English Quarterly* 1,1 (Summer 1968): 23–9.

Mayne, Brian. 'English Studies in an Experimental Arts Programme.' *English Quarterly* 2, 1 (Jan. 1969): 31–9.

Michayluk, J.O. 'Prediction of Freshman Marks in English.' Thesis, U of Saskatchewan, 1961.

Mickleburgh, Brita. 'We Teach English like a Foreign Language.' *Monday Morning* 2, 1 (Sept. 1967): 22–33.

Mullins, Stanley G. 'The Teaching of English-Canadian Literature at Laval University.' *Humanities Association Bulletin* 15, 2 (Autumn 1964): 58–63.

Ontario Institute for Studies in Education. English Study Committee. *English: Four Essays. The Aims and Problems of English in Schools, Community Colleges, and Universities of Ontario*. Curriculum series, no. 3. Toronto: Ontario Institute for Studies in Education, 1968. [See Campbell 1962.]

Peter, John. 'The Critic's Responsibility.' *University of Toronto Quarterly* 29, 2 (Jan. 1960): 109–21.

Priestley, F.E.L. 'The Future of the Humanities in Ontario Universities.' *Humanities Association Bulletin* 19, 1 (Winter 1968): 3–13.

– *The Humanities in Canada: A Report Prepared for the Humanities Research Council of Canada*. Toronto: U Toronto P, 1964. [See Kirkconnell and Woodhouse 1947, and Wiles 1966.]

– 'The Humanities: Specific Needs.' *Scholarship in Canada, 1967: Achievement and Outlook*. Ed. R.H. Hubbard. Op. cit. 11–16.

Scargill, M.H. 'Linguistics and the Teaching of English in Schools.' *Canadian Journal of Linguistics* 6, 2 (Fall 1960): 136–8.

Simpson, Barry. 'Visual Man Flirts with the Electronic Dissolve.' *English Quarterly* 2, 1 (Jan. 1969): 17–21. [response to Mandel 1969]

Squire, James R., ed. *A Common Purpose: The Teaching of English in Great Britain,*

Canada, and the United States: A Report. Champaign, Ill.: National Council of Teachers of English, 1966.

Stevens, Peter. 'Criticism.' ['The Writing of the Decade.'] *Canadian Literature* 41 (Summer 1969): 131–8. Rpt. *The Sixties: Canadian Writers and Writing of the Decade.* Ed. George Woodcock. Vancouver: U British Columbia P, 1969. 131–8.

Thomas, W.K. 'The Medium Helps the Message.' *English Quarterly* 2, 1 (Jan. 1969): 57–62. [teaching on television]

Whalley, George. 'English at School.' *Journal of Education* [U of British Columbia] 4 (1960): 63–73.

Wiles, R.M. *The Humanities in Canada: Supplement to Dec. 31 1964.* Toronto: U Toronto P, 1966. [See Kirkconnell and Woodhouse 1947; and Priestley 1964.]

1970–1979

Association of Canadian University Teachers of English. *Policy on Remedial English Instruction in Universities.* N.p.: ACUTE, 1976. [Gold Report; see Fleck 1976.]

– *Report of Commission on Undergraduate Studies in English in Canadian Universities December 1976.* By F.E.L. Priestley and H.I. Kerpneck. [Toronto]: ACUTE, 1976. [Priestley Report; see Jordan 1978.]

– *Report of Graduate Studies in English in Canada.* N.p: ACUTE, 1975. [Warhaft Report]

– *Unemployment and Underemployment of Qualified University Teachers of English in Canada.* [Vancouver]: ACUTE, 1979. [Rudrum Report]

Barton, Henry Alfred. 'A Study of the Interrelations among Criticism, Literature, and Literary Education in the Thought of Northrop Frye.' Ed. Diss. Harvard U 1972.

Bennett, B. 'The Teaching and Study of Australian Literature in the Universities.' *English Quarterly* 10, 2 (Summer 1977): 49–61.

Bramwell, R.D. 'On Teaching Semantics to Education Students.' *English Quarterly* 12, 4 (Winter 1979–80): 81–94.

'The Canadian Scholar: Roy Daniells.' *English Studies in Canada* 5, 4 (Winter 1979): vii–xix. ['I. Roy Daniells,' by Northrop Frye; 'II. Roy Daniells (1902–1979),' by William E. Fredeman; 'III. Vita and Bibliography,' by Laurenda Daniells]

Clever, Glenn. 'Student Views on Canadian Authors.' *Humanities Association Bulletin* 22, 2 (Spring 1971): 26–9.

Coburn, Kathleen. *In Pursuit of Coleridge.* Toronto: Clarke, Irwin, 1977. [memoirs]

Cole, W.V., V. Rock, and R.L. White. 'A Tentative Report on "American" and

"Canadian" Courses in Canadian University Curricula.' *Canadian Review of American Studies* 1, 1 (1970): 39–47.

Collie, Michael. 'Interdisciplinary Programs.' *English Quarterly* 5, 1/2 (Spring/ Summer 1972): 109–12.

Dawe, Alan, Clarence Tracy, and M.A. Preston. 'Graduate Programs and the Staffing Needs of Post-Secondary Institutions.' *English Quarterly* 5, 1/2 (Spring/Summer 1972): 105-7.

Diltz, Bert Case. *Sense or Nonsense: Contemporary Education at the Crossroads* Toronto: McClelland and Stewart, 1972. [teaching literary appreciation]

Dudek, Louis. 'English in Canada.' *Monday Morning* 6, 2 (Oct. 1971): 18–20. [on teaching]

− 'The Poetry of Reason.' *English Quarterly* 3, 2 (Summer 1970): 6–14. [on teaching]

Duncan, Chester. 'The University of Manitoba as a Literary Environment.' *Mosaic* 3, 3 (Spring 1970): 34–8.

Durant, Geoffrey. 'The New Barbarians.' *In the Name of Language!* Ed. Joseph Gold. Toronto: Macmillan, 1975. 97–130.

Elliott, Maurice S. 'Respecting Our Organs.' *In the Name of Language!* Ed. Joseph Gold. Toronto: Macmillan, 1975. 161–200. [sensory experience and literary education]

Fleck, P. 'The Need for "Remedial English" in Universities.' N.p., ACUTE, 1976. [See Association of Canadian University Teachers of English *Policy* 1976.]

Fogel, Stanley. 'Professors and Professionals.' *Dalhousie Review* 58, 1 (Spring 1978): 63–8.

− 'Teaching the Language of Literature.' *Dalhousie Review* 59, 3 (Autumn 1979): 527–33.

Freedman, Aviva. 'Writing and the University.' *English Quarterly* 12, 1/2 (Spring/Summer 1979): 33–42.

Frye, Northrop [H.N.]. *On Teaching Literature.* New York: Harcourt, Brace, Jovanovich, 1972. Rpt. *On Education.* Toronto: Fitzhenry and Whiteside, 1988. 109–37.

− 'Presidential Address 1976.' *PMLA* 92, 3 (May 1977): 385–91. Rpt. with revisions as 'Teaching the Humanities Today.' *Divisions on a Ground.* Ed. and introd. James Polk. Toronto: Anansi, 1982. 91–101. [on the profession]

− 'The Social Uses of Literature: The Teaching Critic.' Kenosha, Wisc.: Comptron Corp. 1972. [cassette ET- 10.] Rpt. in part as 'The Teaching of Literature.' *Minneapolis 72: Convention Concerns.* Ed. Martha R. Ellison. Urbana, Ill.: NCTE, 1972. 21–2.

− *The Stubborn Structure: Essays on Criticism and Society.* Ithaca, N.Y.: Cornell UP, 1970. [the utility of literary scholarship]

– 'The Teacher of the Humanities in Twentieth-Century Canada.' *Grad Post* 2 (Nov. 1978): 5–7. Rpt. as 'Royal Bank Award Address: Sept. 1978.' *CEA Critic* 42 (Jan. 1980): 2–9. Rpt. abridged as 'The Rear-View Mirror: Notes Toward a Future.' *Divisions on a Ground*. Ed. and introd. James Polk. Toronto: Anansi, 1982. 181–90. Rpt. abridged as 'Thought of a Canadian.' *Report of Confederation* 2 (Nov. 1978): 30–1.

Gold, Joseph. 'Alternatives to the M.A. and Ph.D. Degrees.' *English Quarterly* 5, 1/2 (Spring/Summer 1972): 113–17.

–, ed. *In the Name of Language!* Toronto: Macmillan, 1975.

– 'An Introduction: A Word to the Wise.' *In the Name of Language!* Op. cit. 1–17.

Green, Eric. 'The Possibility of Triumph.' *UBC Alumni Chronicle* 27, 1 (1973): 22–5. [on Roy Daniells]

Gutteridge, D. 'Teaching Structure in English: A Preliminary Essay.' *English Quarterly* 3, 2 (Summer 1970): 37–49.

Hair, Donald S. 'A Checklist of the Publications of F.E.L. Priestley.' *English Studies in Canada* 1, 2 (Summer 1975): 139–43.

Handscombe, Richard. 'Linguistics and Literature in Canada.' *Experimental and Applied Linguistics in Canada / Linguistique expérimentale et appliquée au Canada*. Ed. Pierre R. Leon. Montreal: Didier, 1979. 3–16. [institutionalization of linguistics and stylistics]

– 'Reading Literature.' *English Quarterly* 5, 1/2 (Spring/Summer 1972): 59–66. [training critical readers]

Holden, Michael. 'Literary Theory and the Education of English Teachers: An Analysis of Theories of Literature Presented in Selected Texts on Literature and Its Teaching.' Diss. U of Toronto 1973.

Holmes, Lynn. 'Notes on McLuhan and the Teaching of English.' *Monday Morning* 6, 1 (Sept. 1971): 13.

Horning, Alice. 'Getting Out from Under: A Ready and Easy Way to Teach Freshman Composition.' *English Quarterly* 11, 3 (Fall 1978): 35–44.

Hornyansky, Michael. 'Is Your English Destroying Your Image?' *In the Name of Language!* Ed. Joseph Gold. Op. cit. 71–96.

Jones, L.W. 'Canadian Graduate Studies in American Literature: A Bibliography of Theses and Dissertations, 1921–1968.' *Canadian Review of American Studies* 1, 2 (Fall 1970): 116–29.

Jordan, M. Robert. Review of *Report of Commission on Undergraduate Studies in English in Canadian Universities*. *English Studies in Canada* 4, 1 (Spring 1978): 111–25. [See Association of Canadian University Teachers of English *Report* 1976.]

King, Alan, et al. ['Interface Project.'] *Continuity and Diversity of Courses: The Secondary/Post-secondary Interface. Project III. Nature of Programs.* [Toronto]:

Ontario Ministry of Education and Ministry of Colleges and Universities, 1976. ['English and Anglais,' vol. 1, 57–190, on preparation of students for university English courses; see Morgan 1978.]

King, David B., and Evelyn Cotter. 'An Experiment in Writing Instruction.' *English Quarterly* 3, 2 (1970): 51–6. [Innis College Writing Laboratory, U Toronto]

Kirkham, Michael. 'Teaching Poetry.' *Indirections* [Ontario Council of Teachers of English] 4, 1 (Fall 1978): 5–9.

Kreisel, H. 'Graduate Programs in English in Canadian Universities.' *English Quarterly* 5, 1/2 (Spring/Summer 1972): 95–103.

Lane, Lauriat, Jr. 'Literary Criticism and Scholarship.' *Literary History of Canada: Canadian Literature in English*. Ed. Carl F. Klinck. 2d ed. 3 vols. Toronto: U Toronto P, 1976. 3: 32–62.

Lebel, Maurice. 'Les Humanités dans l'enseignement supérieur au Canada.' *The Undoing of Babel: Watson Kirkconnell: The Man and His Work*. Ed. J.R.C. Perkin. Toronto: McClelland and Stewart, 1975. 50–63. [On *The Humanities in Canada*; see Kirkconnell and Woodhouse 1947.]

Macaree, David. 'Hard Times, Freshman English Today.' *English Quarterly* 5, 4 (Winter 1972–3): 21–6.

McLuhan, Marshall. 'English Literature as Control Tower in Communications Study.' *English Quarterly* 7, 1 (Spring 1974): 3–7.

MacLure, Millar. 'Literary Scholarship to 1960.' *Literary History of Canada: Canadian Literature in English*. Ed. Carl F. Klinck. 2d ed. 3 vols. Toronto: U Toronto P, 1976. 2:53–74.

– 'Teaching and Research in Graduate Programs.' *English Quarterly* 5, 1/2 (Spring/Summer 1972): 119–22.

McMaster, Rowland D. 'The Canadian Scholar: F.E.L. Priestley.' *English Studies in Canada* 1, 2 (Summer 1975): 125–38. [includes Priestley bibliography]

Mardon, Ernest G. *Findings of an Investigation of Graduate Studies in English Literature at Canadian Universities*. Lethbridge, Alta.: [U of Lethbridge], 1970. [includes *Titles of Doctoral Dissertations*]

Mathews, Robin. *Canadian Literature: Surrender or Revolution*. Ed.Gail Dexter. Toronto: Steel Rail Educational Pub., 1978. ['II: Literature, the Universities and Liberal Ideology' 167–204]

– 'Research, Curriculum, Scholarship and Endowment in the Study of Canadian Literature.' *English Quarterly* 5, 3 (Autumn 1972): 39–46. Rpt. *Canadian Literature: Surrender or Revolution*. Op. cit. 181–9.

Morgan, Peter. 'Interface 1978: Relations Between School and University English.' *English Quarterly* 11, 4 (Winter 1978–9): 1–8. [See King et al. 1976.]

Ontario Institute for Studies in Education. English Study Committee. *Rhetoric: A*

Unified Approach to English Curricula. Curriculum Series, no. 9. Toronto: OISE, 1970. [on teaching of rhetoric at all education levels]

Pacey, Desmond. 'The Course of Canadian Criticism.' *Literary History of Canada: Canadian Literature in English*. Ed. Carl F. Klinck. 2d ed. 3 vols. Toronto: U Toronto P, 1976. 3: 16–31.

– 'The Study of Canadian Literature.' *Journal of Canadian Fiction* 2, 2 (Spring 1973): 67–72.

Perkin, J.R.C., ed. *The Undoing of Babel: Watson Kirkconnell: The Man and His Work*. Toronto: McClelland and Stewart, 1975.

Priestley, F.E.L. 'English: An Obsolete Industry?' *In the Name of Language!* Ed. Joseph Gold. Op. cit. 18–45.

– 'Science and the Humanities – Are There Two "Cultures"?' *Humanities Association Bulletin* 23, 4 (Fall 1972): 12–22.

– 'The Uses of Literature.' *Dalhousie Review* 58, 1 (Spring 1978): 5–16.

– and H. Kerpneck. 'Publication and Academic Reward.' *Scholarly Publishing* 8, 3 (April 1977): 233–7.

Robson, John M. *The Hmnnn Retort*. Toronto: New Press, 1970. [satiric account of academic life: 'Criticism and Criticmanship' 84–93]

Ross, Malcolm. 'Critical Theory: Some Trends.' *Literary History of Canada: Canadian Literature in English*. Ed. Carl F. Klinck. 2d ed. 3 vols. Toronto: U Toronto P, 1976. 3:160–75.

Saunders, Peter. 'The Mature Student and an Approach to Teaching Textual Analysis.' *English Quarterly* 12, 1/2 (Spring/Summer 1979): 43–9.

Symons, T.H.B. *To Know Ourselves: The Report of the Commission on Canadian Studies*. 4 vols. Ottawa: Association of Universities and Colleges of Canada, 1975. Abridged version rpt. as *The Symons Report*. [Toronto]: Book and Periodical Development Council, 1978. [Canadian content]

Theall, Donald. 'Innovations in Graduate Programs.' *English Quarterly* 5, 1/2 (Spring/Summer 1972): 123–34.

Titles of Doctoral Dissertations in English Literature Accepted at Canadian Universities 1960–68. [See Mardon 1970.]

Wayman, Tom. 'English: Art or Science?' *University of British Columbia Alumni Chronicle* (Summer 1970): 9–12.

Whalley, George. 'Picking Up the Thread.' *In the Name of Language!* Ed. Joseph Gold. Op. cit. 46–70. Rpt. *Studies in Literature and the Humanities: Innocence of Intent*. Selected and introd. Brian Crick and John Ferns. Kingston and Montreal: McGill-Queen's UP, 1985. 122–44. [literacy]

– 'The Place of Language in the Study of Literature.' *Indirections* [Ontario Council of Teachers of English] 2, 2 (Feb. 1977): 13–31.

– '"Research" and the Humanities.' *Queen's Quarterly* 79 (1972): 441–57. Rpt.

Studies in Literature and the Humanities: Innocence of Intent. Op. cit. 102–21. [See Whalley, 'Picking Up.']

– '"Scholarship," "Research," and "The Pursuit of Truth."' *Proceedings and Transactions of the Royal Society of Canada* 4th ser., 8 (1970) [section 2]: 299–322. Rpt. *Studies in Literature and the Humanities: Innocence of Intent.* Op. cit. 75–101. [See Whalley, 'Picking Up.']

– 'Teaching Poetry.' *The Compass* 5 (Winter 1979): 1–15. Rpt. *Studies in Literature and the Humanities: Innocence of Intent.* Op. cit. 215–29. [See Whalley, 'Picking Up.']

– 'Where Are English Studies Going?' *In the Name of Language!* Ed. Joseph Gold. Op. cit. 131–60.

Woods, Michael J. '"The Buck Stops Here": One Remedy for University Illiteracy.' *English Quarterly* 10, 4 (Winter 1977): 7–13. [Memorial University]

Wright, Vivian. 'The English Language Programme.' *English Quarterly* 11, 2 (Summer 1978): 95–103.

Zanes, John Page. 'Where the Fiddleheads Grow and the Wind Blows Blue: A Consideration of a Canadian Literary Tradition.' Diss. U of Texas 1979. [on University of New Brunswick]

1980–1989

Adamowski, T.H. 'Traditionalism and Its Discontents.' *ADE Bulletin* [Association of Departments of English] 90 (Fall 1988): 68–71.

Aitken, Pat. 'From Reading to Writing: Making It Happen in the University Composition Classroom.' *Show and Tell – 1988. Proceedings from the Conference, April 1988.* Guelph: U of Guelph, 1988. 5–13.

Association of Canadian University Teachers of English. Committee for Professional Concerns. *Guide to Grants and Fellowships for Canadian Graduate Students and Faculty.* [Edmonton]: ACUTE, 1989.

Atwood, Margaret. 'Northrop Frye Observed.' *Second Words: Selected Critical Prose.* Toronto: Anansi, 1982. 398–406. [Frye as teacher]

Ayre, John. *Northrop Frye: A Biography.* Toronto: Random House, 1989. [Frye as teacher]

Balfour, Ian. *Northrop Frye.* Boston: Twayne, 1988. ['The Function of Criticism at Any Given Time: Literature, Education, and Society' 66–77]

Barrett, H.P. *English.* Toronto: U Toronto Faculty of Education Guidance Centre, 1982. Rev. ed. The Student, Subject, and Careers Series, No. 1. Toronto: OISE Guidance Centre / OISE Press, 1988. [careers for English students]

Baxter, Helen. 'The Ph.D., a New Species of Migrant Worker: the ACUTE Report on Unemployment and Underemployment of Qualified University Teachers of English in Canada.' *CAUT Bulletin* [Canadian Association of University Teachers of English] 27, 6 (Oct. 1980): 11.

Beam, Paul. 'Pleasing All the People: Using On-Line Computers in an English Course.' *Computers in Education* 5, 8 (May 1988): 5–8. [University of Waterloo]

Besner, Neil. 'Process against Product: A Real Opposition?' *English Quarterly* 18, 3 (Fall 1985): 9–16.

Bogdan, Deanne. 'Instruction and Delight: Northrop Frye and the Educational Value of Literature.' Diss. U of Toronto 1980.

– 'Is It Relevant and Does It Work? Reconsidering Literature Taught as Rhetoric.' *Journal of Aesthetic Education* 16, 4 (Winter 1982): 27–39.

– '"Let Them Eat Cake."' *English Journal* 70, 7 (Nov. 1981): 33–40. [application of Frye's work]

– 'Pygmalion as Pedagogue: Subjectivist Bias in the Teaching of Literature.' *English Education* 16, 2 (May 1984): 67–75.

– 'A Taxonomy of Responses and Respondents to Literature.' *Paideusis* 1, 1 (Fall 1987): 13–32. [reader response in the classroom; see J. Walsh 1987]

Bonnycastle, Stephen. 'The Crisis in English Studies: The Problem and Our Response.' [Editorial.] *Journal of Literary Theory* 5 (1985): 1–14.

– 'How to Do Reader-Response Criticism in the Classroom: Some Ideas from David Bleich, Norman Holland, and Stanley Fish.' *Journal of Literary Theory* 5 (1985): 47–66.

– 'Why the Academic Literary Community Is in Pieces, and What to Do about It.' [Editorial.] *Journal of Literary Theory* 3 (July 1982): 1–41.

Calder, Robert. 'English on the Rocks.' *CAUT Bulletin* [Canadian Association of University Teachers] 29, 5 (Sept. 1982): 17–18.

Cameron, Barry. 'Problems in the Study of Canadian Literature.' *English Quarterly* 13, 1 (Spring 1980): 59–65.

Campbell, Colin, dir. *Fiddle Faddle*. Videotape. 1988. 26 min. [fictional treatment of ISISS semiotics institute]

Canadian Council of Teachers of English. 'Statement on the Preparation of Teachers in the Area of English and Language Arts.' *Classmate* 15, 2 (Winter 1985): 22–3.

Chambers, Robert D. 'Counting Heads: A Response to a Feminist Metatheory of Literary History.' *Interchange* [Ontario Institute for Studies in Education] 17, 3 (Autumn 1986): 53–5. [response to A. Walsh 1986]

Coman, Alan. 'A Tribute to Northrop Frye.' *Indirections* [Ontario Council of Teachers of English] 13, 3 (Sept. 1988): 5–8.

– 'What Is English? And Why It Matters.' *University of Toronto Graduate* 9, 1 (Sept.-Oct. 1981): 10–11.

Cornell, Pamela. 'The Found Art of Teaching: Northrop Frye: The Better to See.' *University of Toronto Graduate* 6 (Winter 1979): 4.

Cude, Wilfred. 'On the Suppression of Thought by Our Academics: A Presentation. I. Introduction. II. The Canadian Branch-Plant Doctorate: Is It Functioning As It Should Be?' *Journal of Canadian Fiction* 35/6 (1986): 9–43.

– *The Ph.D. Trap*. West Bay, N.S.: Medicine Label P, 1987. [includes criticism of scholarship and graduate training in English]

Demers, Patricia, ed. *The Creating Word: Papers from an International Conference on the Learning and Teaching of English in the 1980s*. London: Macmillan, 1986; Edmonton: U Alberta P, 1986.

Denham, Robert. *Northrop Frye: An Annotated Biliography of Primary and Secondary Sources*. Toronto: U Toronto P, 1987.

Drain, Susan, and Kenna Mannos. 'Testing the Test: Mount Saint Vincent University's English Writing Competency Test (1984).' *English Quarterly* 19, 4 (Winter 1986): 267–81.

Dudek, Louis. 'The Language of Scholarship.' *University of Toronto Quarterly* 58, 4 (Summer 1989): 454–9.

Eggleston, Wilfrid. *Literary Friends*. Ottawa: Borealis P, 1980. [includes Carleton reminiscences]

Falle, George. Interview with George Gray Falle by Valerie Schatzker. 6 sound-tape reels (281 mins.). 1981. Library Oral History Project. [U Toronto Archives B81–0022; English at Toronto]

Fee, Margery. 'Criticism.' In 'Literature in English: Theory and Criticism.' *The Canadian Encyclopedia*. 2d ed. 4 vols. Edmonton: Hurtig, 1988. 2:1228.

– 'English-Canadian Literary Criticism, 1890–1950: Defining and Establishing a National Literature.' Diss. U of Toronto, 1981.

Fekete, John. 'Literature and Politics / Literary Politics.' *Dalhousie Review* 66, 1/2 (Spring/Summer 1986): 45–86. [See Kennedy 1986.]

Feltes, Norman. 'Theory in the Undergraduate Curriculum.' *ACUTE Theory Group Newsletter* 8 (Nov. 10, 1985): [2–4]. [course at York]

Findlay, Leonard M. ['Theory.'] In 'Literature in English: Theory and Criticism.' *The Canadian Encyclopedia*. 2d ed. 4 vols. Edmonton, Hurtig, 1988. 2:1227–8.

Fogel, Stanley. *The Postmodern University: Essays on the Deconstruction of the Humanities*. Downsview, Ont.: ECW P, 1988.

Fredeman, William E. 'New Directions in English Studies.' *Proceedings and Transactions of the Royal Society of Canada* 4th ser., 22 (1984) [transactions]: 227–32.

Freedman, Aviva. 'The Carleton University Writing Tutorial Service.' *Carleton Papers in Applied Language Study* 1 (1984): 77–100.

– 'University Tests of Writing: A Counter Proposal.' *Indirections* [Ontario Council of Teachers of English] 13, 1 (March 1988): 9–24.

- and Ian Pringle, eds. *Reinventing the Rhetorical Tradition*. Ottawa: Canadian Council of Teachers of English, 1980. [proceedings of 1979 CCTE conference 'Learning to Write']

Frye, Northrop [H.N.]. 'Across the River and Out of the Trees.' *University of Toronto Quarterly* 50, 1 (Fall 1980): 1–14. Rpt. *The Arts in Canada: The Last Fifty Years*. Ed. W.J. Keith and B.-Z. Shek. Toronto: U Toronto P, 1980. 1–14. Rpt. *Divisions on a Ground: Essays on Canadian Culture*. Ed. and introd. James Polk. Toronto: Anansi, 1982. 26–40. [development of criticism in Canada]

- 'The Beginning of the Word: OCTE Keynote Address, 30 October 1980.' *Indirections* [Ontario Council of Teachers of English] 6, 1 (Winter 1981): 4–14. Rpt. *On Education*. Toronto: Fitzhenry and Whiteside, 1988. 9–21.

- *Criticism as Education: The Leland B. Jacobs Lecture*. New York: School of Library Science, Columbia U, 1980. Rpt. *On Education*. Toronto: Fitzhenry and Whiteside, 1988. 138–52.

- *Divisions on a Ground: Essays on Canadian Culture*. Ed. and introd. James Polk. Toronto: Anansi, 1982.

- 'Foreword.' *English Studies at Toronto: A History*. By Robin S. Harris. Toronto: U Toronto P, 1988. ix-xii.

- Interview with Northrop Frye by Valerie Schatzker. 7 sound-tape reels (198 mins.). 1982. Library Oral History Project. [U Toronto Archives B86–0046; English at Toronto]

- 'Literary and Linguistic Scholarship in a Postliterate World.' *PMLA* 99, 5 (Oct. 1984): 990–5.

- *On Education*. Toronto: Fitzhenry and Whiteside, 1988.

Gambell, Trevor [T.J.]. 'A New Role for Literature in the English Curriculum.' *Canadian Journal of English Language Arts* 11, 2 (1988): 43–9. [inclusion of national literatures]

- 'A Selected Review of Literature in Canadian Curricula.' *English Quarterly* 19, 2 (Summer 1986): 153–63.

Garson, Marjorie. *ACUTE: The First Twenty-Five Years 1957–1982, a Brief History of the Association of Canadian University Teachers of English*. N.p.: [the Association], [1983].

Godard, Barbara. 'Structuralism/Post-Structuralism: Language, Reality, and Canadian Literature.' *Future Indicative: Literary Theory and Canadian Literature*. Ed. John Moss. Ottawa: U Ottawa P, 1987. 25–52. [overview of criticism]

- 'Theory at York.' *ACUTE Theory Group Newsletter* 11 (May 1988): 2–3.

Gold, Joseph. 'Fiction, Function, and Bibliotherapy: An Introduction to a Theoretical Framework.' *Journal of Literary Theory* 5 (1985): 26–34. [rethinking goals of literary study]

Good, Graham. 'Cultural Criticism or Textual Theory?' *University of Toronto Quarterly* 58, 4 (Summer 1989): 463–9.

Grayson, J. Paul, and L.M. Grayson. 'Canadian Literary and Other Elites: The Historical and Institutional Bases of Shared Realities.' *Canadian Review of Sociology and Anthropology* 17, 4 (1980): 338–56. [university role in forming literary elites]

Halpenny, Francess. 'Scholarly Publishing in Canada.' *Questions of Funding, Publishing and Distribution / Questions d'édition et de diffusion*. Ed. I.S. McLaren and C. Potvin. Edmonton: Research Institute for Comparative Literature, U of Alberta, 1989. 113–31.

Hamilton, A.C. 'The Historical Study of English Literature.' *Proceedings and Transactions of the Royal Society of Canada* 4th ser., 22 (1984) [transactions]: 245–50.

Harris, Robin S. *English Studies at Toronto: A History*. Toronto: U Toronto P, 1988.

Hopkins, Richard. 'The Information Seeking Behaviour of Literary Scholars: Dissertation Summary.' *Canadian Library Journal* 46, 2 (April 1989): 113–15.

– 'The Information Seeking Behaviour of Literary Scholars in Canadian Universities.' Diss. U of Toronto 1988.

Hutcheon, Linda. 'Literary Theory.' *Proceedings and Transactions of the Royal Society of Canada* 4th ser., 22 (1984) [transactions]: 239–44.

– 'The Particular Meets the Universal.' *Language in Her Eye: Views on Writing and Gender by Canadian Women Writing in English*. Ed. Libby Scheier et al. Toronto: Coach House P, 1990. 148–51. [autobiographical account]

Jackel, Susan. 'Canadian Literature in the Secondary Curriculum.' *The Creating Word* ... Ed. Patricia Demers. Op. cit. 197–210.

Jasen, Pat. 'The English-Canadian Liberal Arts Curriculum: An Intellectual History, 1800–1950.' Diss. U of Manitoba 1987.

– '"In Pursuit of Human Values (or Laugh When You Say That)": The Student Critique of the Arts Curriculum in the 1960s.' *Youth, University and Canadian Society: Essays in the Social History of Higher Education*. Ed. Paul Axelrod and John G. Reid. Kingston and Montreal: McGill-Queen's UP, 1989. 247–71. [includes '60s criticisms of English studies]

Johnson, Nan. 'Instruction in Rhetoric: The Present State of the Art.' *Proceedings of the Canadian Society for the History of Rhetoric*. Ed. John Stephen Martin and Christine Mason Sutherland. Calgary: Canadian Society for the History of Rhetoric, 1986. 91–102.

Keefer, Michael K. 'Deconstruction and the Gnostics.' *University of Toronto Quarterly* 55, 1 (Fall 1985): 74–93.

– 'Introduction [to issue on "Literature and Politics / Literary Politics"].' *Dalhousie Review* 66, 1/2 (Spring/Summer 1986): 5–13.

Keith, W.J. 'Canadian Literature.' *Proceedings and Transactions of the Royal Society of Canada* 4th ser., 22 (1984) [transactions]: 251–5. [study of Canadian literature]

– 'The Wood and the Trees: A Personal Response.' *University of Toronto Quarterly* 58, 4 (Summer 1989): 469–74.

– and B.-Z. Shek. 'A Half-Century of *UTQ*.' *University of Toronto Quarterly* 50, 1 (Fall 1980): 146–54. Rpt. *The Arts in Canada: The Last Fifty Years.* Ed. W.J. Keith and B.-Z. Shek. Toronto: U Toronto P, 1980. 146–54.

– and B.-Z. Shek, eds. *The Arts in Canada: The Last Fifty Years.* Toronto: U Toronto P, 1980.

Kennedy, Alan. 'Criticism of Value: Response to John Fekete.' *Dalhousie Review* 66, 1/2 (Spring/Summer 1986): 87–97. [See Fekete 1986.]

– 'Deconstruction Meets the Departments of Englit.' *Dalhousie Review* 64, 2 (Summer 1984): 452–71.

– 'Ubi Sunt?' *University of Toronto Quarterly* 58, 4 (Summer 1989): 474–82. [critics as public intellectuals]

Kirkham, Michael. 'Writing about a Poem.' *Indirections* [Ontario Council of Teachers of English] 6, 2 (Spring 1981): 14–21.

Klingspon, Ron. 'Teaching Shakespeare to Undergraduates: The Professor as Practiser.' *English Quarterly* 17, 2 (Summer 1984): 16–26.

Lawson, Alan. 'The Recognition of National Literatures: The Canadian and Australian Examples.' Diss. U of Queensland 1987.

Lee, Alvin A. 'Victoria's Contribution to Canadian Literary Culture.' *From Cobourg to Toronto: Victoria University in Retrospect: The Sesquicentennial Lectures.* Toronto: Board of Regents Victoria University, 1986. 69–85. [Victoria College writers and critics]

Loss, Archie. 'Experiencing Modern Literature: Approaches in Undergraduate Teaching.' *Highway One* [now *Canadian Journal of English Language Arts*] 9, 3 (Fall 1986): 14–20.

Lunsford, Andrea A. 'The "Old" New Rhetoric and Composition Studies: Yesterday, Today, and Tomorrow.' *Proceedings and Transactions of the Royal Society of Canada* 4th ser., 22 (1984) [transactions]: 265–71.

MacCallum, Hugh. 'A.S.P. Woodhouse: Teacher and Scholar.' *University of Toronto Quarterly* 54, 1 (Fall 1984): 1–16.

MacDonald, Rae McCarthy. 'The Huge Gap between Highschool and University Teaching Styles.' *Indirections* [Ontario Council of Teachers of English] 14, 4 (Dec. 1989): 25–31.

McDougall, R.L. 'Literature in English: Teaching.' *The Canadian Encyclopedia.* 2d ed. 4 vols. Edmonton: Hurtig, 1988. 2:1226–7.

– 'A Place in the Sun.' *Carleton Bulletin 1985* [n.p.]. Rpt. *Essays on Canadian Writ-*

ing 30 (Winter 1984–5): 96–114. Rpt. *Totems: Essays on the Cultural History of Canada.* Ottawa: Tecumseh P, 1990. 259–75. [development of Canadian studies; history of Carleton English department]

MacLulich, T.D. 'What Was Canadian Literature? Taking Stock of the Canlit Industry.' *Essays on Canadian Writing* 30 (Winter 1984–5): 17–34.

McMaster, Rowland [R.D.]. 'Editorial: *ESC* and Its Ways.' *English Studies in Canada* 15, 1 (March 1989): 3–11.

– 'Editorial Review: *English Studies at Toronto.*' *English Studies in Canada* 14, 3 (Sept. 1988): 247–58.

– 'Teaching the Novel: The Creative Word in *Great Expectations.*' *The Creating Word* ... Ed. Patricia Demers. Op. cit. 116–33.

Marchand, Philip. *Marshall McLuhan: The Medium and the Messenger.* Toronto: Random House, 1989. [Toronto departmental history; founding of McLuhan Centre]

Mills, John. 'Festival at Simon Fraser.' *Lizard in the Grass.* Downsview, Ont.: ECW P, 1980. 65–79. [SFU department]

Moore, Michael, ed. *George Whalley: Remembrances.* Kingston, Ont.: Quarry P, 1989.

Morgan, Robert. 'Three Dreams of Language: Or, No Longer Immured in the Bastille of the Humanist Word.' *College English* 49, 4 (April 1987): 449–58.

Mukherjee, Arun P. 'Ideology in the Classroom: A Case Study in the Teaching of English Literature in Canadian Universities.' *Dalhousie Review* 66, 1/2 (Spring/Summer 1986): 22–30. Rpt. *Towards an Aesthetic of Opposition: Essays on Literature, Criticism and Cultural Imperialism.* Stratford, Ont.: Williams-Wallace, 1988. 23–31.

Murray, Heather. 'Women in the Disciplines.' *CAUT Bulletin* [Canadian Association of University Teachers] 35, 3 (March 1988) [Special Publication – Status of Women Committee]: 3–4. [women in English]

Nelson, Sharon H. 'Bemused, Branded and Belittled: Women and Writing in Canada.' *Fireweed* 15 (1982): 65–102. [relationship of women writers to academic institutions]

Neuman, Shirley. 'Women, Words, and the Literary Canon.' *In the Feminine: Women and Words / Les Femmes et les mots.* Ed. Ann Dybikowski et al. Edmonton: Longspoon P, 1985. 136–42.

Olshen, Barry. 'On Teaching John Fowles' *The Magus.*' *ACUTE Theory Group Newsletter* 9 (7 May 1986): 3–4.

Page, Norman. 'Seizing the Shining Reality: The Novel in the Classroom.' *The Creating Word* ... Ed. Patricia Demera. Op. cit. 101–15.

Palmer, David. 'Tests of Writing Competence at Ontario Universities.' *Canadian Journal of Higher Education* 17, 3 (1987): 47–58.

'Paparazzi, Dave.' 'Disseminating Scruples.' *Border/Lines* 9/10 (Fall/Winter 1987–8): 4–5. [ISISS semiotics institute]

Parker, Pat. 'Crossing Boundaries.' *Vic Report* [Victoria College] 14, 2 (Winter 1985–6): 15. [literary studies program]

Polanski, Virginia G. 'Freshman Comp [sic] Students Increase Heuristic Use of Early Drafts.' *English Quarterly* 18, 2 (Summer 1985): 97–106.

Powe, Bruce W. 'The University as the Hidden Ground of Canadian Literature.' *Antigonish Review* 47 (Autumn 1981): 11–15.

Priestley, F.E.L. Interview with 'Felp' Priestley by Valerie Schatzker. 14 sound-tape reels (638 mins.). 1980–1. Library Oral History Project. [U Toronto Archives B81–0019; English at Alberta, UBC, and Toronto]

Robson, John. Interview with John Robson by Valerie Schatzker. 15 sound-tape reels (355 mins.). 1982. Library Oral History Project. [U Toronto Archives B86–0058; English at Toronto]

Rooke, Constance. 'Literary Periodicals: Questions of Funding and Editing.' *Questions of Funding, Publishing and Distribution / Questions d'édition et de diffusion.* Ed. I.S. McLaren and C. Potvin. Edmonton: Research Institute for Comparative Literature, U of Alberta, 1989. 107–12.

Ross, Malcolm MacKenzie. Interview with Malcolm Ross by Valerie Schatzker. 3 sound-tape reels (98 mins). 1983. Library Oral History Project. [U Toronto Archives B86–0083; English at UNB, Toronto, Alberta, Queen's, Manitoba; A.S.P. Woodhouse]

Rowengarten, Herbert. 'The English 100 Exam.' *Update* [Newsletter of the British Columbia English Teachers' Association] 22, 3 (Jan.-Feb. 1981): 5.

Rutland, Barry. 'Theory Based Research Units.' *ACUTE Theory Group Newsletter* 10 (May 1989): [1–2]. [Carleton and Western]

Saddlemyer, Ann. 'Generic Criticism – the Drama.' *Proceedings and Transactions of the Royal Society of Canada* 4th ser., 22 (1984) [transactions]: 257–63.

Sirluck, Ernest. Interview with Ernest Sirluk by Paul A. Bator. 10 sound-tape reels (500 mins.). 1981. Library Oral History Project. [U Toronto Archives B81–0027; graduate English at Toronto; A.S.P. Woodhouse; E.K. Brown]

Skelton, Robin. 'The Teaching of Poetry.' *The Creating Word ...* Ed. Patricia Demers. Op. cit. 86–100.

Smillie, Keith. 'Language, Literature and the Computer.' *The Creating Word ...* Ed. Patricia Demers. Op. cit. 177–96.

Staines, David. 'Canadian Journal Publishing: Notes from a New Editor.' *Questions of Funding, Publishing and Distribution / Questions d'édition et de diffusion.* Ed. I.S. McLaren and C. Potvin. Edmonton: Research Institute for Comparative Literature, U of Alberta, 1989. 103–6.

Steele, Charles R., ed. *Taking Stock: The Calgary Conference on the Canadian Novel.*

Downsview, Ont. : ECW P, 1982. [includes consideration of the canon and teaching]

Stewart, Helen J. 'Northrop Frye's Theory of the Imagination as a Basis for the Study of English, with Particular Reference to the Work of Bert Case Diltz and to Secondary School English in Ontario.' Diss. U of Toronto 1985.

Story, G.M. 'Bibliography and Textual Criticism.' *Proceedings and Transactions of the Royal Society of Canada* 4th ser., 22 (1984) [transactions]: 234–8.

Sutherland, Christine Mason. 'Fundamentals of Communication: Spoken and Written Discourse.' *Proceedings of the Canadian Society for the History of Rhetoric.* Ed. John Stephen Martin and Christine Mason Sutherland. Calgary: Canadian Society for the History of Rhetoric, 1986. 128–35. [course in practical rhetoric at Calgary]

'Symposium: English Studies Today and Tomorrow: The State of the Art.' *Proceedings and Transactions of the Royal Society of Canada* 4th ser., 22 (1984) [transactions]: 225–71.

Thomas, Gillian. 'Lifton's Law and the Teaching of Literature.' *Dalhousie Review* 66, 1/2 (Spring/Summer 1986): 14–21.

'The University and the Arts and Humanities.' *The Mission of the University: A Symposium in Six Parts with an Address by David Chadwick Smith on the Occasion of His Installation as Principal and Vice-Chancellor 25/26 October 1984 Queen's University at Kingston.* Kingston, Ont.: Queen's U, 1985. 58–71. [contains statements on English study by A.C. Hamilton and Margaret Atwood]

University of Toronto Quarterly 58, 4 (Summer 1989) [Special issue: 'Symposium: The Professionalization of Intellectuals'].

Waite, P.B. 'Allan Bevan's Dalhousie.' *Dalhousie Review* 63, 1 (Spring 1983): 7–12. Rpt. as 'The Dalhousie of Allan Bevan.' *Dalhousie Alumni News* (Summer 1984): 29–31.

Walsh, Anne. 'Accountable to the Life of My Tribe, to the Breath of My Planet: Another Scene of Choices.' *Interchange* [Ontario Institute for Studies in Education] 17, 3 (Autumn 1986): 55–60. [reply to Chambers 1986]

– '"The Maps Are Drawn by a Living Choir": Contexts for the Practice of a Feminist Metatheory of Literary History.' *Interchange* 17, 1 (Spring 1986): 1–22. [feminist critique of English studies; see Chambers 1986]

Walsh, Jill Paton. 'A Consideration of Bogdan's "A Taxonomy of Responses and Respondents to Literature."' *Paideusis* 3, 1 (Fall 1989): 5–10. [See Bogdan, 'Taxonomy' 1987.]

Weir, Lorraine. '"Maps and Tales": The Progress of *Canadian Literature, 1959–87.*' *Questions of Funding, Publishing and Distribution / Questions d'édition et de diffusion.* Ed. I.S. McLaren and C. Potvin. Edmonton: Research Institute in Comparative Literature, U of Alberta, 1989. 141–59.

Weiss, Allan Barry. 'The University and the English-Canadian Short Story, 1950–1980.' Diss. U of Toronto 1984.

Whale, Kathleen B., and Trevor Gamble, eds. *From Seed to Harvest: Looking at Literature*. N.p.: Canadian Council of Teachers of English, 1985. [includes contributions from university participants at CCTE conference]

Whalley, George. *Studies in Literature and the Humanities: Innocence of Intent*. Selected and introd. Brian Crick and John Ferns. Kingston and Montreal: McGill-Queen's UP, 1985. [includes Whalley bibliography]

Wiebe, Rudy. 'Creative Writing: Can It Be Taught?' *The Creating Word* ... Ed. Patricia Demers. Op. cit. 134–45.

Willinsky, John. 'From Feminist Literary Criticism Certain Classroom Splendours.' *English Quarterly* 18, 3 (Fall 1983): 35–43.

Woodcock, George. 'Intellectuals and Popular Culture.' *University of Toronto Quarterly* 58, 4 (Summer 1989): 507–12.

– 'When the Past Becomes History: The Half-Century in Non-Fiction Prose.' *University of Toronto Quarterly* 50, 1 (Fall 1980): 90–101. Rpt. *The Arts in Canada: The Last Fifty Years*. Ed. W.J. Keith and B.-Z. Shek. Op. cit. 90–101.

1990–1991

Allemang, John. 'Loose among the Learneds.' *Globe and Mail* (1 June 1991): D1, D4. [includes ACUTE conference]

Association of Canadian University Teachers of English. Committee for Professional Concerns. [With Canadian Association of Chairs of English.] *CACE/ACUTE Questionnaire on Hiring (1990)*. [Toronto]: ACUTE, 1991.

Belladonna, Rita. 'From Thought to Paper: The Writing Workshop as a Pedagogical Tool.' *Italian Literature in North America: Pedagogical Strategies*. Ed. John Picchione and Laura Pietropaolo. [Ottawa]: Canadian Society for Italian Studies, 1990. 296–9.

Bennett, Donna. 'Conflicted Vision: A Consideration of Canon and Genre in English-Canadian Literature.' *Canadian Canons: Essays in Literary Value*. Ed. Robert Lecker. Toronto: U Toronto P, 1991. 131–49.

Bogdan, Deanne. 'The Re-Educated Imagination and the Power of Literary Engagement.' *Journal of Educational Thought* 24, 3A (Dec. 1990): 83–109.

Bonnycastle, Stephen. *In Search of Authority: An Introductory Guide to Literary Theory*. Peterborough, Ont.: Broadview P, 1991. [pedagogic applications]

Bullock, Chris J. 'Changing the Context: Applying Feminist Perspectives to the Writing Class.' *English Quarterly* 22, 3/4 (1990): 141–8.

Cameron, Barry. 'Theory and Criticism: Trends in Canadian Literature.' *Literary*

History of Canada: Canadian Literature in English. Ed. W.H. New. 3d ed. 4 vols. Toronto: U Toronto P, 1990. 4:108–32.

Carpenter, Mary Wilson. 'Eco, Oedipus, and the "View" of the University.' *Diacritics* 20, 1 (Spring 1990): 77–85.

Davey, Frank. 'Critical Response: Canadian Canons.' *Critical Inquiry* 16, 3 (Spring 1990): 672–81. [See Lecker, 'Canonization' 1990; and 'Response' 1990.]

Gerson, Carole. 'Anthologies and the Canon of Early Canadian Women Writers.' *Re(Dis)covering Our Foremothers: Nineteenth Century Canadian Women Writers.* Ed. Lorraine McMullen. Ottawa: U Ottawa P, 1990. 55–76. [critique of academic texts]

Gold, Joseph. *Read for Your Life: Literature as a Life Support System.* Markham, Ont.: Fitzhenry and Whiteside, 1990. [rationale for literary study]

Goldie, Terry. 'Fresh Canons: The Native Canadian Example.' *English Studies in Canada* 17, 4 (Dec. 1991): 373–84.

Graham, Robert J. 'Literary Theory and Curriculum: Rethinking Theory and Practice in English Studies.' *English Quarterly* 22, 1/2 (1990): 20–9.

Halpenny, Francess G. 'From Author to Reader.' *Literary History of Canada: Canadian Literature in English.* Ed. W.H. New. 3d ed. 4 vols. Toronto: U Toronto P, 1990. 4:385–404. [history of publishing]

Hamilton, A.C. *Northrop Frye: Anatomy of His Criticism.* Toronto: U Toronto P, 1990. [educational component of Frye's criticism]

Harms, Dawson C. '(W)riting Deconstruction.' *Journal of Educational Thought* 24, 3A (Dec. 1990): 117–20. [teaching writing]

Harrison, Thomas. 'Deconstruction and Reader-Response: The Pedagogical Essay.' *Italian Literature in North America: Pedagogical Strategies.* Ed. John Picchione and Laura Pietropaolo. [Ottawa]: Canadian Society for Italian Studies, 1990. 131–8.

History of the Affiliated Learned Societies of the Canadian Federation for the Humanities. Ottawa: Canadian Federation for the Humanities, 1990. [brief histories of ACQL, ACUTE, etc.]

Hubert, Henry, and W.F. Garrett-Petts. 'Foreword: An Historical Narrative of Textual Studies in Canada.' *Textual Studies in Canada* 1 (1991): 1–30. [historical account of current disciplinary situation]

Hutcheon, Linda. '"Professionalism" and Professing English.' *ACUTE Newsletter* (March 1991): 3–5.

Keefer, Michael. 'Political Correctness.' *Canadian Federation for the Humanities Bulletin* 14, 2 (Summer 1991): 7–8.

Klinck, Carl F. *Giving Canada a Literary History: A Memoir.* Ed. Sandra Djwa. [Ottawa]: Carleton UP for the U of Western Ontario, 1991.

Lecker, Robert, ed. *Canadian Canons: Essays in Literary Value*. Toronto: U Toronto P, 1991.
- 'The Canonization of Canadian Literature: An Inquiry into Value.' *Critical Inquiry* 16, 3 (Spring 1990): 656–71. [See also Ware 1991.]
- 'Response to Frank Davey.' *Critical Inquiry* 16, 3 (Spring 1990): 682–9. [See Davey 1990.]
Lynch, Michael. 'Last Onsets: Teaching with AIDS.' *Profession 90* [MLA] (1990): 32–6.
McComb, Brenda. 'Literary Criticism and Critical Literacy.' *Italian Literature in North America: Pedagogical Strategies*. Ed. John Picchione and Laura Pietropaolo. [Ottawa]: Canadian Society for Italian Studies, 1990. 281–94.
McDougall, Robert L. *Totems: Essays on the Cultural History of Canada*. Ottawa: Tecumseh P, 1990. [memories of UBC, Carleton and Toronto departments; development of Canadian literary studies]
MacKinnon, Jamie. 'Toward a Canadian Rhetoric.' *Textual Studies in Canada* 1 (1991): 65–76.
McMaster, Rowland ['Hair Teufelsdröckh']. 'Worms, Worms, Was All My Cry.' ['Thinking about the Profession.'] *ACUTE Newsletter* (Sept. 1991): 3–5. [on collegiality]
McWhirter, George. 'Introduction: *A Wildcat Creativity*.' *Words We Call Home: Celebrating Creative Writing at UBC*. Ed. Linda Svendsen. Vancouver: U of British Columbia P, 1990. xxiii–xxvi. [history of the program]
Manos, Kenna. 'On Teaching Composition.' *ACUTE Newsletter* (Dec. 1990): 3–4.
Martin, Robert K. 'Dryden's Dates: Reflections on Canons, Curricula, and Pedagogy.' *English Studies in Canada* 17, 4 (Dec. 1991): 385–99.
Mathews, Lawrence. 'Calgary, Canonization, and Class: Deciphering List B.' *Canadian Canons ...* Ed. Robert Lecker. Op. cit. 151–66.
Michasiw, Kim Ian. 'Psychoanalytic Discourse in the Classroom: Bureaucracy, Hysteria, Mastery.' *Italian Literature in North America: Pedagogical Strategies*. Ed. John Picchione and Laura Pietropaolo. [Ottawa]: Canadian Society for Italian Studies, 1990. 95–104.
- 'Working Past the Canon: Thoughts on a Skills-Based Curriculum.' *English Studies in Canada* 17, 4 (Dec. 1991): 401–20.
Moore, Robert. 'Reading between the Canon and the Curriculum: Issues of Legibility and Legitimacy.' *English Studies in Canada* 17, 4 (Dec. 1991): 421–35.
Morgan, Robert. 'Reading as Discursive Practice: The Politics and History of Reading.' *Beyond Communication: Reading Comprehension and Criticism*. Ed. Deanne Bogdan and Stanley B. Straw. Portsmouth, N.H.: Boynton/Cook, 1990. 319–36.

Murray, Heather. 'Close Reading, Closed Writing.' *College English* 53, 2 (Feb. 1991): 195–208.
– 'From Canon to Curriculum.' *University of Toronto Quarterly* 60, 2 (Winter 1990–1): 229–43.
– 'Resistance and Reception: Backgrounds to Theory in English-Canada.' *Signature* 4 (Winter 1990): 49–67.
Rajan, Balachandra. 'Scholarship and Criticism.' *Literary History of Canada: Canadian Literature in English.* Ed. W.H. New. 3d ed. 4 vols. Toronto: U Toronto P, 1990. 4:133–58.
Slemon, Stephen, and Jo-Ann Wallace. 'Into the Heart of Darkness? Teaching Children's Literature as a Problem in Theory.' *Canadian Children's Literature* 63 (1991): 6–23.
Smith, Rowland. 'Lobbying: The Humanities and the Powerbrokers.' ['Thinking About the Profession.'] *ACUTE Newsletter* (Dec. 1991): 3–5.
Sowton, Ian. 'The Politics of Canonicity.' *ACUTE Newsletter* (Dec. 1990): 4–5.
Steven, Laurence. 'The Grain of Sand in the Oyster: Competency Testing as a Catalyst for Attitude Change at the University.' *Textual Studies in Canada* 1 (1991): 115–44. [testing and instruction at Laurentian]
Surette, Leon. 'Creating the Canadian Canon.' *Canadian Canons.* Ed. Robert Lecker. Op. cit. 17–29.
'Tribute to Northrop Frye.' *University of Toronto Quarterly* 61, 1 (Fall 1991): 1–17. [Frye's influence]
Walker, Laurie. 'Networks and Paradigms in English Language Arts in Canadian Faculties of Education.' *Canadian Journal of Education* 15, 2 (Spring 1990): 115–31.
Ware, Tracy. 'A Little Self-Consciousness Is a Dangerous Thing: A Response to Robert Lecker.' *English Studies in Canada* 17, 4 (1991): 481–93. [See Lecker, 'Canonization' 1990; and 'Response' 1990.]
Wayman, Tom. 'A House without Books: The Writer in Canadian Society.' *Canadian Literature* 130 (Autumn 1991): 62–7. [students' views of writers]

Index

DATE DUE FOR RETURN